"Silverman has done an outstanding job laying out what PR is and isn't, its origins, its purpose, and the useful outcomes it produces. It will be incredibly helpful for newcomers to the field, those thinking of making the transition to PR, and those who are just curious about what PR is. Do yourself a tremendous favor: get and read this book."

Stacey Smith, *APR, Fellow PRSA, Senior Counsel and Partner, Jackson Jackson & Wagner*

"*Public Relations: The Basics* (2nd edition) is the essential resource that today's PR classroom has been waiting for. Students will appreciate the textbook's integrated approach to understanding both the practice and value of PR—beginning with the discipline's early precursors, then focusing on how modern organizations strategically target narratives for optimal communication impact."

Jonathan R. Slater, *SUNY Plattsburgh, USA*

PUBLIC RELATIONS

THE BASICS

This concise and accessible second edition introduces readers to one of the most exciting and fast-paced media industries: public relations—its history and current practice, the types of employment roles available, and practitioner job responsibilities including writing, research, and strategic planning.

Orienting readers to this dynamic and engaging industry, this book gives readers the tools they need to consider career prospects and professional duties. It weaves case studies and practical examples with a brief but foundational look at communication theories helpful to a public relations professional. This edition continues to feature an overview of education for a public relations career, job opportunities, and tips for launching a career in public relations as well as addressing ethics, professionalism, and public relations writing. The four phases of public relations campaigns are also covered: research, strategy, tactics, and evaluation. Updates to this second edition include discussions of artificial intelligence; misinformation and disinformation; crisis communication; diversity, equity, and inclusion; corporate social responsibility; and the use of social media. This edition also incorporates new or updated international case studies throughout the text, ensuring that the book is relevant to a global audience, and features "PR Profiles" of four public relations leaders offering insights on the profession.

Public Relations: The Basics, 2nd Edition is pitched to a variety of audiences interested in learning more about public relations, including general readers, students exploring career options, and guidance counselors and university career advisers.

Deborah A. Silverman, APR, Fellow PRSA, is Chair and Associate Professor of Communication at SUNY Buffalo State University. A former public relations practitioner, she serves as Vice Chair of the national Commission on Public Relations Education in the US. She is the author, with the late Ronald Smith, of *Strategic Planning for Public Relations*, 7th edition, and co-author of *Media Writing*, 6th edition, with Joe Marren and Brian Meyer. Her research interests include PR ethics and service learning in the PR classroom.

THE BASICS SERIES

The Basics is a highly successful series of accessible guidebooks which provide an overview of the fundamental principles of a subject area in a jargon-free and undaunting format.

Intended for students approaching a subject for the first time, the books both introduce the essentials of a subject and provide an ideal springboard for further study. With over 50 titles spanning subjects from artificial intelligence (AI) to women's studies, *The Basics* are an ideal starting point for students seeking to understand a subject area.

Each text comes with recommendations for further study and gradually introduces the complexities and nuances within a subject.

THE HUMAN SKELETON
Steven N. Byers

SIKHISM
Nikky-Guninder Kaur Singh, Eleanor Nesbitt

TRANSACTIONAL ANALYSIS
Mark Widdowson

POETRY
Jeffrey Wainwright

POLITICS AND RELIGION
Jeffrey Haynes

SEMIOTICS (fifth edition)
Daniel Chandler

EDUCATION (second edition)
Kay Wood

SPOKEN ENGLISH
Michael McCarthy and Steve Walsh

BUSINESS START-UP
Alexandrina Pauceanu

ACTING HEIGHTENED TEXT
Catherine Weidner

LIBERTARIANISM
Jessica Flanigan and Christopher Freiman

CLOSE READING (second edition)
David Greenham

FEMINISM
Renee Heberle

MINDFULNESS
Sophie Sansom, David Shannon, and Taravajra

URBAN DESIGN
Tim Heath and Florian Wiedmann

PUBLIC RELATIONS (second edition)
Deborah A. Silverman

EDUCATION STUDIES
Catherine Simon

DRAG
Mark Edward and Chris Greenough

For more information about this series, please visit: www.routledge.com/The-Basics/book-series/B

PUBLIC RELATIONS
THE BASICS

Second Edition

Deborah A. Silverman

NEW YORK AND LONDON

Designed cover image: alexmak72427/Getty

Second edition published 2026
by Routledge
605 Third Avenue, New York, NY 10158

and by Routledge
4 Park Square, Milton Park, Abingdon, Oxon, OX14 4RN

Routledge is an imprint of the Taylor & Francis Group, an informa business

First edition published by Routledge 2014

ISBN: 978-1-032-86075-6 (hbk)
ISBN: 978-1-032-86074-9 (pbk)
ISBN: 978-1-003-52121-1 (ebk)

DOI: 10.4324/9781003521211

Typeset in Bembo
by SPi Technologies India Pvt Ltd (Straive)

CONTENTS

PART I
UNDERSTANDING PUBLIC RELATIONS

Public relations. What do those words mean? For some people, "public relations" means a terrific job in a large city at an agency that communicates on behalf of multiple clients. For others, "public relations" is an equally satisfying career communicating for a nonprofit organization in a small town. For still others, the meaning of "public relations" lies somewhere in between: as a military public affairs officer, an independent consultant, a hospital public relations manager, a university vice president for communication, a publicist for a celebrity, a corporate communication specialist at a bank, a communication director for a sports team … the list goes on and on.

Many of us who work in public relations have strived to explain to our families what we do for a living. This book offers an answer: It's a tremendously rewarding, fulfilling communication career with promising job prospects. In the first part of this book, you'll learn about the benefits of public relations, definitions and the history of public relations, current issues in the profession, ethics and professionalism, settings where public relations is used, public relations writing, and communication theories.

DOI: 10.4324/9781003521211-1

A FIRST LOOK AT PUBLIC RELATIONS

This chapter introduces you to the profession of public relations: What it is and what it isn't. It outlines the benefits that public relations offers organizations and society at large. It also introduces the ethical base of the art and science of public relations.

What is public relations about? Think of the Netflix series "Emily in Paris." A young American communication professional, Emily Cooper, moves to Paris to join the French subsidiary of her American public relations firm. She's a social media whiz kid (think Instagram Stories) who must adjust to life in a multicultural, established PR agency headed by an older French public relations executive, Sylvie Grateau. Viewers learn about pitches for public relations campaigns, social media posts, news releases, special events, ethical dilemmas for the agency, and more. It's a glamorous, glorified look at PR—but there is so much more to the discipline.

This book focuses on public relations, one of the **humanities**. It's an aspect of culture with ethical norms and a social perspective capable of uplifting society and making sense of human experience. As such, it is associated with language and philosophy.

DOI: 10.4324/9781003521211-2

Public relations also is associated with the **arts**, particularly through the important role of design and visual communication in the discipline.

Finally, public relations is a **science**, specifically an applied social science with theoretical models based in research, driven by data, and focused on solving a practical problem.

Together, these concepts of public relations set the stage for looking at a discipline that helps us understand society and human behavior.

WHAT PUBLIC RELATIONS IS

Public relations professionals have spent a lot of time thinking about what "public relations" is. Here are several contemporary definitions by leading public relations organizations.

> *Public relations is a strategic communication process that builds mutually beneficial relationships between organizations and their publics.*
>
> Public Relations Society of America

> *Public relations is the discipline that looks after reputation, with the aim of earning understanding and support and influencing opinion and behaviour. It is the planned and sustained effort to establish and maintain goodwill and understanding between an organization and its publics.*
>
> Chartered Institute of Public Relations, United Kingdom

> *Public relations is the strategic management of relationships between an organization and its diverse publics, through the use of communication, to achieve mutual understanding, realize organizational goals and serve the public interest.*
>
> Canadian Public Relations Society

> *Public relations is a decision-making management practice tasked with building relationships and interests between organisations and their publics based on the delivery of information through trusted and ethical communication methods.*
>
> International Public Relations Association

> *Public relations is the deliberate, planned and sustained effort to establish and maintain mutual understanding between an organisation (or individual) and its (or their) publics. It's the key to effective communication in all sectors of business, government, academic and not-for-profit.*
>
> Communications and Public Relations Australia

> *Public relations is the management, through communication, of perceptions and strategic relationships between an organization and its internal and external stakeholders.*
>
> Public Relations Institute of Southern Africa

> *Public relations is a strategic discipline that focuses on reaching and influencing an organization's stakeholders.*
>
> Middle East Public Relations Association

Notice the emphasis in these definitions on strategic management, relationships, mutual understanding, planning, goodwill, and public interest.

Contemporary public relations has several attributes that apply equally to corporations, nonprofit organizations, and social causes, both large and small.

First, public relations operates on a principle of *mutual benefits*; it seeks not only to assist the sponsoring organization but also to benefit its publics. It's committed to the *public interest* and the betterment of society.

It adheres to high *ethical standards* of honesty, accuracy, decency, and truth. Many organizations have clear *codes of ethics* outlining such commitments.

Public relations operates with *transparency* in an open environment, aligning itself with *democratic ideals* of the right of people to know the source of messages and to accept or reject those messages. It appreciates *diversity* and the cultural distinction of its publics, and particularly respects the rights and dignity of minorities within its publics.

Organizations must be *accountable* to their publics. Most publics are increasing their expectations for *quality performance* and *open communication.* Organizations can succeed only when they perform at a high level, delivering quality products and services. All organizations operate in a *competitive environment.* Publics sought by competitors will remain loyal only to those organizations that earn their loyalty consistently and continuously.

As part of the *management function* within an organization, public relations counsels organizational leaders. It brings to the decision-making table *theories* born of ongoing *research* and both original and existing *data* to drive decisions through *strategic planning*. It seeks to develop systematic, sustained communication to address issues in common with its various publics. This communication is rooted in the organization's mission as lived out through its *bottom line*, which goes beyond money earned or raised; it focuses on the organization's fundamental purpose. Public relations strategists plot courses, set objectives, and measure results.

Public relations maintains a *proactive*, *two-way*, *ongoing dialogue* with the organization's various publics. Such dialogue seeks to represent one to the other and to nurture an environment in which each can influence the other. This involves *listening*, not only hearing but also understanding another perspective. In this *boundary-spanning capacity*, public relations can assist the organization in *adapting* its products, services, and ideas toward the interests of its publics.

Within an organization, effective communication involves *cooperation* between public relations and other organizational functions such as marketing, legal, human resources, quality control, and fundraising. Each discipline should have an effective and equal voice around the boardroom table.

Mergers, downsizing, and restructuring have led both businesses and nonprofits to seek ways to operate with *leaner resources*, and the duplication that exists when marketing is isolated from public relations is too great a price for organizations to pay.

Many *media changes* are affecting the way organizations communicate. Digital and social media have made it easy for organizations to bypass the traditional news media "gatekeepers," although news media remain useful as communication tools. Increasing advertising costs and tighter budgets have led organizations to look at more cost-effective owned media, such as websites and email, as well as social media.

Organizations are successful to the extent that they enjoy a strong *reputation*, which results from neither accident nor luck. Strategic planning can identify and evaluate an organization's visibility and reputation.

Organizations are realizing the need for long-term, *mutually beneficial relationships* between the organization and its various publics. Public relations practitioners have long recognized this; more recently marketing has expressed this idea as *relationship marketing*.

Not surprisingly, public relations is one of the fastest-growing professions and one of the most competitive. Universities find that the number of students wishing to study public relations often exceeds their ability to hire enough faculty to keep pace with the enrollment trend. Employers report receiving hundreds of viable applications for a single job opening.

This signals a healthy future for public relations, and for people who are willing to develop their skills in communication and problem-solving, making themselves competitive in a profession that knows few boundaries.

WHAT PUBLIC RELATIONS IS NOT

Many misunderstandings surround public relations. Some result from confusing, outdated, or partial information. Other misunderstandings seem more deliberate, the result of willfully looking only at the dark side and assuming that the worst example is the norm.

Let's look at these **fallacies**—*erroneous statements*—so that we can glimpse the positive side of public relations.

Fallacy: PR equates to lying, hype, and exaggeration.

Reality: Truth is a foundation of public relations. "That's just PR" overlooks the standard of verifiable performance and sees only the illusion of smoke and mirrors. If public relations was so negative, it couldn't last. Public relations is about accuracy and honesty.

Fallacy: PR is just a form of propaganda.

Reality: Propaganda lives in a world of half-truths, innuendo, misrepresentation, and hidden bias. Public relations focuses on the polar opposites. Years ago, the terms "propaganda" and "public relations" were used interchangeably, so it's not hard to understand that some people have not updated themselves on the nuances of the terms or the fact that no reputable public relations professional engages in anything like propaganda.

Fallacy: PR is secretive and insidious.

Reality: Public relations professionals work with journalists and others to tell an accurate and timely story about their organizations. But much of the work of public relations is behind the scenes: researching, advising, counseling, strategizing, planning. So it is generally off the radar for most journalists and other observers. However, secretive means uncommunicative, and public relations is anything but. Open, honest, and timely communication is at the heart of public relations.

Fallacy: PR tries to keep the public ignorant about what's really happening.

Reality: Public relations flourishes only in a democracy, where many voices participate in debate on public issues. It enables people or organizations with different viewpoints to advocate and argue toward consensus—or, if that isn't forthcoming, at least toward a fair policy in which the majority accommodates the concerns of the minority.

Fallacy: PR tries to control unsuspecting people.

Reality: Public relations definitely does not try to control anyone. It couldn't even if it tried, because mind control doesn't work, at least not in the public arena. Public relations does, however, seek to influence. It does this by building relationships to add value to organizations by increasing willingness of publics to support rather than oppose those organizations. And that's more than a semantic difference between control and influence.

Fallacy: PR is only about spin, making bad guys look good.

Reality: The term "spin" is wrong on so many levels. It suggests a hired gun who tries to make bad things look good, or at least less bad. Public relations serves the public interest by providing a voice for all in the court of public opinion. It advances society just as does its legal parallel, in which even people charged with a crime and presumed by some observers to be guilty deserve a vigorous defense by ethical attorneys. The court of public opinion isn't always fair. Both sides may not have equal representation, and there's no wise judge, no impartial jury to deliberate. Still, public relations gives every party an opportunity to present its case to perhaps the only jury that really matters—the public.

> Fallacy: PR works only for powerful groups with deep pockets: corporations, government, lobbyists, and others who work against the best interests of average people.

Reality: Public relations enhances democratic values by providing for multiple voices in the marketplace of ideas. For every cereal manufacturer advertising sugary food to kids, dozens of nonprofit groups use public relations to educate parents on childhood nutrition, expose the false claims of marketers, and advocate for effective public oversight on marketing practices. The same is true for issues ranging from climate change to women's reproductive rights.

> Fallacy: PR is only publicity.

Reality: Publicity accounts for only a small slice of the public relations pie. Thanks to ever-evolving digital and social media, organizations now can go directly to their publics without needing the assistance of journalists. "Mere PR" inaccurately dismisses the profession as being inconsequential and unnecessary. It also misses the point that—in addition to being skilled writers, social media specialists, and so on—public relations practitioners also are experts in strategy, management, and other problem-solving aspects of organizational life.

> Fallacy: Anybody can do PR.

Reality: It's true that public relations doesn't require a license as do dentistry, law, and funeral services. So anybody can call himself or herself a PR person, and who's to disagree? But public relations is a profession rooted in research, ethics, strategic planning, and evaluation, as well as effective written, spoken, and visual communication. It is based on a course of study. So it's more accurate to say that anyone who has acquired the skills and adopted the ethical standards can do the work of public relations.

> Fallacy: PR is the guy with the shovel following the elephants in a circus parade.

Reality: Sometimes public relations is asked to clean up the mess caused by others, usually managers who made bad decisions with even worse consequences, often because they failed to consider public relations perspectives before they acted. But rather than being the Band-Aid, public relations has become the wellness program and preventative medicine that helps avoids the problem in the first place.

> Fallacy: PR has a dark history, such as campaigns to get women to smoke and books that guided the Nazi propaganda machine.

Reality: In the past, research sometimes looked at how the uneducated masses could be influenced and manipulated. That's where research was in the early 20th century. But theory and research also have developed, as has the rest of society. It's true that an early public relations campaign aimed for social acceptance of women smokers. That was when society discriminated overtly against women and when even doctors and nurses smoked, before we learned of the associated dangers. So it's more accurate to point out that public relations, from its early foundations as a profession, has been used in many ways to uplift society and help people who have been oppressed and marginalized—and yes, to sell cigarettes and all the other consumer products that corporations provide.

It's easy to criticize any organization if you focus only on the excesses, exaggerations, and aberrations rather than the best practices, high standards, and good work. Schools? Look at all the dropouts, cost-inefficiencies, bullying, and poorly-educated graduates. Focusing only on such negatives is an exercise in paranoia. It may be fun for people who enjoy reading about conspiracy theories, but it's not useful for understanding real-world relationships.

ADVANTAGES OF PUBLIC RELATIONS

Public relations helps society at large, as well as the organizations and people within society, in a number of ways:

- *Financial Well-being.* Businesses and nonprofit organizations can save money with programs that retain customers, increase productivity, and influence legislation. They can make money by generating new customers and by attracting interest in new products and services, as well as by enhancing the support of stockholders and donors.

- *Health*. Public relations can lead to healthy lifestyles with education and advocacy programs such as those that encourage people to control obesity, eat more nutritious meals, exercise regularly, and check for early signs of disease.
- *Safety*. Public relations can save lives through programs advocating behaviors related to seatbelt use, bicycle helmets, organ donation, child abduction, and more.
- *Civic Awareness*. Government agencies and lawmakers promote programs and services to their constituents. Military units use public relations to recruit, foster public support, and report their progress to members, families, and legislators.
- *Recreation*. Public relations within the sports and entertainment worlds can help people enjoy their leisure time. Sports teams, entertainers, recreational facilities, and travel destinations use public relations to publicize events and engage fans. Every leisure activity from gaming to football, bird watching to painting engages in public relations.
- *Community Service*. Nonprofit organizations such as schools, churches, and charities promote their services and share their expertise. Hospitals and medical organizations promote health literacy and thus help people make healthy choices.
- *Reputation*. Public relations helps organizations to gain support and minimize opposition by generating favorable publicity, encouraging alliances with other groups, and testing plans against the interests of the organization's publics.
- *Survival*. Public relations helps organizations weather crises, survive lawsuits, and reverse negative opinions.

THE PUBLICS OF PUBLIC RELATIONS

When public relations professionals talk about the organizations and the people they engage, they sometimes use the language of **systems theory**, *theory that explains an organization's relationships with its publics*.

The concept of open or closed systems indicates the extent to which an organization interacts with its environment. **Open systems** *interact frequently and easily*; **closed systems**, not so much. Public relations generally operates best with open systems; that is, with organizations that are ready, willing, and able to engage their many publics.

Systems theory offers the idea of **linkages**, *patterns in which an organization interacts with its various publics*. Every public can fit into one of four linkage patterns: **customers**, *publics who use the product or service*; **producers**, *publics who make it, such as employees, volunteers, suppliers, and financial backers*; **enablers**, *publics who help an organization exist and prosper, such as opinion leaders, regulators, allies, or media*; and **limiters**, *publics who undermine an organization's success, such as competitors, opponents, unfriendly media, watchdog organizations, and opinion leaders who hold negative views of the organization.*

Let's take a university as an example. Among the customer publics, students and potential students are obviously important as primary customers. But don't stop there. Secondary customers include graduate schools that eventually will receive applications from graduates of the university and organizations that eventually will hire the graduates.

Producer publics would include the university's employees. These can be subdivided: faculty and staff, longtime and new employees, tenured and non-tenured faculty, full-time and part-time instructors, volunteer members of university boards, and so on. Then add the important people that help the university produce its "product" (i.e., education): alumni, donors, foundations, state and federal grants, book suppliers, and state legislators in the case of public universities.

Enabler publics provide support and foster a positive environment. For the university, this category includes opinion leaders such as parents and career counselors who help students make academic choices. It includes regulators such as state education departments, educational oversight agencies, and accrediting organizations—groups that can create a positive academic environment—and news media that can distribute the university's message to other publics.

Community colleges that serve as feeder programs for transfer students and other universities that function as colleagues are also enabler publics. Enablers also include the surrounding community—neighbors, local government, police agencies, restaurants, bookstores and entertainment sites, and landlords providing off-campus housing.

Limiter publics, on the other hand, are groups that may negatively impact the university, such as news media that disseminate negative stories, activists who are critical of the university's position on controversial topics, or other universities competing for the same students. Limiters also can be threatening environmental factors, such as high interest rates on student loans or demographic factors such as fewer people of high school and college age.

Each of these groups is in a relationship not only with the university but also with each other and with additional groups unrelated to the university. Thus, each is a player on the public relations stage.

HOW ORGANIZATIONS USE PUBLIC RELATIONS

What types of organizations use public relations? All kinds. It's hard to think of any organization that doesn't engage in public relations in some way. Some practitioners work for departments within corporations or nonprofit organizations. Others work for public relations agencies that are hired by corporations or nonprofits to handle particular public relations needs.

In either setting—in-house or agency—the work generally falls into one of several categories. Here's a look, along with related case studies.

CORPORATE PUBLIC RELATIONS

Corporate public relations *provides the vehicle for businesses to publicize products, gain customers, motivate productivity and workplace safety, and maintain a communication link with investors, regulators, and industry colleagues.*

Public relations is an everyday aspect of business in most corporations, such as the fashion, automobile, and pharmaceutical industries; small businesses such as garden centers and corner cafes; service providers from hair salons to hospitals; and leisure entities such as sports teams, hotels, and travel agencies. Even public relations agencies, newspapers, and television stations have their own public relations professionals to engage their customers, attract new business, and promote their role within the community.

Today, most corporate public relations professionals are engaged in **integrated marketing communication**, *a blend of public relations and marketing that allows organizations to strategically use every possible* *communication tool to engage and communicate with their customers and other significant publics.*

Practitioners who work in corporate public relations are committed to helping their businesses. They also understand that the ethical practice of public relations is, in the long run, in the best interests of their company. They have observed that corporations that hide behind pseudo public relations to deceive customers, or mask corporate wrongdoing, inevitably find themselves in the public spotlight.

Consider these well-publicized instances of corporate misconduct: Facebook allowing harvesting of data from its users without their consent, German financial services company Wirecard overreporting its cash balances, Chinese coffee chain Luckin Coffee reporting large sums in fraudulent transactions, Enron hiding debts, Volkswagen cheating on emissions tests, and many other scandals involving corruption, bribery, tax evasion, illegal political contributions, sex scandals, and environmental offenses. Usually, the stonewalling and attempted (and always unsuccessful) cover-up is the greater crime, at least in the court of public opinion.

Thus for both ethical and pragmatic reasons, public relations practitioners often find themselves as the corporate conscience and voice of reason, urging companies to operate with transparency, integrity, and accountability.

7-ELEVEN SLURPEES

As a legacy brand, 7-Eleven needed to sustain its growth into the next 50 years by targeting Gen Z and young Millennials. The challenge: to create a culturally relevant new vibe and point of view for the company's iconic Slurpee drink to usher in a new generation of Slurpee fans across its 13,000 stores.

Research found that consumers view 7-Eleven as a nostalgic brand, even if they didn't grow up with it, and that they have strong affinities for specific cultural fandoms: gaming, fashion, music, and sports.

The public relations strategy was to keep the nostalgic drink dominating news and social media feeds all summer long with a steady drumbeat of news targeting the music and fashion fan communities. "The Summer of Slurpee" kicked off with an announcement of the Slurpee rebrand, pitched to national news media. Next, Slurpee teamed with rapper Flo Milli to release her "Anything Flows" song, featuring Slurpee-inspired verses and cameos from rising stars Kari Faux, 2Rare, and Maiya the Don on streaming platforms. Slurpee invited consumers to submit lyrics to the track's open verse. The top entry would land a spot on the song's remix that would drop at the end of the summer. Consumers who weren't ready to step up to the mic could win custom pieces of Slurpee-inspired jewelry from King Ice or the chance to be an extra in a Lyrical Lemonade music video.

Everything culminated with the brand's biggest day of the year—July 11, 7-Eleven's Slurpee Day. In addition to the brand's traditional offer of free Slurpees on that day, for this campaign, the company revealed an 11-day extended timeframe and three extra opportunities to get a free Slurpee, limited edition birthday merch on its website, and an exclusive birthday digital collectible.

The successful campaign earned coverage in trade and consumer publications. It generated nearly 1.65 billion media impressions and 813 media placements. The release of the single by Flo Milli earned over 2.5 million streams on Spotify. The news around Slurpee Day surpassed 5 billion impressions, including coverage on top morning TV shows like TODAY and Fox & Friends. A post-campaign survey found that 96 percent of consumers are more likely to purchase a Slurpee after seeing the campaign.

GOVERNMENT RELATIONS AND PUBLIC AFFAIRS

Government relations *involves an organization's efforts to build and maintain a working relationship with elected or appointed government officials*. Organizations present information to government officials and sometimes use **lobbying**, *persuasive campaigns to support, defeat, or amend legislation that's necessary to an organization's own interests*. From small nonprofits to large corporations, all organizations sometimes mount public relations campaigns for or against various issues such as health care, business regulation, product safety, and more.

Related to government relations is **public affairs**, *efforts by government agencies to inform their publics about programs and services, to* *respond to inquiries, and gauge public opinion.* From the White House to Whitehall, every government agency throughout the world has to communicate with constituents; see the government health campaign described below.

PREVENT OVERDOSE WA

The United States is experiencing a drug overdose epidemic fueled by the proliferation of potent synthetic opioids containing fentanyl. In the state of Washington alone, overdose deaths involving opioids increased more than 160 percent between 2018 and 2022, and thousands more struggle with opioid use.

To address this problem, the Washington State Department of Health and its PR agency, C+C, created a campaign to reduce overdose deaths by building awareness about the opioid crisis and "harm reduction" to motivate people to take steps to reduce the likelihood of overdose deaths.

The campaign, which recruited people who use opioids into the research, included six research phases: secondary research, stakeholder interviews, message testing, concept testing, a statewide survey, and evaluation of ad recall.

This research helped the team narrow its campaign focus to the most immediate behavior that can help save lives: getting more people to know how to use naloxone, a nasal spray that can reverse an opioid overdose. Research also identified two key publics: people who use opioids and their "care networks," people who have a close relationship with an opioid user. Four campaign objectives were defined: 1) Increase the number of people who are aware of, carry, and know how to use naloxone; 2) Drive orders for free naloxone in the 13 Washington counties with the highest overdose rates; 3) Increase the number of people who feel confident intervening if they encounter someone experiencing an overdose; 4) Address stigma through a compassionate and non-judgmental approach.

The resulting campaign in English and Spanish, Prevent Overdose WA/No más sobredosis WA, gave people information to identify an overdose and how to stop it. Tactics included using media to raise awareness of naloxone with a website containing information about signs of an overdose, and promoting easy mail order access to naloxone. A video told the story of someone using naloxone to save a friend's life. Digital video, digital audio, TV, Snapchat, TikTok, Facebook, Instagram, and billboards targeted key publics.

The campaign achieved all of its objectives and it began to address stigma through a compassionate, non-judgmental approach.

PUBLIC DIPLOMACY

Public diplomacy is related to government public relations. Formal state-to-state diplomacy usually is conducted in secret. **Public diplomacy** *is the overlap area in which governments use the power and influence of the media to impact public opinion in another country or perhaps within a nongovernmental organization, corporation, political faction, or non-profit organization.*

There have been many times when, during a civil war or internal uprisings in various countries, an outside government would float ideas and allow leaks to encourage the strife-torn country to accept internal reform, make peace with warring factions, or otherwise resolve the conflict. Sometimes, the public diplomacy has been directed toward a third country with influence over the leaders of the conflicted nation, encouraging them to make the necessary concessions or allow the needed reforms. For example, in 2016, Carnival Corporation worked behind the scenes with the US and Cuban governments to secure approval to become the first US cruise company since the Kennedy administration to sail to Cuba.

Public diplomacy tools include traditional publicity vehicles, social media, opinion leaders, and public appeals to religious and cultural leaders.

US-KOREA CONNECT

After the US-Korea Free Trade Agreement (KORUS FTA) was put into effect, the Korean government wanted to make sure that American businesses knew about the free trade agreement and benefits of trade with Korea. So the Embassy of the Republic of Korea hired FINN Partners to create an awareness campaign with two strategies: creation of content about the benefits of trade with Korea and development of a national network of businesses interested in US-Korea trade under the new agreement.

Program messaging highlighted the importance of Korea as an American trading partner and addressed the positive economic and strategic impact of the agreement. Content included monthly newsletters, state trade fact sheets, business success stories, blog posts, KORUS FTA trade data brochures, media coverage, op-eds, social media content, and the US-Korea Connect website. Network development programming included social media, business events, Embassy of the Republic of Korea receptions, trade delegations, and cultivating relationships with key international trade thought leaders.

The US-Korea Connect program has been a resounding success. It established the Embassy of Korea as the resource for information on the US-Korea Free Trade Agreement. The campaign built awareness of Korea's role as an essential US trade partner.

POLITICAL PUBLIC RELATIONS

Political public relations *focuses on the process of getting elected and staying in office.* Practiced by ethical professionals, political public relations can positively impact public opinion and generate support for candidates and issues. Though the environment may be highly partisan and the players often confrontational, nevertheless, there is an important role for civic-minded experts with skills in polling, issue analysis, strategic planning, and writing.

The day-to-day work of political public relations involves research into a candidate's image and constituents' take on public policy issues. It deals with publicity for candidates and their positions.

Two types of tactics are common in political public relations: special events such as press-the-flesh rallies and public debates, and media relations with an increasing emphasis on social media. Fundraising and political advertising also play a huge role.

Unfortunately, political public relations also exemplifies many of the most egregious excesses and irregularities associated with public relations. In too many situations, political public relations involves negative strategy (name calling, dirty tricks, attack ads, vilification of opponents, misrepresentation, and outright lying). It is public relations stripped of its ethical base, commitment to honest communication, and any vision of mutual benefits and social responsibility.

WRITE-IN CAMPAIGN

It's almost impossible to buck the system when it comes to party endorsements in US politics. But a strong public relations plan fed an upset when Lisa Murkowski became the first write-in candidate in 56 years to win a US Senate seat.

Murkowski, a Republican, had been a US senator from Alaska. She was beaten in a primary, largely because of opposition from the Tea Party faction of her party. But when polling showed that she had strong voter support, she launched a write-in campaign. The task had all of the expected goals related to funding, visibility, and appeals to voter interests, plus one additional factor. Write-ins require proper spelling of the candidate's name, and Murkowski isn't your typical Brown, Smith, or Jones. So the campaign distributed 50,000 bracelets with Murkowski's name.

Other than that, the public relations plan relied heavily on social media, which was especially effective in countering Tea Party opposition messages. It also featured the standard fare for political public relations: news releases, speeches, TV and newspaper interviews and news reports, meetings with editorial boards of newspapers, issue papers, televised debates, e-mails and phone calls to voters, websites with frequent updates and redesigns to attract repeat visitors, and downloadable videos.

The result was that Murkowski received 10,000 votes more than her nearest rival, the party-endorsed Republican.

NONPROFIT PUBLIC RELATIONS

Nonprofit public relations *involves a wide variety of organizations: education, health care, cultural and religious groups, human service agencies and charitable organizations, and membership organizations such as unions and professional groups.* The nonprofit sphere also involves travel and tourism, entertainment, and some aspects of sports and recreation.

A key element of nonprofit public relations is that journalists in both traditional news media and social media are more likely to be supportive. Consider these typical activities by nonprofit organizations:

- Introduction of a fundraising campaign for a new hospital wing to extend cancer treatment.
- Announcement of a grant based on promising research into a childhood disease.
- Appointment of a new religious leader for a denomination with many members in the community.
- Final preparation in staging a benefit performance by a touring musical artist.
- Creation of a foundation for inner-city children by a sports celebrity who just signed a multi-million-dollar contract.

Reporters don't cover these news stories with the same skepticism and watchdog mentality with which they approach corporations and politicians. That is one reason that many practitioners prefer nonprofit public relations, particularly because they can deal every day with causes that serve the public good and contribute to a better society.

Like corporations, nonprofit organizations have faced reputational damage, social media attacks, funding losses, or threats to organizational safety after taking public stands on social issues such as abortion access, immigrant rights, LGBTQ rights, Palestinian rights, or diversity, equity, and inclusion (DEI). In response, many nonprofits have adopted strategies to insulate their programs and staff, such as increasing security measures and making programmatic changes.

TEN LIVES CLUB

Like many nonprofits, Ten Lives Club in Buffalo, NY has partnered with professional athletes as spokespersons. Buffalo Bills place kicker Tyler Bass, a cat lover, was showcased in a Ten Lives Club fundraising campaign.

Months later, when Bass was harshly criticized on social media after missing a critical field goal in a Bills game against the Kansas City Chiefs, resulting in the Bills' elimination from the playoffs,

Ten Lives Club came to his defense. "We stand with Tyler Bass. Don't bully our friend. He's an excellent football player and an even better person who took the time to help our organization and rescue cats last year," said the club on social media. That triggered a flood of donations to Ten Lives Club, many people donating $22 in honor of Bass's jersey number, 2. Within a few weeks, Ten Lives Club had raised $400,000 (£320,903; €381,075), and after its public relations manager was interviewed on national television about the donations in Bass's name, still more donations poured in.

PUBLIC RELATIONS FOR SOCIAL REFORM

Public relations for social reform has an ancient history. It sometimes overlaps with nonprofit public relations and nongovernmental organizations, but it differs in that it generally is movement-based rather than linked to a specific organization. For example, Amnesty International focuses on international social reform on behalf of prisoners of conscience and political prisoners.

Yet the movement for fair treatment of political prisoners is broader than that one organization. It involves many educational institutions, religious groups, legal organizations, and human rights entities all working toward a similar end, but without the coordination of a single organization.

One of the most significant social reform movements involved the abolition of slavery or the slave trade in many countries—England, France, Australia, the US, and many European colonies and possessions. Public relations played a major part in the abolition cause with publicity, speeches, books and pamphlets, lobbying, advertising, and eventually newspapers, radio, and television.

Such anti-slavery campaigns have been so successful over the past two centuries that institutional slavery is now banned throughout the world. But dark shadows remain: human trafficking, child slavery, and the sex trade. Public relations practitioners use not only traditional tactics but social media on behalf of their cause to eradicate the remnants of such captivity and abuse.

Other reform movements similarly have benefitted from public relations support: domestic violence, suffrage campaigns for the right of women to vote, safety standards for food, animal rights, educational reform, reduction of gun violence, humane treatment of the mentally ill, elimination of child labor, pro-peace/anti-war campaigns, and elimination or regulation of prostitution, smoking, drugs, and alcohol.

Today the public relations fight continues with activism on many issues such as women's reproductive rights, environmental protection, religious freedom, LGBTQ rights, rights of aboriginal/native peoples, abolition of the death penalty, pornography, and gambling.

"HE'S COMING HOME"

Women's Aid, a British charity dedicated to ending domestic violence against women and children, launched its "He's Coming Home" campaign during the World Cup in 2022. The campaign aims to shine a light on the darker side of major football championships, which could lead to an increase in domestic violence.

Women's Aid partnered with UK creative agency House 337. Their research found that cases of domestic abuse rise by 38 percent during major sporting events, intensifying during football tournaments like the European Football Championship, known as the Euros.

The multi-channel campaign, which went viral, appeared on billboards, was featured in a film, posted across social media, and received widespread news media coverage. The campaign got attention from political figures such as Prime Minister Keir Starmer, the Home Office, national police authorities, policymakers, and local councils. It generated 23 million TikTok views and extensive sharing across social media platforms. As a result, Women's Aid saw a 78 percent increase in traffic to its website and a 44 percent rise in visits to its "Donate" page.

The 2024 installment of the campaign, coinciding with the Euros 2024 tournament, featured specially created football scarves imprinted with well-known football chants revised to highlight the domestic abuse crisis, such as "No More Years of Hurt." The campaign has enabled Women's Aid to enlist key figures in politics and football as allies along with celebrity ambassadors and is credited with raising awareness of domestic violence as an issue.

PUBLIC RELATIONS, PERFORMANCE, AND ADAPTATION

"Actions speak louder than words." You've probably heard this saying, which applies to public relations practitioners. Act appropriately and strategically, and the words will follow.

Public relations involves the notion of helping organizations adjust to the social environment. This builds on the advice of Edward Bernays, a founding father of the public relations profession, who advised that the "engineering of consent" rests on information, persuasion, and adjustment by the organization to its publics.

Some organizations see the difference between performance and pronouncements, between word and deed.

Narcotics Anonymous, for example, says "our public relations policy is based on attraction rather than promotion." That's a good formula even if you are not an addict in recovery, because it reflects the humility and transparency that underlies any good public relations program. Trustees of the organization note that "most addicts will only hear of us through media reports and announcements, through professional referral, or through direction given by members of the community-at-large—or they won't hear of us at all." For that reason, says Narcotics Anonymous, cooperative relationships within the community are necessary to the organization's ability to help people in need.

Some groups go out of their way to engage critics. Ford Motors has been applauded by the Sierra Club for developing a hybrid SUV, but the same environmental group also denounced Ford for having the most gas-guzzling cars in the industry. Yet Ford meets regularly with the Sierra Club, noting that such interaction gives it signals of what consumers want and expect. Even if they can't agree on everything, both sides see the engagement as a positive.

EXAMPLES OF ADAPTATION

An important strategy in public relations is **adaptation**—*the ability of an organization to make changes on the basis of what its publics want and need.* Adaptation is a critical component of organizational performance. Such changes in the way an organization does business can help it thrive in a competitive marketplace.

Here are some examples of adaptation:

— Netflix: Originally known for DVD rental by mail, it transitioned to a subscription-based streaming service, then began producing original content like *The Crown* and *Stranger Things*, becoming a global leader in streaming and entertainment.
— Amazon: From its origins as an online bookstore, Amazon expanded into a diversified e-commerce platform, cloud computing, and digital streaming, revolutionizing the retail and cloud computing industries.
— IBM: It shifted focus from hardware manufacturing to software, computer services, and consulting, with an emphasis on AI and cloud computing, becoming a major player in enterprise IT solutions and AI development.
— Tesla: First known for its electric sports cars for niche markets, Tesla expanded to mass-market electric vehicles, clean energy solutions, and autonomous driving technologies, impacting the automotive and renewable energy industries.
— Disney: The film production, television, and theme park giant—originally an animation studio—transformed by launching Disney+, focusing on direct-to-consumer streaming alongside its traditional businesses and establishing itself as a major competitor in the streaming space.

PUBLIC RELATIONS, IMAGE, AND REPUTATION

A squirrel is a rat with good public relations. This statement lightheartedly links public relations with reputation. What people know and think of something—whether that something is an organization, a person, or a rodent—is important with regards to how they treat it. Reputation spells the difference between like and dislike, support and opposition, feeding the cute critter, or setting a trap for it.

But the squirrel-rat allusion misses much of what reputation is about. While part of reputation is based on image, a bigger part is based on action. Reputation is rooted in how a person or organization (or rodent) acts. Regardless of the cuteness quotient that Disney gives squirrels, any farmer or gardener knows that destructive behavior means that the furry beast is no friend.

Reputation *is the general, overall, and long-term impression of an organization on a specific public.* Reputation is rooted in what people know, or think they know, about an organization and what attitudes they hold based on that information.

Reputation management *is the process of seeking to influence the way publics view and understand the organization.* It begins with tracking and identifying what others say and feel about an organization, with a focus on building and maintaining a desired reputation with key publics. In critical times, reputation management can be part of crisis communication, with the organization attempting to recover from a negative environment.

From a public relations perspective, reputation is the result of what you do, what you say, and what others say about you. One reason for the continuing growth of public relations is that organizations are paying more attention to this, realizing that what people say affects the bottom line.

Reputation is probably the single most-important asset an organization has. Consider Apple, the world's most valuable brand worth $516 billion (£411 billion, €495 billion). The company's reputation and branding have made it a worldwide leader for products and services such as smartphones, personal computers, tablets, and Apple Music.

Warren Buffett, one of the world's most successful business investors, famously told employees of the scandal-riddled Salomon Brothers investment bank: "If you lose money for the firm by bad decisions, I will be very understanding. If you lose a shred of reputation for the firm, I will be ruthless."

Reputation is built up with consistent action over time, but it can be lost with a single bad decision. For example, Penn State decided not to report or investigate charges of child abuse. Attempting to avoid bad publicity, the university jeopardized its 157-year heritage, destroyed its place in the football record books, and risked its future as an athletics program, while earning an immediate $60 million (£48 million, €57 million) football fine and the likelihood of perhaps $500 million (£398 million, €480 million) in legal costs and fines.

Some confusion exists about the relationship between reputation and image. **Image** *is a short-term evaluation of an organization's messages,* *drawn from the way an organization projects itself toward its various publics.* Image is what people think about the organization based on both word and deed; that is, on the planned and unplanned verbal, visual, and behavioral messages that come from an organization and leave an impression. Not all publics receive the same messages or process them the same way, so image can be inconsistent and can vary from one public to another or from one time to another.

Reputation is interactive and closely associated with public relations; image is linked more with advertising and the production/presentation of branding messages.

Several additional terms are connected to the concepts of reputation and image. **Positioning** *is a process of managing how an organization distinguishes itself with a unique meaning in the mind of its publics.* A concept drawn from marketing, positioning is the organization's competitive posture.

Organizational **identity** *is the way an organization consciously projects itself visually as an expression of its personality.* An **identity system** *involves tools used by an organization to project its identity, including name and logo, uniform use of color, brochures, news releases, advertisements, social media sites, and other means of communication.*

UNITED TO BEAT MALARIA

Orkin, a leading pest-control company, has positioned itself as a protector of public health with many marketing and educational materials to help homeowners guard against mosquitos and other pests.

As part of a reputation-enhancement campaign, Orkin became a sponsor for the United Nations Foundation's "United to Beat Malaria" program, formerly called "Nothing But Nets." Since 2006, the global grassroots campaign has brought together a diverse set of partners from around the world to take action to end malaria, which kills a child nearly every minute. United to Beat Malaria prioritizes families with young children, pregnant women, displaced populations, remote communities with little to no healthcare access, and frontline healthcare workers who are fighting malaria in those communities.

United to Beat Malaria has helped to protect vulnerable people from malaria by raising funds to purchase and distribute mosquito bed nets and other life-saving tools. Its grassroots donor and major donor fundraising campaigns incorporate a wide array of communication tactics including community events across the globe, digital marketing, news releases, blogs, social media, an annual Leadership Summit, and successful advocacy efforts to lobby for funding from the US Congress and other governments.

Orkin's plan, called "Fight the Bite," focused largely on its employees, using print and social media to prepare employees as communicators about the benefits of mosquito netting. The Orkin campaign also reached customers through a media relations component and participation in United to Beat Malaria community events.

Orkin is one of dozens of United to Beat Malaria sponsors, which also include NBA Cares, the charity of the basketball league; MLS Works, the community outreach program of Major League Soccer; and *Sports Illustrated* magazine.

In recent years, donations from individuals have supported malaria projects in African nations such as Nigeria, Madagascar, Ethiopia, the Democratic Republic of the Congo, and South Sudan as well as malaria elimination efforts across 17 Latin American and Caribbean countries.

To date, United to Beat Malaria has helped protect over 40 million people from malaria in 61 countries and has raised over $75 million (£60 million, €72 million) in its fight to end malaria.

ETHICS AND PROFESSIONALISM

One of the hallmarks of public relations is a strong ethical base and a commitment to contribute to the public good while also serving the interests of the boss or client. Ethics is the distinguishing characteristic between a real public relations practitioner and someone with communication skills merely pretending to do public relations work.

The professional organizations in many countries of the world are strong upholders of ethical practice. Living as we do in a borderless world, the practice of public relations spans the globe, extending ethical norms that developed in North America, Western Europe, and Australia into new areas, such as the former Soviet Bloc republics and emerging democracies in Africa and the Middle East.

These codes of ethics emphasize professional values such as honesty, responsible advocacy for one's clients, responsible use of expertise, objective counsel, loyalty to one's clients, and fairness in dealings with clients, employers, and others. The codes also offer guidelines pertaining to the free flow of information, fair competition among public relations professionals, disclosure of information, safeguarding confidential information gained from clients, avoiding conflicts of interest, and working to enhance the public's trust in the public relations profession.

Because of their size, the professional organizations in the US, Canada, and UK are among the most influential across the globe. Their ethics codes are similar. For example, the Public Relations Society of America's ethics code resembles the code of conduct of the Chartered Institute of Public Relations in the UK and the code of professional standards of the Canadian Public Relations Society.

Additionally, professional standards are established by several wider organizations. The Global Alliance for Public Relations and Communication Management's code of ethics serves as a worldwide model.

Use a search engine to find the websites of professional groups associated with the Global Alliance. Altogether, nearly 100 national organizations exist to promote the work of ethical and effective public relations. Here's a partial list of countries with professional public relations organizations:

- In Europe: Czech Republic, Estonia, Finland, France, Germany, Greece, Iceland, Ireland, Italy, Latvia, Lithuania, Norway, Poland, Portugal, Slovenia, Spain, Sweden, Switzerland, Ukraine, and the United Kingdom.
- In the Middle East: Azerbaijan, Israel, Syria, and Turkey.
- In Asia: Bangladesh, China, India, Indonesia, Japan, Malaysia, the Philippines, Singapore, South Korea, and Vietnam.
- In the Americas: Argentina, Brazil, Canada, Cuba, Mexico, the United States, and Venezuela.
- In Africa: Egypt, Kenya, Nigeria, South Africa, and Sudan.
- In Australia and Oceania: Australia and New Zealand.

A question sometimes comes up: Why isn't there some kind of **licensing** to make sure that people who call themselves public relations practitioners actually know what they are doing and are committed to working ethically? After all, it requires a license to do acupuncture and physical therapy, to practice law or medicine, to be a teacher or pharmacist, and to operate a funeral home or work as a landscape architect or a realtor. Some of the licenses come from governments, others from professional groups. Most have educational requirements and testing.

All of these professions impact the people whom they serve, making licensing a reasonable rule. But public relations is different. As noted earlier in this chapter, public relations serves the public good. But it's also part of the wider issue of human rights. The United Nations and most countries have provisions for freedom of expression, open communication, free and generally unrestricted speech, and freedom of opinion. Allowing governments to limit these to people in a certain profession generally has been considered an unwarranted intrusion into individual liberties.

But the public relations profession has devised a middle ground between no limits and government approval for doing public relations: **accreditation**, *a process that involves the public relations profession setting and maintaining its own standards, rather than having them imposed from outside.*

In some countries, the professional organization has created a program of study, testing, sponsorship, and/or portfolio review. Practitioners voluntarily submit themselves for the accrediting process in return for the right to be acknowledged as an accredited practitioner of public relations.

In the United States, the Universal Accreditation Board oversees three credentials. The Accreditation in Public Relations (APR) designation serves as a mark of distinction given to public relations practitioners by public relations practitioners, attesting to the demonstrated expertise and commitment to the profession and its ethical standards. The Accreditation in Public Relations and Military Communications (APR+M) is for those working in military public affairs as members of US armed forces and civilian employees of the US Department of Defense. The Certificate in Principles of Public Relations is an entry-level credential for those entering the field.

The Universal Accreditation Board includes the Public Relations Society of America, several regional public relations groups, and discipline-specific groups such as the National School Public Relations Association, Religion Communicators Council, and the National Association of Government Communicators.

Public relations associations in Canada, Australia, India, the United Kingdom, and the Philippines have their own accreditation processes. Additionally, professional groups in many countries including the US, Ireland, the UK, and Australia have a voluntary process to certify universities that offer public relations programs.

WORKS CITED

Iyer, D. & Douglas, J. (Oct. 24, 2024). *Sounding the alarm: Nonprofits on the frontlines of a polarized political climate.* Building Movement Project. https://buildingmovement.org/blog/new-report-sounding-the-alarm/

MacIndoe, H., Faulk, L., & Kim, M. (Oct. 29, 2024). *Rising partisanship is making nonprofits more reluctant to engage in policy debates—New research.* The Conversation. https://theconversation.com/rising-partisanship-is-making-nonprofits-more-reluctant-to-engage-in-policy-debates-new-research-231225

Thompson, I. (Nov. 12, 2024). *Nonprofits face backlash for "controversial" work, report warns.* Nonprofit Quarterly. https://nonprofitquarterly.org/nonprofits-face-backlash-for-controversial-work-report-warns/

2

PUBLIC RELATIONS PAST AND PRESENT

This chapter provides an overview of the history and evolution of public relations as well current issues today. Rooted in social interaction throughout history, public relations has come into its own as a legitimate profession contributing to the improvement of society.

Public relations is as ancient as clay tablets in Mesopotamia and as modern as digital tablets. It is as traditional as a political speech in the public square and as cutting edge as an international social media campaign for human rights.

HISTORICAL ANTECEDENTS OF PUBLIC RELATIONS

Public relations is a natural, essential, and recurring element of human social interaction. It's part of what makes us human. As such, it's one of the oldest and most foundational aspects of society. It's difficult to imagine a society in which effective communication and information, advocacy, and positive relationships are not among the most basic components of everyday life.

Edward Bernays, one of the founding fathers of contemporary public relations, observed that "The three main elements of public

DOI: 10.4324/9781003521211-3

relations are practically as old as society: informing people, persuading people, or integrating people with people." Thus, understanding the evolution of public relations gives us glimpses into what the profession has become in today's world.

It's not accurate to say that this look back through the centuries reveals people who were consciously practicing public relations as we understand it today. But it does show that the various elements of public relations have been present in society since the earliest of times. In this chapter, these elements are printed in italics, so you can better observe some aspects of public relations throughout the ages.

Be forewarned: this look back also reveals that some past practices were unethical by today's standards. Traces of some of these remain today, generally disavowed by public relations practitioners but, nevertheless, part of the underbelly of persuasive communication and the contentious battle for public opinion.

PUBLIC RELATIONS IN CLASSICAL ANTIQUITY

The antecedents of modern public relations practice lie in the ancient world.

We can begin in Mesopotamia, the land of contemporary Iraq. Archaeologists have discovered building inscriptions that are artifacts of a public relations campaign to boost the reputation of the kings. Clay tablets dating to 1,800 BCE served as *bulletins* and *brochures* that instructed farmers how to sow crops, irrigate fields, and increase their harvests. What today we call *consumer affairs* was important to kings and other rulers, who knew that governmental stability depended on subjects who were well fed and prosperous.

Two of the oldest-known pieces of literature—the *Iliad* and the *Odyssey*, ascribed to the Greek poet Homer about 850 BCE—feature examples of effective *persuasive speeches*. Odysseus convinces the Cyclops not to eat him; Paris entreats Helen to leave her husband and go off with him; Hector and Achilles give stirring speeches to pump up their troops.

Earlier (though difficult to date) pieces of literature—the Pentateuch of the Hebrew Bible and the Sumerian epic of Gilgamesh—also have passages with strong persuasive rhetoric, again positioning advocacy as an important drive for both individuals and groups.

To enhance the *credibility* of communication, ancient Egyptian stories often were written as advice from a father to a son, generally implying that the wisdom had been handed down for many generations.

In China in the 4th century BCE, Confucius elevated the concept of *eloquence* in speech, persuasion based on the elegant use of language and expression of emotions. Chinese culture, as well as the related cultures of Korea and Japan, emphasizes *interpersonal relationships* and the role of *personal influence* in the civic and professional spheres. Other aspects of Northeastern Asian rhetoric show the value of *silence* as a tool of communication.

In the 3rd century BCE in Athens, Socrates and Plato taught that effective communication should be *based on truth*. Plato's student Aristotle analyzed persuasive communication and taught others how to be effective speakers, specifically by developing *compelling and ethical arguments* that offer verbal proofs.

PUBLIC RELATIONS IN GOVERNMENT

In antiquity, poems and stories often were written to bolster the reputation of kings and military leaders. The pharaohs of classical Egypt commissioned statues and built temples and pyramids to impress their people. Court advisers in Egypt 2,400 years ago told the pharaohs to *communicate truthfully* and *address audience interests*.

From the period of classical Greece, the teachings of Aristotle are still important today because he sought to equip his students with the persuasive skills to function effectively in a *democracy*. These skills have become increasingly useful as the world moves toward giving all citizens a voice in their civic life.

In the 5th century BCE, the biblical Joseph (Yosef ben Yaakov in the Hebrew Bible, Yusuf ibn Ya'qub in the Quran) functioned in the role of *public relations adviser* in Egypt, analyzing trends and counseling the pharaoh as he developed a campaign to educate farmers about gathering food for a seven-year famine.

Philip of Macedonia and his son, Alexander the Great, used public relations tactics as they extended Greek rule throughout Northern Africa and the Middle East into Central Asia and India. They employed tactics such as *public monuments*, *commemorative stamps* and *coins*, and *named buildings* and *stadiums*.

Elsewhere in the classical Mediterranean world, others also were studying communication. Corax of Syracuse wrote about *persuasive speaking*. Rome's most acclaimed orator, Marcus Tullius Cicero, developed the earlier Greek rhetorical methods for presenting *persuasive arguments* in public.

Julius Caesar wrote the first *campaign biography* to publicize his battlefield exploits as military governor of Gaul, successfully making the case that he was the best candidate to rule Rome. After maneuvering himself to be proclaimed "dictator in perpetuity," Caesar ordered the posting of the first public *newsletter* to keep his citizenry informed.

Later, the first Roman Emperor, Octavian Augustus Caesar (the adopted great-nephew of Julius), actively courted *public opinion*, realizing that he needed the support of the people in order to reign successfully. One of his tactics was to commission the poet Virgil to write an epic poem (The *Aeneid*) depicting Caesar as being ordained by the gods to rebuild Rome. This gave *credibility* to the emperor as a legitimate ruler of his people as a successor to the Roman republic.

In pre-Islamic Arabia, poets played a role in news and public relations, often commissioned by tribal chiefs to create poetry and stories that influenced public opinion.

In 9th-century Persia (present-day Iran), caliph Harun al-Rashid (Aaron the Just) engaged in international *diplomacy*, sending emissaries to the European court of Charlemagne, the Chinese court of the Tang dynasty, and the Pala empire of present-day Bangladesh. His internal public relations included what today would be called *constituent research* and *community relations*. *The Thousand and One Nights*, a collection of Middle Eastern folktales, recounts his practice of wandering among his subjects in disguise to learn how his government administrators were working for the benefit of his subjects.

Civil society and religion intersected in 1215, when the archbishop of Canterbury, Stephen Langton, used tactics of *lobbying* and *government relations* to persuade influential English barons to join him in demanding that King John recognize the rights of both the barons and the church. The result of this successful persuasion was the Magna Carta, the document that laid the foundation for constitutional government not only in England but also, eventually, around the world.

Whereas Western rhetoric focused on persuasion, communication in Asia often valued *consensus*. Hindu philosophy developed the concept of *dialectics* particularly during the Gupta Empire around the 4th century. This is a form of *dialogue* and *conflict resolution* in which participants with different points of view discuss a topic not to persuade each other but together to reach a common understanding, which is very much in line with a contemporary approach to public relations. The message often had an underlying theme, such as supporting rulers and social elites.

India also had the experience of sutradhars, who had a role much like the more musical troubadours of medieval Europe. Both were traveling storytellers, narrators who interpreted the story, often with a message or moral with a bit of humor.

PUBLIC RELATIONS AND RELIGION

Much of the history of public relations, like so many other aspects of Western society, is connected with religion.

The Hebrew scriptures depict Aaron as a great public speaker who served as the *spokesman* for his brother Moses. In the Christian scriptures, John the Baptist was shown as the advance man in what became a new religion, *generating interest* and preparing the way for Jesus Christ. Jesus himself was a great storyteller who used *parables* and other *short stories* with strong, simple, and easy-to-understand messages to teach moral lessons.

Indeed, all of the major religious scriptures associated with Judaism, Christianity, and Islam as well as the texts of Hinduism and Buddhism reveal the importance of *storytelling* as an essential ingredient in communication on religious, moral, and spiritual topics.

In the mid-1st century, St. Peter and St. Paul (Saul of Tarsus) led the Christian apostles in using many persuasive techniques: *speeches*, *staged events*, *letters*, and *oral teaching*. Their aim was to increase interest in Jesus, recruit for the new religious movement, and maintain morale and order among church members. Paul's letters, in particular, are examples of the *eloquence of the written word*.

The gospel writers Matthew, Mark, Luke, and John used the strategies of *interpretation* and *audience segmentation*, each presenting the same story in four different versions to appeal to the interests, experiences, and needs of four different audiences (Matthew writing for Jewish Christians, Mark for non-Jewish Greeks, Luke for non-Jewish Christians, and John for nonbelievers and later the network of Christian communities spreading throughout the Eastern Mediterranean).

The Roman Emperor Nero used the strategy of *orchestrating events* when he blamed the burning of Rome on the Christians, already the social scapegoats of his empire. It was a classic example of *framing*: telling one side of the story first so that any other versions are received as being different from what people already have heard.

The early Christian Church preserved and enhanced the concepts of *rhetoric*. In Roman Africa, the 5th-century philosopher-bishop Augustine of Hippo developed the art of preaching, insisting that *truth is the ultimate goal* of such public speaking. He had great influence in both civil and religious practice. Later in Northern Europe, the 8th-century Saxon theologian Alcuin reinterpreted Roman rhetorical teachings for the Emperor Charlemagne and his medieval court.

Use of public relations strategies and tactics was not limited to Christianity. In 6th-century Northern Africa, the prophet Mohammed sometimes retired to an out-of-the-way place to ponder problems facing his people, eventually to emerge with writings that he identified as the word of Allah. These writings, assembled as the Quran, thus received a *credibility* that encouraged acceptance by his followers.

In the Middle Ages, church leaders applied principles of *persuasive communication* in an effort to recapture the lands of Christian origin. Pope Urban II in 1095 sent his message throughout Europe using the only efficient communication system of the times—the network of monasteries and dioceses. He used a *sustained approach* that involved all the communication tactics of the times: *writing*, *public speaking*, *word of mouth*, *slogans*, and *symbols*. The role of *opinion leaders* and the influence on *public opinion* was effective, attracting thousands of volunteers for the first in a series of crusades.

During the eclipse of Western civilization, the classical teaching of Aristotle had virtually been lost to European society. It was Muslim scholars, Christian Arabs, and Arabic-speaking Jews who, during the 9th century, kept alive the study of Aristotle in the Middle East. One of the less-unfortunate consequences of the Crusades was the subsequent introduction of this Arab scholarship to the West, such as the "science of eloquence" associated with the Persian scholar Abd al-Jurijani.

In the 15th century, Franciscan friar Bernardino of Siena overcame a speech impediment and became respected for his skills in *public speaking* and *preaching*, as well as the now-recognized public relations roles of *conflict resolution* and *reconciliation*. Bernardino became so well known that he successfully negotiated a peace settlement between warring factions in Italy and later participated in negotiations to reunite Greek and Roman branches of Christianity.

Soon the printing press made possible greater *literacy* and with it an interest in reading the Bible. This laid the foundation for the Protestant Reformation and the subsequent Catholic Reformation. When friar Martin Luther tacked on the cathedral door his argument against various church practices, he was using a common technique for *public discussion* during that time in history.

That era led to the Catholic Church's establishment of the Congregatio de Propaganda Fide (Congregation for the Propagation of the Faith) to educate and support missionaries and advance the religion as Europeans pursued new openings in Asia, Africa, and the Western Hemisphere.

The term "propaganda" comes from that organization, later applied to any group set up to spread a doctrine or promote a principle. In its original form, *propaganda* was the common word used to describe what today is public relations. Until the 1950s, both terms were used interchangeably, but propaganda increasingly took on negative connotations by its association with the propaganda ministry of the Nazi regime and other totalitarian governments. It came to indicate manipulative communication, hidden motives, and half-truths. (With that in mind, American public relations pioneer Edward Bernays quipped that he practiced propaganda and not im-propaganda.)

In religions beyond Christianity, there are other aspects of public relations, some of them suggesting additional approaches to communication and relationships.

For example, as Buddhism extended throughout Eastern Asia between the 6th and 12th centuries, it lifted up literature and poetry as elements of communication. Until recent times in Asia, imperial rule and social cohesion were the norm, and the Eastern social environment had little need for public discussion of issues and *persuasive discourse*. In Japan and China, Buddhism emphasized the unity of speaker and audience. Communication often was based on *relationships*. *Silence* and *nonverbals* often are more important than words.

Meanwhile, religious and cultural traditions for centuries intermingled in African society and among indigenous people of Australia and the Americas. These communities often emphasized the value of *storytelling*, the graceful use of language, the development of *consensus*, and the communicative value of *silence*.

All of these concepts of communication and social relationships have practical relevance for today's public relations practitioner.

PUBLIC RELATIONS IN COLONIZATION

Public relations also played a role in European expansion and colonization of newly discovered lands.

In the 10th century, Vikings landed on an uninhabited island of ice and snow in the North Atlantic. Led by Erik "The Red" Thorvaldsson, they used creative *labeling*. The *Saga of Erik the Red* is explicit: "[which] he called Greenland, as he said people would be attracted there if it had a favorable name." Erik was successful, attracting 5,000 or so immigrants from Norway and Iceland (which, ironically, is warmer than Greenland). Pleasant labeling aside, it was the harsh climate change and unfriendly newcomers (the Inuits) that caused them to abandon the Greenland settlements five centuries later.

In the 16th century, Sir Walter Raleigh employed *positive messaging* when he sent glowing reports to England about Roanoke Island off present-day North Carolina. Compared to England, this new land had better soil, bigger trees, and more plentiful harvests, as well as friendly Indians—so he said when recruiting settlers. *Promotional leaflets* with wild exaggerations attracted settlers and financial backers, but the claims didn't match reality. The island was largely swamp, food was scarce, sickness was prevalent, and harsh treatment by the colonists turned the native people hostile. The colony was abandoned after two years, giving evidence of another axiom of public relations: Mere words are ineffective when they do not reflect reality.

In other parts of the hemisphere, conquistadores sent similarly enthusiastic reports to Spain about cities of gold and fountains of youth. Neither were found, but the stories helped spur immigration to the Americas. In French Canada, public relations tactics were less exaggerated. Tactics included a *book* by Samuel de Champlain in order to "lure settlers," as well as a campaign to recruit young women from France as wives of the immigrants already in New France, most of them single men.

For more than 150 years, England had sent convicts and its Irish or Scottish prisoners of war as cheap labor to the American colonies. After the Revolutionary War ended in 1783, other destinations had to be found. At the same time, the war displaced thousands of American loyalists who found themselves no longer welcomed in the fledgling United States. Coincidentally, English explorers had recently claimed Australia, a potential haven for disaffected American colonists. At a time when reformers in England were demanding better conditions for prisoners, Australia also was a likely successor as a penal colony. A potential *win-win situation* was developing.

Again, *positive messaging* with romantic descriptions of Australia was sent back to England: fertile soil, mild climate, exquisite beauty, and friendly Aboriginals—though the facts didn't always match the claims. Shipping corporations encouraged immigration. *Newspaper ads* back in England promised free land and representative government.

In the 17th century, the first Europeans in Australia were convicts being resettled, but soon other immigrants came of their own will, lured by *publicity* and *advertising* promising land opportunities. Germans responding to similar *advertisements* went to Australia to escape religious conflict in Europe. Later, in the mid-1800s, looking for a cheap source of labor in the Northern Territories, Australia advertised in Chinese and Malaysian newspapers for immigrants.

This early aberration of public relations—exaggerated promises and unfounded claims—popped up once again in North America. The Western expansion in the US brought a *glorified view* of life on the frontier. The *legend* of Davy Crockett and *stories* about Calamity Jane and Buffalo Bill Cody were among the persuasive messages developed to encourage expansion.

Corporations began using public relations to stimulate westward migration. The Southern Pacific Railroad, for example, hired a *publicity agent* to promote Southern California and *commissioned artists* to paint romanticized images of the Southwest. Land companies hired *promoters* to attract settlers, and the federal government hyped the California Gold Rush to foster *public opinion* for the war against

Mexico. After the American Civil War, the Burlington Railroad promoted land grants for army veterans along its route in the northern plains. It even took out *newspaper ads* in Germany, Scandinavia, and The Netherlands to attract European immigrants.

Who knows? Future generations may find similar exaggerations about undersea colonies or the first settlements on the moon.

PUBLIC RELATIONS IN REVOLUTION

The American Revolution stands as an example of the power of *public opinion* and the role that public relations can play.

Samuel Adams, the chief *strategist* for the independence movement, used many public relations strategies and tactics. He encouraged *organizing groups* such as the Caucus Club and the Committees of Correspondence. He created *activist organizations* such as the Sons of Liberty.

Adams organized *staged events*, most notably the Boston Tea Party, which was part of the resistance movement designed to satirize the British tea tax and symbolize colonial defiance. The in-your-face tactic shocked not only the British but also many colonists as well, and the propaganda machine went into high gear. *Sketches* and *pictures* were circulated depicting the fight with inaccurate details that inflamed the colonists. *Brochures* (many of them anonymous) were distributed in America and in England, describing—against the facts—an unprovoked attack on peaceful citizens.

In an example of *framing*, the colonists got their "official" version of the story of the Boston Tea Party across the Atlantic before pro-British loyalists could be heard. Benjamin Franklin, in residence in London, lost no time in being the first to circulate the revolutionary version of the event throughout the city.

Meanwhile, the rebel colonists were using persuasive messages including *songs* of protest and patriotism, *symbols* such as the Liberty Tree, and *slogans* ("Taxation without representation is tyranny").

They also became adept at *orchestrating the message*, such as their elaboration of the Boston Massacre—hardly a massacre, but rather, a riot caused by a drunken colonial mob. But *poems*, *essays*, and *engravings* memorialized the event throughout the colonies (except in New

York, where the story was suppressed by colonial leaders because of their continuing rivalry with Boston).

The colonists also built *alliances* with American Indians, though most tribes sided with the British because England recognized their lands and protected them from encroaching colonists.

The independence movement also had some of the darker elements that sometimes have been associated with public relations. It *demonized the opposition*, ridiculing King George and his representatives in the colonies. More seriously, it *ostracized sympathizers* of the opposition, such as in the *plays* and *poetry* of Mercy Otis Warren ridiculing loyalists in the colonies, and the Patriot Committee in each colony that harassed loyalists (real and suspected), including confiscation of their land, torture, even murder. Such actions caused most of the loyalist colonists to flee to Canada or relocate to Australia or elsewhere. (The term "lynching" derives from Judge Charles Lynch of Virginia, who, without trial, beat and jailed colonists accused of being loyal to their king back in London.)

Another negative strategy of the independence movement capitalized on people's *fears* and *bigotry*. The notable example of this was the anti-Catholic prejudice fanned in the colonies after England promulgated the Quebec Act. That law allowed Catholics in the former French colony of Quebec (recently conquered by the British) to practice their faith, something not permitted in most of the American colonies. The colonial leaders fueled the revolutionary sentiment against England by playing to anti-Catholic bigotry in what essentially were Protestant colonies.

Many public relations tactics were employed during the American Revolution, including the use of anniversaries of events as news pegs for publicity, letters to opinion leaders, town and county meetings, petitions in colonial (later state) legislatures, leaks to the press, use of all existing communication tools (a multimedia campaign), and *The Federalist Papers*, a collection of 85 articles and essays written by Alexander Hamilton, James Madison, and John Jay under the pseudonym "Publius" to promote the ratification of the Constitution of the United States.

In addition, the rebel colonists' tactics included more than 1,500 booklets and pamphlets in the 20 years of the independence movement, ghostwritten articles and letters (e.g., Samuel Adams wrote under 25 different aliases), newspaper essays and editorials, speeches and sermons, personal correspondence, word-of-mouth communication during visits to taverns and other public gathering places, meetings, parades, and posting of notices in public places.

Consider the following observations regarding the influence of public opinion and the power of public relations during the Revolutionary War:

1. Despite the political rhetoric, colonists were not an oppressed people. In fact, they generally paid no taxes. Because of the distance from Mother England, they were already autonomous in most practical day-to-day matters.
2. Most of the colonists were not in favor of separation from England. Many families and even entire communities moved through New York and across the Niagara River into Canada or north through New England into the Maritime Provinces. About 100,000 colonists escaped to Canada, returned to England, or fled to the Bahamas, Australia, or other British territories.
3. The colonies were not united. Indeed, there were serious and deep divisions and hostile suspicion among them. For example, the Boston Massacre was not reported in New York because of intra-colony feuding, and the issue of slavery nearly scuttled the ability to find common ground among the colonies.
4. The colonial experience had not been about freedom and equality for everyone, and the American Revolution did not seek to change that. The very people who founded the colonies had introduced human trafficking and slavery, and many leaders of the independence movement owned slaves. The colonists confiscated Native American lands that had been protected under British rule. Most colonies excluded Jews and Catholics. Voting and other legal privileges were denied to women and to all men except white Protestant landowners, a very small percentage of the colonial population.
5. Yet the independence movement was successful, because *public opinion* ultimately is stronger than legal right or military might. And public relations lies at the heart of public opinion.

MODERN HISTORY OF PUBLIC RELATIONS

While history shows aspects of public relations as a constant element of human interaction, it has been only in recent times that society has recognized and begun to practice what can be called the profession of public relations. Jobs have been created for public relations functions. Education has been developed to support this. Research has been undertaken to better understand the new discipline.

American scholar James Grunig is associated with a framework showing a four-phase evolution of modern public relations. These phases can be called the publicity era, information era, advocacy era, and relationship era.

PUBLICITY ERA (1800s)

- Focus: Dissemination and attention-getting
- Nature of Communication: One-way
- Ethics: Full truth not considered important
- Research: Little
- Current Use: Entertainment, sports and marketing

Sometimes called the public-be-damned era, this is seen as the dawn of public relations as a contemporary profession. The focus is on *dissemination of information* and *gaining attention.* This **publicity model** is an aspect of public relations that exists today, particularly in entertainment, sports, and marketing.

In the 1820s, Kentucky newspaper editor Amos Kendall became essentially the first presidential press secretary, though with more power and influence than is associated with that position today. Kendall assisted Andrew Jackson during his election campaign and his terms as president. He conducted *polls*, drafted *speeches*, wrote *news releases* and *editorials*, distributed favorable *reprints*, and advised Jackson on *image* and *strategy*.

As a member of the president's Kitchen Cabinet, Kendall helped Jackson play to populist elements and overcome his most controversial issue, his brutal and lifelong campaign of ethnic cleansing against Native Americans. He also helped arrange for financial backers to make loans to editors and buy newspaper ads to guarantee *positive publicity*.

Meanwhile, Jackson's political opponents fought back. They raised up a backwoodsman Tennessee congressman with a larger-than-life *reputation*. Armed with *ghostwritten speeches* and even a *book* penned by someone in his name, Davy Crockett was elected to Congress, where he unsuccessfully opposed Jackson's policies, particularly the Indian Removal Act. His public relations handlers and financial backers launched him into an unsuccessful re-election campaign.

After leaving Washington, Crockett went to Texas, later to gain fame by dying at the Alamo.

Once again, *propaganda* of the day wasn't constrained by facts. It was the Mexicans who were defending their country against the Texans seeking a breakaway territory where they could own slaves. In Disney's version of the story, Crockett died fighting, though weeks after the battle stories circulated that he and several other Texans had surrendered and were later executed.

As with Kendall, much of this early activity in public relations centered on individuals. William Seward, Lincoln's secretary of state, engaged in *media relations* by speaking frequently with newspaper editors. "They have a large audience and can repeat a thousand times what I want to impress on the public," he said.

Meanwhile in England, Georgiana Cavendish, Duchess of Devonshire, was an influential socialite a century before women achieved the right to vote. She was well known as a sort of *publicist*, *lobbyist*, and *campaigner* for Charles James Fox, a Whig statesman in the late 1800s.

The opening of the American West provided opportunities for *persuasive messages* to influence migration. Many of the tactics were inspired by promoters such as P.T. Barnum, who successfully publicized circuses, concerts, museums, theaters, and other entertainment venues.

Though exaggerated, many of the messages were effective. The legend of Daniel Boone and hyped stories of Buffalo Bill Cody, Wyatt Earp, and Calamity Jane induced settlers to the territories west of the Mississippi. Railroads commissioned artists to paint romanticized pictures of the West, complete with peaceful-looking Indians and fertile lands.

As with the American experience, railroads became a prime business for doing public relations in other countries. The modern practice of the profession in India and Canada, for example, began with promotion of the railroads. The Great Indian Peninsular Railways developed a *communication campaign* directed toward England, then the occupying nation of the subcontinent. Attempting to attract tourists, the railroad's *publicity bureau* distributed *press releases* and purchased *advertising* in British newspapers. It introduced a traveling *film* for fairs and festivals.

Social reform in the second half of the 19th century also relied heavily on classic publicity techniques. Harriet Beecher Stowe *personalized* the issue of slavery with her influential novel *Uncle Tom's Cabin*, and Harriet Tubman gave face and voice to the abolitionist movement. Both were part of a massive public relations movement involving *opinion leaders*, *public meetings*, *lectures*, *sermons*, *religious tracts*, *petitions*, and other tactics all loosely coordinated to end slavery.

The temperance movement to abolish liquor and the suffrage movement to gain women the right to vote were other successful social reform movements that relied heavily on public relations strategies and tactics.

It was during this formative period that the term "public relations" came into use. Dorman Eaton seems to have first used the term in 1882 when he addressed Yale Law School graduates on "The Public Relations and Duties of the Legal Profession." The Association of American Railroads apparently was the first organization to use the term in print, in the *1897 Yearbook of Railway Literature.*

Public relations played a role in the "War of the Currents" between Westinghouse and General Electric over the relative merits of alternating current (AC) and direct current (DC) as the better technology for making electricity available to the masses.

Thomas Edison and his General Electric business associates supported DC by conducting a *scare campaign* against exaggerated dangers of AC. Edison used *mudslinging* and *false advertising* as he *lobbied* lawmakers. He wrote *letters to the editor* attacking his opponents and hired false "experts" to speak on behalf of his DC cause. Attempting to shock audiences, Edison used AC to electrocute hundreds of animals, including dogs and horses. He even created a *special event* by arranging for the electrocution of a convicted murderer, a tactic that turned out so gruesome that it effectively lost the case Edison was trying to make.

Meanwhile, Westinghouse countered with calm, logic, and appeals to reason, winning the argument with what is generally considered a more *strategic public relations campaign*. Today Westinghouse's AC is standard throughout the world. This war of the currents of the late 1880s and early 1890s is a prime example of the movement from the publicity model into the information era.

INFORMATION ERA (EARLY 1900s)

- Focus: Honest and accurate dissemination of information
- Nature of Communication: One-way
- Ethics: Accuracy and truth considered important
- Research: Readability and comprehension
- Current Use: Government, nonprofit organizations, and business organizations

The transition from the public-be-damned era into a public-be-informed approach centered on a new standard of honest and accurate dissemination of *newsworthy information*. Truth telling became a public virtue. This **information model** is prevalent today in many businesses, nonprofits, and government agencies.

This time period saw a maturing of public relations to add a stronger *ethical base* to public relations tactics. *News releases* were now expected to be *accurate*, and speeches *truthful*.

As Europe was discovering with its nobility, America was seeing parallel truths about business potentates: The public matters. Ex-journalist Ivy Ledbetter Lee, often called the "father of public relations," bucked the prevailing business feeling associated with the empire builders and the Gilded Age, telling clients such as John D. Rockefeller, Walter Chrysler, and George Westinghouse that the *public could no longer be ignored*.

Lee issued a Declaration of Principles calling for *honest communication* on behalf of clients and telling newspaper editors that he would offer them *newsworthy information* promptly, accurately, and in the open. When one of his clients, the Pennsylvania Railroad, experienced a train crash, Lee advised the company to tell what had happened, bring reporters to the scene, and let them report the story firsthand.

This era saw many "firsts": the first public relations agencies, first university publicity bureau, first employee newsletter, first public relations journal, and the first public relations departments for groups as disparate as churches, military, unions, charities, nonprofit organizations, and corporations.

Public relations saw parallel growth around the world. In Canada, public relations departments and agencies also were developing, beginning with Bell Canada. Railroads, banks, and other companies hired publicity specialists to create effective *government relations* programs at the beginning of World War I.

Government agencies were created in the UK, France, and the US during World War I to manage the flow of information, looking for citizen support for the military efforts.

The Indian government set up a publicity board during World War I as a link between the government and the press. In monitoring media criticism of the government, the board provided *feedback* to government strategists. The board later morphed into the Indian Ministry of Information and Broadcasting, which today coordinates public relations, publicity, advertising, and film policy.

During the build-up to World War I, the German propaganda ministry produced *books* and *pamphlets*, *speeches*, and even *children's books*. It established the German Information Bureau to influence Americans to remain neutral, a position supported by public opinion before April 1917, when the US entered the war.

One week after declaring war, President Wilson created the Committee on Public Information. The agency, headed by George Creel, sought to garner public opinion supporting a role for America in the war, *framing* it as a positive force for democracy.

Creel said that its purpose was to coordinate "not propaganda as the Germans defined it, but propaganda in the true sense of the word, meaning the 'propagation of faith'." The committee used all the tools at its disposal: *posters* and *newspapers*, *telegraph* and *radio*, *film* and *speeches*. Volunteers gave 7.5 million succinct four-minute speeches to audiences totaling 314 million people.

Meanwhile, England's theme was that it was a matter of duty to help France and Belgium, threatened by Germany. *Posters* asked, "Daddy, what did you do in the Great War?" Recruiting *advertisements* asked women about their sons and husbands, "Is he to hang his head because you would not let him go?" Toward the war's end, the Ministry of Information pulled together the work of several different government agencies dealing with various aspects of media, news, and public opinion.

In Australia, opponents to the government ban on drafting soldiers to fight in Europe mounted a national referendum on the law as a sort of *public opinion*. The referendum was twice defeated, but publicity about the vote led 400,000 Australians to volunteer to help the Mother Country after England entered the war.

Not all public relations had good intentions. Two Atlanta publicists of this time, Edward Clarke and Bessie Tyler, gained a footnote in public relations history because of their immense success in *recruiting* and *fundraising*. They took a group from a few thousand members in 1920 to nearly 4 million in 1923. The group was the Ku Klux Klan, America's most notorious vigilante terrorist organization. This revival of the short-lived post-Civil War KKK reframed the klan as a patriotic nativist group and extended its traditional hostility toward Blacks by adding Catholics, Jews, and unions to its hate list.

Clarke and Tyler used many common public relations strategies and tactics: all kinds of *publications*, *speeches*, and *symbols*, such as the burning cross. Most of the success was in the US, but the anti-Catholic message played in Canada as well.

The story of this second KKK shows the power of *negative strategy*, appeals to fear and hatred, and other divisive methods that can enjoy short-term success. But the story isn't complete without noting that this klan fizzled out and disbanded within 20 years, adding another lesson for public relations: Hate groups inevitably implode from their inability to sustain rabid negativity.

ADVOCACY ERA (MID-1900s)

- Focus: Modify attitudes and influence behavior
- Nature of Communication: Two-way
- Ethics: Transparent research and communication
- Research: Attitude and opinion
- Current Use: Competitive business organizations, causes, and movements

By the mid-20th century, people were attempting to reconcile new facts on the international social consciousness: genocide in Armenia and popular German support for the Holocaust, along with behavioral theories such as conditioned reflex, cognitive dissonance, and scapegoat theory. The thinking was: If people could be induced to do evil things, how can they be persuaded to do good?

The focus of this **advocacy model** was on *modifying attitudes* and *influencing behavior.* It introduced social research into the practice of public relations, establishing a role for *demographics* and developing techniques for *surveys* and *opinion polls* as well as *focus groups* and *content analysis.*

These are aspects of public relations still used today in competitive business organizations promoting products and services, as well as in advocacy causes and movements such as public health, welfare, and human rights. Perhaps the largest field for this has been that of electoral politics and public policy issues.

This era is associated with Edward Bernays, the second founding figure for public relations along with Ivy Lee. An Austrian-American and the nephew of Sigmund Freud, Bernays gave public relations a base in *social psychology* as he engaged the profession on behalf of an international list of clients.

Among his achievements were assisting President Wilson with the Creel Committee to encourage public support for American involvement in World War I. He later promoted water fluoridation as a public health issue and helped to introduce orange juice as a common breakfast beverage. One of his most noteworthy and controversial successes was a campaign on behalf of Lucky Strike cigarettes (which he labeled "torches of freedom") to make it socially acceptable for women to smoke in public, something he later came to regret as health literacy increased.

Bernays also wrote the first book on public relations (*Crystallizing Public Opinion*) and taught the first university course (at New York University) in the new discipline. It was Bernays who introduced the term "public relations counsel."

Bernays said public relations was about the "engineering of consent"—not by force or manipulation, but by carefully orchestrated strategies that were *based on theory* and *informed by research*, with a strong *ethical undertone.* Bernays remained a leading figure in public relations until he died in 1995 at the age of 103.

Doris Fleishman, Bernays' wife and professional colleague, used her public relations skills for feminist causes. She became the first married American woman to receive a passport in her maiden name.

Another key figure in public relations during this time period was Arthur Page. He became the first known in-house corporate public relations strategist when he accepted a job as vice president of AT&T, after negotiating that he would be a corporate adviser and decision maker rather than a publicity voice. Page insisted that his staff observe seven principles: Tell the truth; prove it with action; listen to the customer; manage for tomorrow; conduct public relations as if the whole company depends on it; realize a company's true character is expressed by its peoples; and remain calm, patient, and good humored.

During the middle and latter parts of the 20th century, much of public relations (both research and practice) was built on the advocacy model. Organizations tried to influence the *attitudes and behaviors* of their publics. Governments around the world tried to nurture support for World War II, and *information as a weapon* (including *misinformation*; that is, lying and deception) became part of the Cold War, paralleling military might with communication-based campaigns to win the hearts and minds of people. Britain and the US used news and information to build support and later post-war propaganda campaigns. Other research was related to brainwashing and *social manipulation*.

Social reform movements continued to use public relations, attempting to change attitudes on issues such as child labor, worker rights, prostitution, food safety, and regulation of big business.

Former journalist Elmer Davis headed the Office of War Information during World War II, coordinating public information from the military, mobilizing public support for the war effort, and undermining enemy morale. Davis successfully campaigned against efforts to strip US-born Japanese-Americans of their citizenship and place them in internment camps for the duration of the war. He urged President Roosevelt to allow Japanese-Americans to enlist for military service, even while their parents were forcibly removed from their homes and placed under military internment. Davis has been acclaimed as one of the "unsung forefathers" of the all-Japanese 442nd Regimental Combat Team that became the most decorated infantry regiment in American history. After the war, Davis returned to his career in radio, using that as a platform to campaign against Senator Joseph McCarthy's Communist witch hunt.

It is interesting to note the language surrounding government and public relations. Totalitarian regimes often have used the *propaganda* label, such as Hitler's Ministry of Public Enlightenment and Propaganda, the Soviet Department for Agitation and Propaganda, and both the Office of Foreign Propaganda and the Communist Party Propaganda Department under China's Chairman Mao.

Democratic countries, on the other hand, have been more likely to use the *information* title, as with the Ministries of Information in Britain and Israel and the US Committee on Information and the US Information Agency. Today, most nations have abandoned the propaganda label for government agencies dealing with information, news, and public relations.

RELATIONSHIP ERA (LATE 1900s TO PRESENT)

- Focus: Mutual understanding and conflict resolution
- Nature of Communication: Two-way
- Ethics: Balance and symmetry in relationships
- Research: Perception and values
- Current Use: Regulated business, government, nonprofit organizations, and social movements

In recent decades, public relations has assumed a focus toward programming aimed at mutual understanding, organizational adaptation, and conflict resolution.

This **relationship model** today often is associated with social movements, as well as with nonprofit organizations, government agencies, and corporations, especially regulated businesses that often interact with both government and social advocates.

Consumer-rights groups have drawn attention to a variety of health and safety issues, such as automobiles, airplane travel safety, clean water, and children's sleepwear. Much of this activity has been spurred by social advocates such as Rachel Carson, a marine biologist whose book *Silent Spring* spurred a global environmental movement, and Ralph Nader, whose book *Unsafe at Any Speed* focused attention on auto safety in North America and beyond. In each of these cases, government and industry responded to *public opinion* supporting oversight and quality reform. Regulations were put in place as consumers adopted many pro-environment and pro-safety habits, often with government encouragement through public relations campaigns.

Meanwhile, speeches such as "I Have a Dream" and "I've Been to the Mountain Top" by Martin Luther King Jr. led not only to legal guarantees of civil rights but also to the personal transformation of many individuals toward celebration of racial and ethnic diversity. President Obama's second inaugural address referenced themes precious to marginalized groups, including his reference to the Stonewall riots (foreshadowing the gay rights movement) with parallel icons such as Seneca Falls (women's rights) and Selma (civil rights).

The relationship model, whether it involves advocacy groups or the companies and agencies dealing with their issues, drives public relations strategists toward helping their organizations listen to consumers and adapt their products and services to meet their needs.

Sometimes this means researching consumer interests or communicating more with publics. Often it also means making internal changes to deliver a better product or service. Organizations of all types have come to realize that, in order to be successful, they need to listen to consumers and adapt their products and services to meet their needs.

Thus the hallmark of the relationship model is *adaptation*, an organization's willingness to respond to publics and make meaningful change to create a *mutually beneficial* environment for both the publics and the organization.

This new relationship model is built on the principles of *communication as listening* and is focused on *conflict resolution* and the search for *mutual benefits* for both organizations and their publics.

Internationally, this relationship approach has been seen in concepts such as *détente* and *rapprochement*. In the business environment, *public-private partnerships* and the courting of consumers are becoming common.

In the religious world, the *ecumenical movement* and *interreligious dialogue* are examples of the relationship model. The documents from the Catholic Church's Vatican Council II in the 1960s—particularly the statements on the church's relationship with other Christian denominations, with Jews, and with non-Christian religions—show the application of the relationship model to interreligious matters.

In all of these situations, public relations has become *research based*. It is more a function of the management and leadership of an organization, rather than simply the implementation of communication tactics. Meanwhile, new technologies associated with the internet allow organizations to communicate directly with their publics and to offer *information-on-demand* in an interactive consumer-driven environment. These technologies, combined with the *fragmentation* of the so-called *mass media*, are creating new opportunities for public relations practitioners.

It is important to remember that the relationship model complements earlier visions of public relations focused on publicity, information, and advocacy. Organizations will always need a publicity model for some of their public relations purposes, such as announcing new products and services and promoting upcoming events. Society will continue to use the information model that disseminates honest and reliable facts on which to base personal and civic decisions. The advocacy model will always be enshrouded as part of human nature, which frequently nudges us toward promoting a cause and fostering our beliefs. And the relationship model will continue to find favor wherever society values dialogue in an atmosphere of mutual respect toward win-win solutions that benefit everybody.

PUBLIC RELATIONS TODAY

Why the history lesson? Because it provides insights into the development of a profession that is still evolving. As noted in Chapter 1, misperceptions about public relations are based on incorrect or outdated information. Understanding the profession's development, as outlined here, helps us to better appreciate where public relations is today and where it seems to be heading.

Looking country by country, we see a clear link between social structure and public relations. The profession has an obvious connection with democracy, in which public opinion is needed for leaders to gain the consent of the citizenry, and with capitalism, an economic system based on competitive markets and voluntary exchange between buyer and seller.

While many activities that we associate with public relations have become nearly universal, scholars and historians around the world agree that the practice of public relations as a profession began in the United States. It quickly spread to other English-speaking democratic societies, particularly Canada, Australia, and the United Kingdom, as noted in the previous section.

The discipline is so much rooted in North America that the English words "public relations" or direct translations ("relations publique," in France, "relaciones públicas" in Spain) are used almost universally rather than homegrown phrases. A German term "Öffentlichkeitsarbeit" sometimes translates as "publicity campaign," but the English term is more commonly used in German-speaking settings. In Japan, the common term is "pee-ah-roo" or sometimes "paburikku rireshon."

Though the name may be the same, the role of public relations is not uniform throughout the world. The understanding presented here is consistent with professional practice in North America and in English-rooted cultures around the world.

In much of Europe, the focus is more on promotion and communication tactics but less on strategic management issues, and the relationship between advertising and public relations remains unsettled. In many Asian cultures, public relations is focused on international companies trying to navigate domestic peculiarities in government and media. Arab culture sometimes equates public relations with social relations and hospitality.

Scholars have observed that public relations came late to totalitarian states, giving evidence to the observation by scholars that propaganda is a phase, a stepping-stone along the path toward open communication. In countries such as Chile and the Philippines—until recently associated with totalitarian governments—public relations still has not been completely severed from propaganda. This isn't surprising. The US has had more than two centuries of practice with democracy. Canada, Australia, and the UK likewise have a long history with social and economic freedom. Yet even in these countries, there are remnants of deceptive propaganda.

Public relations by necessity requires literacy and higher levels of education. It is not surprising that countries with low literacy rates and education levels are ill equipped to generate a functional public relations profession. There is little opportunity to practice public relations in African nations such as Mali, South Sudan, and Chad, where less than 35 percent of adults are literate, or in Afghanistan, where the literacy rate is only 37 percent.

Additionally, cultural differences come into play. In Japan, for example, it is considered impolite to ask questions at a press briefing; instead, reporters hold their questions for follow-up one-on-one interviews. The International Communications Consultancy Organisation has offered some observations on how public relations practitioners engage European journalists: Germans want small media briefings, but in the UK one-on-one interviews are preferred. Italian reporters like breakfast meetings, not too early. In Belgium, journalists prefer to get their news over lunch or dinner served with beer.

Despite these cultural differences, public relations professionals around the world are confronting many of the same issues today. Here is an overview.

THE RISE OF ARTIFICIAL INTELLIGENCE

Artificial intelligence (AI), *the ability of a computer or computer-controlled robot to perform tasks commonly associated with human beings*, is revolutionizing the public relations workplace, as it is in industries worldwide. AI is enhancing efficiency and effectiveness for public relations professionals for mundane, time-consuming tasks such as content creation and repurposing content for different platforms, media monitoring and analysis, and reporting and measurement.

For example, you can use ChatGPT or Claude to draft news releases or social media posts—then add your "human touch" to finalize the item and get suggestions for repurposing the content for other platforms. Otter is helpful for meeting notes or agendas, while DALL-E can aid with image creation.

Media monitoring and analysis—sorting through many news articles, online mentions, and social media posts to track brand sentiment and possible crises—can be simplified with AI tools, greatly reducing the number of hours spent by PR professionals on media monitoring and catching more relevant mentions in the media.

Reporting and measurement, which involves compilation of vast amounts of data from many sources, creating reports, and extracting insights on the value of public relations, can benefit from AI tools as well.

In the future, public relations professionals expect that AI will offer the potential for advanced predictive analytics—the ability to predict the success of a public relations campaign or predict what might become a crisis for a PR client.

AI tools offer exciting possibilities, but they also present ethical issues. For example, AI-generated content may be inaccurate, exhibit bias, inadvertently share proprietary information, plagiarize, or infringe on copyrights. Professional organizations such as the Public Relations Society of America's Board of Ethics and Professional Standards (Staley et al., 2023), the Chartered Institute of Public Relations (Valin & Gregory, 2020), the PR Council (Green & McClennan, 2024), and the International Communication Consultancy Organisation (2023) offer guidance on such issues. This includes checking for accuracy and inadvertent plagiarism, using caution when putting confidential client information into an AI tool, watching for any biases in writing or imagery incorporated into AI-generated output, and disclosures to clients about use of AI in any part of the creative process.

AI isn't replacing humans who work in public relations, but rather, augmenting their work, offering a range of new jobs for public relations graduates in data and analytics, AI prompt design, identification of misinformation and disinformation, and more.

DEI (DIVERSITY, EQUITY, AND INCLUSION)

Diversity, equity, and inclusion (DEI) has become a major concern for businesses and nonprofits alike in recent years, especially after the 2020 murder of African-American George Floyd, which sparked national protests over systemic racism. DEI centers around *the idea of appreciating human differences* (**diversity**), *treating all people fairly* (**equity**), and *ensuring that individuals in organizations and communities feel valued* (**inclusion**). Organizations that embrace DEI principles are seen as socially responsible, which can enhance their reputation and help them to connect with underrepresented or marginalized communities.

As organizations prioritize their DEI initiatives, their public relations professionals are expected to integrate those principles into their campaigns. Storytelling that highlights stories from underrepresented groups can help campaigns resonate with diverse audiences, building trust and loyalty to an organization. In addition, public relations professionals frequently work with the organization's human resources department to promote internal DEI initiatives, which can boost employee morale and retention.

However, there has been pushback to DEI, particularly since US President Donald Trump's return to office in January 2025. Within hours of his inauguration, he signed two executive orders seeking to end what he called "illegal DEI" programs and policies in the federal government. Those orders hastened an ongoing DEI retreat across corporate America, because some private companies are federal contractors who are subject to the executive orders, and other companies are seeking US government approval for business dealings.

Many organizations, including colleges and universities, are removing DEI references from websites, ending bonuses tied to increasing the number of employees who are women or minorities, or eliminating diversity-related policies and programs. Other organizations are renaming DEI initiatives as programs that foster equal opportunity, creating environments where every person feels respected, valued, and able to fully participate. But some companies are standing up for DEI policies for now, including Marriott, Delta, and Cisco. Marriott's CEO Anthony Capuano received 40,000 "thank you" emails from employees after publicly stating, "We welcome all to our hotels and we create opportunities for all—and fundamentally those will never change. The words might change, but that's who we are as a company."

Public relations professionals are playing a key role in shaping their organizations' communication in this fast-changing policy and regulatory landscape surrounding diversity, equity, and inclusion.

MISINFORMATION, DISINFORMATION, AND FAKE NEWS

Public relations professionals are dealing with an increase in **disinformation** (*false information intentionally created to confuse, misinform, and harm a person or group*); a type of disinformation called **fake news** (*purposefully crafted, sensational, emotionally charged, misleading, or totally fabricated information that mimics the form of mainstream news*); and **misinformation** (*false information though not created with negative intent*). Whether on social media or through traditional news media, disinformation (including fake news) and misinformation make it more difficult for public relations professionals to ensure their messages are accurate and trustworthy.

CRISIS MANAGEMENT

Today, crises can unfold in real time on social media, so organizations need to develop crisis management strategies that can address issues instantly and with transparency. AI predictive tools play an increasing role in identifying a problem before it becomes a crisis for an organization.

NAVIGATING THE SOCIAL MEDIA LANDSCAPE

Instagram, TikTok, and newer social media platforms like Bluesky and Threads are reshaping how organizations are engaging with their key publics (The Chi Group, 2024). Social media strategies that succeeded last year might fail this year, thus requiring public relations professionals to track emerging social media platforms used by their key publics and revise strategies as needed. The rise of influencers also is reshaping the communication landscape; organizations are increasingly collaborating with influencers who align with their values to amplify messages and nurture authentic connections with key publics.

VIRTUAL ENGAGEMENTS AND THE METAVERSE

The **metaverse**, *a virtual-reality space in which users can interact with a computer-generated environment and other users*, has become an important platform for brand engagement. Public relations campaigns are increasingly leveraging virtual spaces to host press events, interactive experiences, and product launches. Organizations can use **virtual reality** (*a three-dimensional, computer-generated digital and real space in which users interact, while also creating their own experiences*) and **augmented reality** (*a technology that superimposes a computer-generated* *image on a user's view of the real world, thus providing a composite view*) to create immersive storytelling experiences for their key publics. For example, NASA offers a virtual-reality tour of Mars. Snapchat, a popular multimedia messaging app that digitally imposes filters on a user's face, is an example of augmented reality.

CORPORATE SOCIAL RESPONSIBILITY AND SUSTAINABILITY

Given the urgency of climate change and social responsibility, consumers increasingly are aligning with organizations that demonstrate a commitment to **corporate social responsibility**, *an aspect of community relations and strategic philanthropy in which an organization contributes to the betterment of society*, and **sustainability**, *development that meets the needs of the present without compromising the ability of future generations to meet their own needs*. Public relations professionals are crafting messages that showcase their companies' social, environmental, and ethical initiatives to build trust and loyalty with their publics. **Greenwashing**, *dissemination of misleading publicity by an organization with the aim of presenting an environmentally responsible public image*, will fail.

FOCUS ON DATA PRIVACY

Data-driven communication has become the norm, resulting in greater scrutiny regarding data privacy. Stricter regulations on data usage will require transparent communication about how consumer data is collected, stored, and used. PR campaigns should highlight compliance with data privacy regulations.

WORKS CITED

Aspan, M. (2025, May 19). *Verizon ends DEI policies to get FCC's blessing for its $20 billion Frontier deal*. NPR. https://www.npr.org/2025/05/19/nx-s1-5402863/verizon-fcc-frontier-dei-trump

Carter, A. (2024, September 19). *By the numbers: These are the best AI tools for marcomm tasks, according to Edelman*. PR Daily. https://www.prdaily.com/best-ai-tools-for-marcomm-tasks-according-to-edelman/

Dietrich, G. (2024). *How AI in PR is revolutionizing how you work*. Spinsucks.com. https://spinsucks.com/communication/ai-in-pr-how-you-work/

Green, A. & McClennan, M. (2024). *Ethical guidelines for generative AI update*. PR Council. https://prcouncil.net/advocacy/policies/ethical-guidelines-for-generative-ai-update/

International Communication Consultancy Organisation. (2023, November). *ICCO principles for ethical use of AI in public relations*. https://iccopr.com/wp-content/uploads/2023/11/ICCO-Guidelines-for-Ethical-Use-of-AI-in-Public-Relations-Agencies.docx.pdf

Lutz, A. (2025, April 18). *Marriott's CEO spoke out about DEI. The next day, he had 40,000 emails from his associates*. Fortune. https://www.msn.com/en-us/money/companies/marriott-s-ceo-spoke-out-about-dei-the-next-day-he-had-40-000-emails-from-his-associates/ar-AA1DbDle?ocid=msedgntp&pc=DCTS&cvid=dbec2f2ff22f45c2a08c358ab8d600eb&ei=18

Pawlak, H. (2024, March 15). *The biggest challenges facing the PR industry*. Brandpoint.com. https://www.brandpoint.com/blog/author/hpawlak/

Staley, L., Dvorak, M., Ewing, M.E., Hall, H.K., Hoeft, J.R., & Myers, C. (2023, November). *Promise & pitfalls: The ethical use of AI for public relations professionals*. Public Relations Society of America. https://www.prsa.org/docs/default-source/about/ethics/ethicaluseofai.pdf

The Chi Group. *Top public relations trends to watch in 2025* (2024, November 30). https://thechigroup.co/articles/2024/11/30/top-public-relations-trends-to-watch-in-2025

Torossian, R. (2024, December 23). *Public relations in 2025: Navigating the future of communication*. RonnTorossianUpdate.com. https://ronntorossianupdate.com/public-relations-in-2025-navigating-the-future-of-communication

Toth, E.L. & Bourland-Davis, P.G., eds. (2023). Chapter 2: The Future of the Public Relations Workplace. In *Navigating change: Recommendations for advancing undergraduate public relations education—The 50th anniversary report* (pp. 27–28). Commission on Public Relations Education. https://www.commissionpred.org

Valin, J. & Gregory, A. (2020, August). *Ethics guide to artificial intelligence in PR*. Chartered Institute of Public Relations and Canadian Public Relations Society. https://www.cipr.co.uk/CIPR/Our_work/Policy/AI_in_PR_/AI_in_PR_guides.aspx

3

TYPES OF PUBLIC RELATIONS

Public relations work is varied and diverse. This chapter gives you an overview of the various types or categories of public relations, along with case studies of each.

Ask three people working in public relations what they do, and you are likely to hear about three very different jobs. That's because public relations is a wonderfully diverse discipline. All kinds of organizations practice public relations, which itself has many different subcategories, with overlap among the various specialty areas. Here are some of these specialty areas.

- Strategic counseling
- Consumer relations
- Employee relations
- Community relations
- Global communication
- Investor/donor relations
- Public affairs and government relations
- Special events and promotion
- Media relations
- Crisis communication

DOI: 10.4324/9781003521211-4

STRATEGIC COUNSELING

The top priority for every public relations practitioner should be **strategic counseling**, *a management function that involves research, analysis and planning, execution of tactics, and evaluation.*

This function is often described as **issues management**, *the process by which an organization tries to anticipate emerging issues and respond to them before they get out hand.* However, the term **strategic counseling** suggests not only attention to issues, but a major role for public relations as part of an organization's leadership team. This counseling also is associated with **risk management**, *the process of identifying, controlling, and minimizing the impact of uncertain events on an organization*, and **crisis communication**, *the process by which an organization plans for, deals with, and communicates in out-of-control issues.*

Public relations practitioners aim to advise other organizational leaders on communication strategies, not simply to carry out communication tasks assigned to them by others who may not have the insights that practitioners have to focus on long-term relationships between the organization and its publics.

This anticipatory practice helps organizations detect issues in which they potentially may be out of step with their publics. Ideally, they learn this early enough to do something to prevent or at least minimize any negative impact.

For example, fast-food companies such as Subway, McDonald's, Wimpy, MOS Burger, and Burger King took note of public comments about healthy food and introduced more salads, fruits, and vegetables. That didn't spell the end of the Happy Meal, but it gave a choice to customers and a forum for the companies to promote their social responsibility.

An example of poor issues management is the US auto industry, which made large cars while Americans were buying smaller imports from Germany and Japan, and which today lags behind other countries in electric and hybrid vehicle technology.

ROYAL CARIBBEAN GROUP

The COVID-19 pandemic dealt a serious blow to the cruise industry in 2020, with America's Centers for Disease Control and Prevention (CDC) issuing a "No Sail Order" until spring 2021.

The stock of Royal Caribbean Group (RCG) fell 80 percent from a near-record high. How could the company navigate a safe return to cruising, working with the CDC, to restore confidence among consumers, investors, media, travel partners, and employees?

RCG partnered with marketing communications agency Weber Shandwick on a communication plan. Their primary research, including consumer insights and in-depth interviews in international markets with policymakers, medical providers, investors, and community leaders, found that the 2020 outbreaks didn't inflict irreparable harm to the cruise industry's credibility, cruising's core consumers never lost confidence, and the industry's COVID response was seen as too slow. Their research indicated that messaging needed to visualize safety protocols (such as social distancing) to increase confidence in cruising, showing that health and safety protocols outweighed speed for returning to service, and expressing confidence in cruising's future.

RCG created a Healthy Sail Panel (HSP) comprised of scientific, medical, maritime operations, and former government leaders. The panel, which collaborated with the CDC, had unfettered independence to make recommendations on how cruise ships could operate safely, resulting in 74 detailed "best practices." RCG developed messaging to address key concerns identified in research, including testing for all on board, highest cleanliness standards in travel, 100 percent fresh circulated air with upgraded and new technology, expert medical care, and safe destinations.

Tactics included Q&As, messages, news releases, media briefings, and media trainings, with RCG's CEO Richard Fain, an experienced cruise industry leader, as spokesperson, resulting in positive media coverage. RCG also rallied around its travel partners, providing financial help to prevent those small business owners from going out of business. This generated significant trade media coverage.

The result: the CDC accepted the HSP's recommendations as standards for a "Conditional Sail Order" in May 2021, with RCG's Celebrity Edge as the first ship approved by the CDC to sail. Broadcast, business, and trade media attended the inaugural cruise, with Fain conducting more than 100 interviews, including media outlets such as Bloomberg and Yahoo! Finance to reach the investor community.

Financial media cited RCG's leadership during the pandemic in lifting the entire cruise industry, further instilling investor confidence in the company's future and resulting in a nearly four-fold increase in RCG's stock price. Consumer interest in cruises nearly returned to levels last seen at the start of the pandemic.

CONSUMER RELATIONS

Every organization should have a program of **consumer relations** targeting **consumers**, *the people who obtain and use the products or services of the organization.* Consumers include fans, patients, students, members, voters, parishioners, clients, and shoppers as well as former consumers.

The relationship between these consumers and the organization is interdependent: consumers want or need the organization's products, services, or ideas; and the organization depends on the consumers' money, time, and support for its survival.

Thus consumer relations (also called **customer relations** or **consumer affairs**) warrants the careful and considered attention of the organization. Because it often is the front line dealing with customer fears and complaints, consumer relations should involve well-trained people who can create and maintain the best possible relationship between the organization and its customers.

Research into consumers' knowledge, attitudes, opinions, and behaviors is a major part of consumer relations. Tactics associated with consumer relations include advisory boards, brochures and other print or online literature, informational videos, direct mail, position papers, conferences, public relations advertising, social media, and media relations tactics.

Though interrelated, consumer relations differs from marketing in that it is focused primarily on people, with a mission to foster a mutually beneficial relationship based on understanding. Marketing is more about products and sales. But concepts such as **relationship marketing** signal a conscious adoption by marketing of the public relations principles of long-term engagement, mutual benefits, and transparency. Additionally, classic public relations is frequently used to launch new products, often under the name of **marketing public relations**.

XBOX

Xbox wanted to target football fans in the UK and Germany to turn them into Xbox fans, encouraging them to play EA Sports FC (formerly FIFA) on Xbox and encouraging loyalty to Xbox through gaming rewards.

The company turned to global communications firm Edelman, which created a campaign strategy to reach key publics both in real life at football stadiums and on dedicated football platforms on social media by hiding gaming reward codes in real life locations on match days, including stadiums across the UK and Germany. Fans could find codes on merchandise, hot dog buns, and even on the security team—and trade them in for gaming advantages online. The codes also could be shared by fans on social media.

Xbox's Hidden Fan Codes campaign was highly successful, with 100 percent of the 216 hidden codes being claimed by fans. The campaign resulted in a reach of 25 million, 9.2 million views, and 350,000 engagements.

EMPLOYEE RELATIONS

Employees are the first public of an organization. They make the product, perform the service, create the ideas, and generate information that "sells" the organization to its various consumers and others. They ensure safety in the workplace and quality in the product.

Employee relations (sometimes called **internal relations**) means that *an organization is likely to be successful when employees are informed, motivated, and on board with its mission.* Employee relations is often a liaison between employers and workers. Most organizations have policies that encourage open, honest, and transparent job-related communication, supported by ongoing employee research and assessment.

No organization will be successful without the cooperation and involvement of its employees, its volunteers, and often, its retired employees and families of employees. Significant category distinctions among employees include union and management for some organizations; for others, distinctions may center on tenure, line or staff function, length of service, rank, and work shift.

In some organizations, groups such as boards of directors or trustees function both as employee publics and as extensions of the employer. Sometimes employers are only loosely connected with an organization, such as physicians who work at, but not for, a hospital.

Employee relations often involves internal communication programs designed to motivate and educate employees. Communication tactics include employee meetings with their immediate supervisors, town hall meetings with company leaders, intranet sites, email, digital newsletters, bulletin boards, picnics and holiday parties, brochures, social media, and **blogs**, *websites featuring short articles called blog posts, often with videos, photos, and links to other blogs or websites, with reader comments*. Research activities include focus groups, surveys, and content analysis.

This specialization of public relations also involves recognition programs to reward employees for good work as well as employee volunteer programs. Research shows that employees who are encouraged to participate in volunteer work, some of it on company time, ultimately are more productive and have lower turnover rates and fewer sick days.

MUTUAL OF OMAHA

When unsolicited feedback from employees found that internal communications weren't hitting the mark, insurance company Mutual of Omaha took action. It created an internal communication campaign based on results of surveys and focus groups of employees.

Goals were to create a centralized location for all communication channels, report news and updates in real time, establish credible senders, increase senior leader visibility, determine the level of employee interaction with published communications through readership and viewership metrics, and reinforce the purpose within each communication.

The company developed a robust intranet site that houses all news stories, videos, podcasts, social media feeds, events, and announcements in one centralized location, with a notification system for employees who don't frequent the intranet site and a weekly wrap-up email featuring news stories published that week.

The visibility of senior leaders was increased by featuring them in news stories, as guests on podcasts, participants in videos, holding Q&A sessions during associate meetings, participants in manager meetings, and sending out packages to employees' homes. Mutual of Omaha also created a metrics dashboard to determine which content drove the highest views and days/times for greatest interaction.

The campaign was a success on all counts. The company saw an increase in viewership to the intranet site, increases in the frequency and readership of news stories, and involvement of senior leadership twice per month rather than a few times per year. The metrics dashboard indicated which times and days of the week drove the highest engagement and what type of news people enjoyed the most. A post-campaign employee survey showed that 92 percent of employees stated they are a strong fit for the company culture, 83 percent understood the organization's plans for future success, and 92 percent would recommend the organization as a great place to work.

COMMUNITY RELATIONS

Community relations is *an organization's planned and ongoing engagement with people who live in the neighborhood or community in which it operates*, to enhance its environment and foster a mutually beneficial relationship between the organization and the community.

Community relations involves the civic role of an organization and its contribution to the quality of life in a community. It impacts other areas of public relations involving employees and volunteers, regulators and government agencies, donors, and others.

Thus, community relations projects might involve recycling, beautification, restoration, and other environmental programs. It also plays out in sponsorships of academic teams, athletic sponsorships, children's activities, science competitions, and other engagements with schools, as well as in cultural interaction such as visual and performing arts.

This specialty also involves professional relationships gained by participating in business and civic groups such as Rotary, hosting meetings and events by outside groups, and buying locally.

Another aspect of community relations programs is **corporate philanthropy**, which involves financial, operational, or administrative support for charity drives and scholarships. **Employee volunteer programs** also form part of an organization's community relations program, as well as part of employee relations as noted previously.

Why should organizations spend time and money for community relations? It serves as a type of insurance, building up goodwill for when a crisis occurs or when bad news attaches itself to the organization. It also can smooth the way when zoning variances or construction permits are needed and can help create an environment that is attractive to potential new employees.

KAISER PERMANENTE

Soaring rents and home prices in San Francisco's East Bay have largely priced even middle-income families out of the housing market, resulting in long commutes and seriously impacting the health of families. Kaiser Permanente (KP), one of the region's largest employers and healthcare providers, knew how important safe, affordable housing is for overall health, so it sought to unite business and political leaders to prioritize affordable housing.

KP conducted a literature review, research on the fiscal and sociological impacts of scarce affordable housing, an employee survey, and in-depth interviews with potential partners. The research showed that while there was much concern about the lack of affordable housing, there was little coordinated effort to bring together the diverse forces needed to make an impact. KP stepped up to convene key publics (city, business, and community leaders) in a series of meetings while mobilizing KP employees as advocates. KP also sought a partner to build an affordable housing community.

Campaign objectives included: (1) Raising awareness about the importance of affordable housing by repeatedly reaching 20 percent of the county's residents; (2) Engaging 25 businesses and seven politicians to marshal resources to address the issue; (3) Mobilizing 100 KP employees as volunteer advocates; and (4) Elevating KP's reputation as a driving force to address the health of its members and community.

KP met with the region's most influential leaders to raise awareness of the advantages of affordable housing, coalesce partnerships, and identify strategies. KP also partnered with Habitat for Humanity to build Esperanza Place, a 42-unit townhome community. A website highlighted partners and construction progress, supplemented by online advertising and social media posts. A quarterly digital newsletter kept partners, the media, KP employees, and the community updated. KP hosted monthly volunteer opportunities for KP employees and partners to work at the construction site. Finally, KP hosted a "Sneak Peek" event for civic and political partners, business leaders, and housing advocates to tour the nearly completed site.

KP succeeded with all of its original objectives. The campaign garnered 5 million traditional and online media impressions, far exceeding the campaign goal of reaching 20 percent of the county's 1.1 million residents. KP recruited 77 leading business partners (triple the campaign's objective) and 14 politicians (double the campaign's objective) to support the initiative.

Building Esperanza Place was the crystallizing element of the campaign, serving as the region's focal point for ongoing efforts to address affordable housing. The campaign motivated over 200 KP employees (double the objective) to donate nearly 2,000 volunteer hours during Build Days.

Finally, by taking leadership on this issue, KP's respect among partners, employees, and the broader community increased dramatically. A coalition of 258 civic leaders and organizations voted to present Kaiser Permanente with the coveted East Bay Leadership Medal, the region's highest honor for outstanding service, specifically noting KP's leadership on affordable housing.

GLOBAL COMMUNICATION

Economic globalization and the resulting increase in global communication are connecting the world as never before, providing more opportunities for public relations. Many multinational organizations launch public relations campaigns that span the entire globe, often in partnership with public relations professionals "born into the culture."

To succeed, public relations professionals need to be aware of different **value systems**—*what people value or place importance on*—and a particular nation's cultural identity. **Culture**, *how people live their lives, includes shared experiences and activities such as language, religion, dress, food, the environment, history, and government that binds a region or country together as a distinct social system.*

Although well-known American brands, such as McDonald's, are present in many nations, there are concerns about the dominance of US culture and values, leading some nations to maintain their native cultures by enacting policies and regulations to dampen US influence. Sensitivity to, and appreciation for, cultural differences is critical for multinational organizations to build trusting relationships with key publics. For example, KFC (Kentucky Fried Chicken) is very successful in Asia, where it uses local ingredients and regional dishes on its menus.

It's important for public relations practitioners who are developing partnerships in another country to learn that country's culture and language. All translated messages, including brand names, should be reviewed by native speakers and tested within the target market before a campaign is launched. Coors learned this the hard way when it launched its "Turn It Loose" campaign to the Spanish-language market – discovering that it translated as "Suffer from Diarrhea." Likewise, Clairol and Estee Lauder had to rename their Mist Stick curling iron and Country Mist fragrance, respectively, for German customers because "mist" is slang in German for "manure." Oops!

Organizations also need to consider demographics, such as education and literacy rates, and whether technology is widespread in a country when developing their communication strategies.

Also, although many citizens of many countries enjoy freedom of speech and freedom of assembly, these aren't enjoyed universally. Limits on free speech can adversely affect an organization's ability to communicate freely, especially with news media. In some parts of the world, "cash for editorial" is common—meaning organizations pay to get a story in the news media. Governments can shut down unauthorized websites. Limits on freedom of assembly also can pose problems when planning a public relations campaign if gathering people for meetings, events, or demonstrations can be monitored or stopped by the government.

DOUBLETREE BY HILTON

DoubleTree by Hilton's guests around the world are welcomed with a warm chocolate chip cookie at check-in, a gesture synonymous with the brand's commitment to providing guests with a comfortable stay. The cookie's popularity soared to even greater heights after a company social media team tweet about a luxury car's launch into space, which resulted in an offer to make the cookie the first food ever baked in space.

The goal of the Cookies in Space campaign was to position the brand as the most welcoming in the world. Research showed that space-related news was a timely, trending topic. That, plus the company's partnership with Zero G Kitchen, which was working to develop a functioning kitchen in space, gave DoubleTree by Hilton the credentials to create a program that resonated with its key publics and the news media.

The campaign targeted DoubleTree by Hilton's markets around the world including the United States, Asia, Europe, the Middle East, and Africa. Tactics included a launch announcement, introduction of a space-themed cookie recipe book on National Chocolate Chip Cookie Day, the launch of the cookie into space, public reveal of the results of the cookie baking experiment onboard the International Space Station, a student contest and partnership with Scholastic Magazines, and a live Q&A call for more than 300 students to speak with a NASA astronaut aboard the International Space Station. All efforts drove consumers to CookiesInSpace.com. Digital content for mobile devices was created along with videos, blog posts, and photos created by DoubleTree by Hilton's social influencers. Employees were informed through internal newsletters, property celebration toolkits, and a team member contest.

The campaign yielded more than 1,123 earned online placements and 7.4 billion earned online impression globally, more than 24 times the company's initial goal. DoubleTree by Hilton saw a 6-point increase in unaided brand awareness and a 422 percent increase in social media brand conversation during the week of launch.

INVESTOR/DONOR RELATIONS

Investor relations, also called **financial public relations**, is a *specialty within public relations that manages an organization's relationship with shareholders, regulators, financial journalists and bloggers, investors, and both sell-side and buy-side analysts.* It requires expertise not only in public relations but also knowledge of finance and economics, as well as the ability to follow detailed legal requirements associated with mergers, stock options, public disclosure, and related matters.

Investor relations specialists conduct research on attitudes toward the company and then develop communication programs for shareholders, including large-group investors such as pension programs, mutual funds and unions, and individual investors—who often have very different interests and needs. These public relations professionals also communicate with regulators, financial journalists and bloggers, and both sell-side and buy-side analysts. Specifically, they create presentations for these publics, write speeches, prepare print and digital information, and work with financial media. They deal with information associated with mergers and acquisitions, both friendly and hostile.

Investor relations specialists oversee the company's annual stockholder meetings. They prepare the annual report, which generally is a sophisticated print and online presentation of the company's financial situation and outlook.

Investor relations also deals with **corporate social responsibility**, *a commitment by many companies to contributing to the betterment of society* while earning money for stockholders.

For nonprofit organizations, the financial field includes **donor relations**, *a specialty within public relations, similar to investor relations, that manages the organization's relationship with donors and with regulators and watchdog organizations.* Often part of a wider fundraising and development program, donor relations calls for tactics similar to those used for stockholders.

GENERAL MOTORS

General Motors (GM) has delivered consistent financial performance quarter after quarter, but its stock was regarded as a safe bet rather than a company with growth potential, especially among younger investors such as millennials, who are increasingly taking to social networks to share their views.

So GM partnered with global PR agency FleishmanHillard to target millennials. Research showed that GM's focus on electric vehicles, autonomous vehicles, and clean energy technologies was more likely to increase investment appeal. Message testing found that GM's aspirations needed to be backed by tangible products, such as "By 2025, GM will have more EVs on the market than anyone else."

The campaign plan leveraged millennial investor influencers with large social media audiences, including Grant Sabatier, creator of the website Millennial Money, and Tonya Rapley, founder of My Fab Finance, a financial education and lifestyle blog. GM also partnered with Cheddar, a popular news source for millennial investors, on a six-segment pilot series about GM's goals for an all-electric future and clean energy.

The Cheddar series featured subject matter experts on GM's electric vehicle strategy. Both influencers produced content to educate their audiences on reasons why GM is a smart investment choice, including a 10-minute YouTube video from Sabatier and blogposts from Rapley.

To evaluate the campaign, the team compared millennial investors with the Cheddar audience aged 18–44 who did not see the content. They found that of those exposed to the campaign:

— 71 percent have a "very" or "somewhat favorable" opinion of GM, 27 percent higher than those not exposed;
— 70 percent would consider investing in GM, compared to only 47 percent of those who weren't exposed;

— 67 percent intend to invest in GM within the next six months, a 116 percent increase compared to those who didn't see the content;
— 82 percent are more interested in GM after having engaged with the PR campaign, a 257 percent increase from the non-engaged group;
— 82 percent reported being more interested, compared to only 23 percent of the non-engaged group.

The campaign was so effective that it has become part of the regular communication strategy for the GM investor relations team.

PUBLIC AFFAIRS AND GOVERNMENT RELATIONS

Most organizations deal with regulatory agencies and government entities. Corporations often have oversight groups looking at safety issues. Nonprofit organizations sometimes interact with legislators, and advocacy groups often focus on public policy issues.

Public affairs or **government relations** is *an organization's efforts to build and maintain a working relationship with elected or appointed government officials.* The tasks associated with public affairs include research and information-gathering, interactive activities such as conferences and meetings, and communication techniques including print and online materials, as well as social media and media relations.

This category includes **lobbying**, *persuasive campaigns to support, defeat, or amend legislation that's necessary to an organization's own interests*, as organizations promote their interests to lawmakers and government regulators, hoping to obtain votes or support. Increasingly, both businesses and nonprofits are involved in both nonpartisan issue advocacy and in the highly partisan electoral process, especially on the funding side.

Government agencies also practice **intergovernmental relations**, *engaging their counterparts in other nations.* This practice, sometimes called **public diplomacy**, differs from regular diplomacy in that the latter often is conducted in secret, whereas public diplomacy generally is more transparent and involves the use of news media and social media to foster positive relationships between nations.

The term **public affairs** can be misleading, because many government agencies use this term for their entire public relations program. At one time, Congress refused to fund public relations activities, fearing that other branches of government would try to manipulate public opinion. But it does fund **public information**, *media relations by government agencies and the military*, through press secretaries, public information officers, and public affairs staffs.

Practitioners in this field hold news conferences, maintain press rooms, produce videos, seek publicity, and perform all the other tactics associated with public relations. During the Iraq War, coalition forces (led by the US and including the UK, Italy, Poland, and several other nations) launched a YouTube channel where videos showing aspects of the military operation attracted more than 9 million views.

Despite their occasional need for secrecy and tact, government and public relations practitioners generally try to be seen as open and transparent.

Over the years, governments have created commissions on public information and supported the use of information as a strategic element of defense and diplomacy. The Australian Army Public Relations Service, for example, provides support for strategic communication objectives. In Britain, the Royal Air Force includes active journalists in its reserve units, many working in the Public Relations Squadron that, among other things, provides media training.

IKEA CANADA

In Canada, a 13 percent Harmonised Sales Tax (HST), a blend of federal and provincial tax, is applied to every sales transaction, including second-hand items. Those items have lost their original look, packaging, and price, but never lose their tax. This double taxation generates $720 million Canadian ($501.2 million American, £402.6 million, €477.6 million) for the federal government amid a nationwide affordability crisis.

IKEA wanted to reinforce its role as a leader in affordability and environmental stewardship, so it partnered with global PR agency Edelman on an awareness campaign. Research showed that 45 percent of Canadians were concerned about their finances, many purchasing second-hand items to make the most of every dollar. As a result, IKEA created the SHT (Second Hand Tax), meaning customers pay zero percent tax when shopping the IKEA second-hand marketplace. This idea was designed to earn attention from consumers as well as government and business stakeholders who had the power to make change in federal tax policy.

IKEA sent digital letters to top federal and provincial leaders about the SHT idea. Letters appeared in newspapers read by Canadian business leaders such as *The Globe and Mail*, *Financial Post*, *Toronto Star*, and *Ottawa Citizen*. IKEA distributed a news release across the Canadian Newswire, created a broadcast chatter sheet, and did targeted pitching to gain awareness of the initiative, drive traffic to IKEA's second-hand marketplace, and spur petition signatures.

The campaign was a huge success. IKEA was the first consumer brand in Canada to propose changes to tax laws. The petition drive resulted in more than 35,000 petition signatures, a 192 percent increase in IKEA second-hand sales, and the Canadian government agreed to meet with IKEA to discuss a policy change to end the double tax.

SPECIAL EVENTS AND PROMOTION

All kinds of organizations engage in **special events**, *activities created by an organization mainly to provide a venue within which to interact with its publics*. They are designed to generate publicity, increase understanding, and generate support for the organization's services, products, or causes. In-person events have made a strong comeback since the 2020 pandemic, but virtual events, especially for educational purposes, and hybrid events remain popular. Organizations may hold an open house for customers, host recognition luncheons for employees, or sponsor appreciation events for donors and other supporters.

Such events should be potentially newsworthy, cost-effective, and linked to the organization's mission. For this reason, men's clothing stores sponsor golf tournaments, healthcare organizations support marathons, and museums recreate historical events. Cities bid to host the Olympics, Stanley Cup, and other international events to promote tourism and trade. Resorts and restaurants often have large staffs to help plan special events for guests.

In 2021, the global events industry market was valued at $736.8 billion (£594 billion, €713.4 billion) and it is expected to reach $2.5 trillion (£2.02 trillion, €2.42 trillion) by 2032, according to Allied Marketing Research.

Special events require planning to ensure the right fit between the organization and event, and also much attention to detail months in advance. Special events may include selecting a date and venue, choosing a menu, speakers, entertainment, and decorations, creating digital and print materials, managing registration, and handling social media and news media. Planners need to consider whether enough parking and toilets are available, and that menus consider people who are vegans or have food allergies.

PAWS & CLAUS

Many animal shelters maintain a no-kill policy, ensuring that no domestic animals are euthanized due to prolonged stays or capacity constraints. But what happens when there's an influx of dogs and cats that strains the shelter's capacity?

Seminole County Animal Services (SCAS) in Lake Mary, Florida promoted pet adoptions through a new holiday event, Paws & Claus. Its research found that 23 percent of dogs and 31 percent of cats find their forever homes through adoptions from an animal shelter, and narratives about animals rescued from difficult situations can evoke sympathy and a desire to provide a loving home.

Armed with this information, SCAS created a public relations strategy to complete at least eight pet adoptions during its event, obtain at least ten earned local media spots, reach a social media audience of 100,000, strengthen partnerships with local vendors and rescue groups by inviting them to table at the event, raise the name recognition of SCAS, and create community goodwill.

SCAS shared photos and videos on social media and event details on its website, created a Facebook event, held a promotional photo and video shoot at the shelter with Santa Claus, distributed flyers to participating vendors and rescues, had an electronic billboard on a prominent highway, and provided unique opportunities to local TV stations.

Paws & Claus surpassed all of its objectives. It adopted out 37 pets, exceeding its initial objective of eight pets. Social media posts reached 137,152 viewers, exceeding the objective by 37 percent. Twenty-one local media spots featured the event, surpassing the objective of spots, and 40 vendors participated, exceeding the objective of 30 vendors.

MEDIA RELATIONS

An organization's engagement with news media is the best-known part of public relations. In fact, many people think only of this instead of the wider array of public relations activities.

Media relations is *a specialty within public relations through which an organization communicates through various media.* Those media include print media such as newspapers and magazines, and broadcast and cable media including television and radio, both in their traditional form and online. The media also include digital venues, including blogs and websites, and social media such as Facebook, Instagram, X, YouTube, TikTok, and LinkedIn.

One premise of effective media relations is the mutually beneficial relationship between organizations and media. Organizations rely on media to help them communicate with their publics, while the media rely on organizations for newsworthy information to share with their audiences.

Research for media relations involves knowing media audiences as well as media **gatekeepers**, *the editors, reporters, or news directors who determine what gets reported in the media.*

Commonly used tactics for media relations are **fact sheets**, *brief, generally one-page outlines of information usually presented as bulleted items*, and **news releases**, *news-type articles written by public relations practitioners and given to media gatekeepers.* News releases are sometimes incorrectly called **press releases**—*implying releases only for print media*, or **handouts**, *an inappropriate slang term for news release.* News releases and fact sheets may be disseminated by mail or email and posted online for journalists and others.

There are many variations on news releases. They can be general or local, depending on the organization, its publics and the news being presented. They may include photos for print media or they may be directed to broadcast media with audio or video news releases, supported by voice actualities or video B-rolls. They may have a multimedia focus or interactive features (for example, visit the PR Newswire website at https://www.prnewswire.com/news-releases/videos/).

Feature releases, *news releases that emphasize personalities and human-interest angles rather than hard news*, are another option. They include biographies, interviews with individuals, histories of organizations, product overviews, question-answer pieces, and **how-to articles** (also called **service articles**) *that tell readers how to accomplish a certain task*. Feature releases may be written as a narrative or as a series of questions and answers or action steps.

Media relations also provides an outlet for organizational opinion. Opinion statements can be incorporated into blogs or as quotes in news and feature releases. Others are presented more formally as **position statements** (also known as **white papers**), *the formal, public position of an organization on a particular topic*, which include **position papers** and shorter **position paragraphs**. Opinions also can be expressed as **letters to the editor** or as **guest editorials**, *opinion pieces published as a solicited or approved editorial presenting the view of a person or organization not affiliated with the publication.* These are similar to **op-ed commentaries**, *opinion pieces not necessarily solicited by the publication*.

Many organizations gather their media relations materials at an **online newsroom**, *a set of web pages within a website that provides resources for journalists*. Examples of good online newsrooms include IBM, Netflix, Nike, Anheuser-Busch, Microsoft, United Nations, the British Royal Family, and the Australian Department of Immigration and Citizenship.

Media relations involves inviting and responding to requests for one-on-one interviews with journalists, along with organizing **news conferences**, *group interviews in which an organizational spokesperson makes a newsworthy announcement and reporters ask follow-up questions*. But journalists are very competitive with each other and do not favor news conferences, instead preferring to question news sources in private.

12 PRINCIPLES OF EFFECTIVE MEDIA RELATIONS

1. A relationship is both inevitable and necessary between an organization and the media. The actions of the organization will determine if this relationship is good or bad.
2. The organization should publicly speak with one voice by designating and preparing a single spokesperson (or multiple spokespersons with a coordinated message).
3. The person closest to the situation should be the designated spokesperson or at least be in close communication with the spokesperson.
4. "No comment" is never an option. Every bona fide question should be addressed.
5. The organization should look upon reporters as allies in reaching various publics rather than as intruders or enemies.
6. The organization should consider itself accountable to all of its various publics, internal as well as external. This includes customers, employees/volunteers, stockholders/donors, supporters, and the community. Further, it should view the news media as one of the vehicles available for communicating with these constituencies.
7. The organization should not expect to control the media's agenda or their assessment of what is newsworthy. But it can help add issues to that agenda.
8. The public/media relations office should always be "in the loop" in all newsworthy situations, especially those with negative potential.
9. Reporters should be accommodated with professional assistance such as parking permits, access, and a functioning media room.
10. The organization should expect that it occasionally will "take a hit" in the media. Its response should be to accept this, try to understand it, and get over it as quickly as possible.
11. Media skepticism and scrutiny can be more bearable when the organization interacts with reporters in a timely manner and with openness, accuracy, and candor.
12. Media coverage is considerably more credible than advertising. The effective use of the news media gives an organization a believable voice in the community.

IRELAND'S ENVIRONMENTAL PROTECTION AGENCY

The Irish Environmental Protection Agency wanted to make teenagers more aware of the environmental impact of items they use every day, so it hired Walsh, a Dublin-based public relations agency. Walsh developed the "Story of Your Stuff" campaign, which challenged teens to create a short film or documentary about the lifecycle and environmental impact of something they use on a daily basis.

With its focus on sustainability, waste management, climate action, and environmental protection, the competition asked young people to think, talk, and make small changes that can have far-reaching impacts. The students then had a chance to win €500 ($518; £418) for themselves and €500 ($518; £418) for their school. There also was a special "climate topic prize" as well as a prize for the best Irish language entry.

The campaign enlisted ambassadors such as the young filmmaker Christian Tierney and world-class surfer and environmentalist Easkey Britton to engage with the audience and inspire entries.

The campaign also developed content tailored specifically for schools, including a microsite, class lessons, video tutorials, photography, and tips on how to create a winning entry.

Much of the content was repurposed for a successful media relations campaign that achieved extensive national broadcast, print, online, and regional coverage.

For two consecutive years, the campaign far exceeded its goals in terms of driving traffic onto the website and the number of competition entries that were received.

CRISIS COMMUNICATION

A **crisis** *is a major, negative, public, sudden, and unpredicted event that can seriously disrupt an organization's activity and potentially hurts its bottom line or mission.*

Because crises can and eventually do affect every type of organization, **crisis communications** programs are a standard component of the wider public relations agenda. Because a crisis occurs in a public environment, even private businesses and nonprofit organizations cannot shield themselves from the expectation of being accountable to their publics.

By its nature, a crisis invites outside scrutiny and jeopardizes the organization's reputation. An organization can find itself in the role of either culprit or victim in a crisis situation. Regardless of the cause, if a crisis is handled properly, it offers the organization an opportunity to create a positive impression with its key publics.

Public relations professionals engage in crisis communication in various stages. The **pre-crisis** time is *one of anticipation and prevention*. Effective practitioners look for warning signs, undergo media training, and develop response plans for worst-case scenarios—all to be ready for events they hope will never occur.

The **acute stage** is *when the crisis breaks forth on the public stage*. It is a time to contain the problem, work with regulators and the media, and begin investigating the cause. In the **post-crisis stage**, the *focus is on recovering: returning to normal, assessing the extent of both physical and reputational damage, and planning to prevent a recurrence of the crisis*.

The court of public opinion is a common reference with public relations, and a new subspecialty of crisis communication merges this concept with actual legal courts. The media historically have covered lawsuits primarily with information from law enforcement and prosecutors. **Litigation public relations** provides *a tool for defense attorneys to manage communication before and during legal disputes* in an effort to impact the outcome of the case.

Generally, this area focuses on pre-trial publicity, which makes sense because most lawsuits are settled before trial. Specifically, it involves seeking balanced media coverage, counteracting negative publicity, strategically releasing information or inviting the media to give voice to a client's viewpoint, wordsmithing legal language for maximum impact with publics, and helping the media and their audiences understand legal complexities. It sometimes is able to influence the prosecution to bring a lesser charge.

Litigation public relations also is related to **reputation management**, *the process of seeking to influence the way publics view and understand the organization*.

Public relations practitioners are careful to protect the integrity of both the legal and communication processes, particularly because pre-trial publicity involves both factual and emotional messages.

Litigation public relations generally enjoys the attorney-client privilege of confidential interaction and thus has some specific regulations.

Tactics associated with litigation public relations include courthouse news conferences, attorney participation in talk shows, and daily media briefings by the prosecution. But it also involves behind-the-scenes activity.

Some observers have noted that this area is growing, particularly in the US and the UK, where the media are increasingly covering legal cases. Because the legal process is adversarial and creates a win-lose situation, the public information and advocacy models of public relations are most in play in the litigation area.

SEVEN PRINCIPLES OF CRISIS COMMUNICATION

Principle of Existing Relationships. Communicate with employees, volunteers, stockholders, donors, and other constituent groups. Keep them informed, because their continued support will be important in rebuilding after the crisis.

Principle of Media-as-Ally. Organizations in crisis should treat the news media as allies that provide opportunities to communicate with their key publics. If the media are intrusive and/or hostile, it may be because the organization has not been forthcoming in providing legitimate information to the media and, through them, to the organization's other publics.

Principle of Reputational Priority. After safety issues, the top priority is to shore up the organization's reputation by setting objectives to maintain and/or restore credibility. Focus on doing what's best for all publics—not only managers and stockholders, but also employees, customers, neighbors, and others.

Principle of Quick Response. There's a one-hour rule: Within one hour of learning about a crisis, the organization should have its first message available to its publics, particularly the media. Details about injury or death should be delayed until families are notified.

Principle of One Voice. A single spokesperson should be designated to speak for the organization. If multiple spokespersons are needed, each should be aware of what the others are saying, and all should present a coordinated message and work from the same set of facts.

Principle of Full Disclosure. Without admitting fault, organizations in crisis should work from the premise that they should share everything they know with their publics, subject to specific legal or other strategic justification for not releasing certain information.

Principle of Message Framing. This means that the organization maintains some level of control over how the story unfolds. This can be accomplished by seizing an opportunity early in a crisis by being accessible and providing information that sets the tone for subsequent reporting. The premise is that, if the organization does not tell its own story, that story will be told by others who probably have less knowledge of the facts and certainly less interest in the organization and its reputation.

MAYOR OF LONDON'S VAX-CAM

Organizations throughout the world dealt with a common crisis in 2020, the COVID-19 pandemic that has killed millions of people. When vaccines became available in 2021, government agencies sought ways to persuade people to get the vaccine, including the Office of the Mayor of London.

The Mayor's Office teamed with global communications agency Ketchum on a campaign to convince young Londoners ages 18 to 35 to get vaccinated. The "Vax-Cam" digital campaign was inspired by the success of the National Basketball Association's "Kiss Cams," where couples are picked out from the crowd at basketball games and shown on giant screens. The "Vax-Cam" campaign showed real Londoners getting the vaccine in a series of short digital vignettes. As they celebrated their world opening up, the screen filled with joyous animations as cartoon stickers, with phrases such as "Happy Jab Day."

The campaign was shown on selected cinema screens and digital billboards across London, including iconic locations such as The Oval cricket ground and Piccadilly Circus. Most of the digital billboards and cinema screens showed the vax-cam free of charge to help increase vaccinations in London.

A mix of earned, owned, and paid channels was used to promote the campaign. Messages emphasized the vital role the vaccine played in easing restrictions, getting both doses of the vaccine as soon as possible, and that getting vaccinated was quick and easy.

The results: one in two London residents saw the ad, and hesitancy on getting the COVID-19 vaccine dropped in London from 11 percent in March 2021 to 7 percent in July 2021. The campaign led to a 15 percent increase in vaccinations among young Londoners.

WORKS CITED

Allied Market Research. (December 2024). *Events Industry Market Size, Share, Competitive Landscape and Trend Analysis Report, by Type, by Revenue Source, by Organizer, by Age Group, by Origin of Attendees, by Event Location: Global Opportunity Analysis and Industry Forecast, 2024–2035.* https://www.alliedmarketresearch.com/events-industry-market

4

PUBLIC RELATIONS WRITING AND THEORIES

To be successful in public relations, practitioners need to be excellent writers and understand communication theories. This chapter focuses on those foundational elements of success.

If a public relations career only involved hosting parties and posing for photos, a fabulous wardrobe and movie-star looks would probably be assets. But that's not the case for most public relations practitioners. It's a profession that calls for solid writing skills and knowledge of communication theories that can be used in a public relations campaign, the focus of the second half of this book.

This chapter will explore those necessary ingredients for a successful career in public relations. Let's look first at writing.

WRITING SKILLS

When employers are surveyed about the skills they want in an entry-level public relations employee, good writing tops the list as an absolutely crucial skill. That's no surprise, given the importance of writing in so many public relations jobs, whether one is posting on the company's social media sites, creating news releases, or writing speeches

DOI: 10.4324/9781003521211-5

for a university president. Public relations deals with language: clarity, brevity, and accuracy. It calls for subtlety, understanding the nuance in choosing not just an OK word but the exact right word. Writing deals with strategy, knowing why you are sitting in front of a blank computer screen. It involves knowing what you want to accomplish, the audience you are writing for and its wants and needs, and what impact you hope to make.

Is it necessary to love writing? Probably! Most people who are successful in public relations genuinely like to write. They enjoy the process as much as the outcome. They like researching a topic and then strategically crafting the relevant information into a piece that is persuasive or newsworthy to achieve a certain purpose.

It's beyond the scope of this book to provide a comprehensive emphasis on public relations writing; entire books are available on the topic. But it's helpful to understand the nature of "news" and how to prepare a news release.

The news release format is the versatile foundation for writing for broadcast and print media, social media, and other online venues such as blogs and email. Its principles even enhance advocacy and fundraising pieces.

WHAT IS NEWS?

What are some of the principles of good news releases?

We begin with **news**, *significant information relevant to a local media audience, presented with balance and objectivity and in a timely manner.* We can simplify things with the acronym **SiLoBaTi + UnFa**, *a convenient acronym to identify elements of news—significance, localness, balance, timeliness, unusualness, and fame.*

- **Significance**. First, news is information of importance, consequence, and magnitude. It has meaning to many people, even those beyond the organization. It overcomes the "So What?" question that meets information of lesser importance.
- **Local**. News deals with information relevant to the local area, as defined by the coverage area of the news medium featuring the information, or to the special interests of an audience. "Local"

might be defined geographically for a community newspaper or focused on the interests of a particular audience such as a Hispanic newspaper.

- **Balance**. News is information presented with objectivity and balance. While the public relations practitioner uses information to promote the organization or client, it should not be packaged merely in a promotional manner. Rather, it should be presented with the air of detachment and neutrality that is associated with credible news venues. It is not hyped or exaggerated.
- **Timeliness**. The final key ingredient in news is that it is current and timely, being connected with contemporary issues, especially those high on public and media agendas.

In addition to these four key elements, newsworthiness is magnified by two other factors that public relations strategists strive for:

- **Unusualness**. News interest is enhanced when the information deals with unusual situations. This is what writers call human interest, that hard-to-define quality involving rarity, novelty, uniqueness, milestones, or slightly offbeat occurrences.
- **Fame**. News interest also is enhanced when the information involves fame. "Names make news" isn't idle chatter. Well-known or important people can add interest to a newsworthy situation. Sometimes their involvement can take an otherwise routine event and elevate it to the status of news.

There are different types of news. **Hard news** *is information that deals with momentous events: accidents, crime, death, disaster, scandals, and activities with immediate results such as elections, trials, and sporting events.* **Breaking news** is *hard news that is happening even as the media are covering it.* Both hard and breaking news often throw public relations practitioners into the area of crisis communication in a reactive mode.

Two other categories of news lend themselves more to proactive public relations. **Soft news** is *lighter information dealing with upcoming events and new programs, trends, and developments without major consequences.* **Specialized news** is *information of importance to particular publics and particular segments of the media.* This includes news about business, religion, sports, the arts, agriculture, science, health, home, fashion, and other interest areas.

Sometimes, news spontaneously occurs within organizations, usually in crisis scenarios. But in a more proactive way, public relations practitioners know how to generate newsworthy information that will interest both their publics and the media. Sometimes this involves a **news peg**, *linking the organization's message to something already being reported by the media.* For example, if a celebrity announces that he or she is dealing with mental illness, health advocacy organizations may be quick to engage reporters on news and feature stories about how to identify the illness in loved ones or the kinds of treatments available.

Other ways that organizations can generate news include giving an award, holding a contest, announcing personnel changes, addressing a local need, issuing a report or localizing a wider existing report, launching a campaign, giving a speech, involving a celebrity, and addressing a public issue.

NEWS RELEASE: THE BASIC TOOL

There has been speculation about the importance of news releases in the practice of public relations. The news release is dead, proclaim some observers. They base that declaration on the fact that fewer people read newspapers and that newspapers have less news and therefore use fewer news releases than they once did. But news releases also can be written to serve the format needs of both broadcast media and social media.

Knowing how to write effective news releases also helps public relations practitioners write advocacy and fundraising letters, position statements, and annual reports. It also assists with less formal writing associated with blogs and other interactive forms of media.

Here are the basic components of a news release:

- The **lead** (pronounced LEED) is *the most important paragraph in a news release.* It is the gateway to the entire story, the basis on which editors will decide to use the release and readers will decide whether to read it. The most common type is a **summary news lead**, a *lead that provides a one- or two-sentence report of the most interesting facts.* Details such as names and dates will come later, but the summary lead announces that corporate profits are up, that a new executive director has been selected, or that a new program or product will be available soon.

- The **benefit statement**, *a statement that clearly articulates the benefit or advantage that a product or service offers to a public*, is the biggest difference between a news release and a journalistic report. A news release always includes information indicating how this newsworthy information will be useful to people. One of the smoothest ways to highlight the benefit statement is to develop it as a quote or narrative explaining the advantage.
- Another component in news releases, but not necessarily in news reports, is the **information-action statement**, *a way to mobilize readers and viewers*. It gives the audience how-to instructions on obtaining more information or acting on the information provided in the release, such as buying a product, visiting a museum, or making a donation. This may highlight a website, phone number, or public meeting.
- **Secondary details** *amplify information in the lead*. For example, the lead may note that a biology teacher with 20 years of service to the local school district has been appointed assistant superintendent for science education. Later in the release would be biographical information about the teacher, organizational information about how science is taught throughout the district, and possibly information about the selection process.
- **Background information** *provides context for a news release*. In the education scenario noted above, background information might deal with a statewide report on science education.
- Some news releases include an optional section with **organizational identification**, *a paragraph with standard wording about an organization that routinely is dropped into a news release, usually at the end*. It often deals with corporate structure, such as by identifying a company as a subsidiary of a larger corporation and noting the industry ranking or the business. Organizational IDs are seldom published, but they alert reporters to useful information. They also become part of the report when the news release is posted on the organization's website.

Within this structure, public relations writers follow the basic journalistic guidelines for proper news reporting—in particular, focusing on objective presentation of newsworthy information. Other standards for news writing include using short sentences with simple language, and attributing quotes and all paraphrases that deal with opinion to a news source. Releases for newspapers generally are one or two pages long.

Like reporters, public relations writers follow a journalistic stylebook such as the *Associated Press Stylebook* in the US, the *Canadian Press Stylebook*, and *Reuters Handbook of Journalism*, used in many other English-speaking parts of the world. These stylebooks outline standard ways to use names and titles, abbreviations, capitalization, punctuation, governmental and military references, numbers, and other details of writing.

Public relations practitioners know that journalists often do not use news releases verbatim. But the information they contain often becomes part of the story produced by reporters. Additionally, practitioners routinely archive news releases at an online newsroom or media page at their organizational website.

Types of news releases include the **announcement release**, *which announces an upcoming activity or a new program or product*; the **follow-up release**, *a news release in which the organization responds or adds to prior news reporting*; and **interview notes**, *a news release that provides reporters with an unedited transcript of an interview that they can use to develop a story.*

BROADCAST NEWS RELEASE

Releases tailored for broadcast media are more conversational, writing that is professionally casual, with contractions, "you" references, and short sentences written for the ear rather than the eye.

Broadcast releases generally use stylebook variations developed specifically for radio and television. Generally, this means omitting middle initials, avoiding leads with names unfamiliar to audiences, avoiding courtesy titles (Mr, Mrs, Ms), using long titles only after names, and using attribution at the beginning of a quote or paraphrase rather than at the end.

Broadcast releases also assist reporters with pronunciation. They include **pronouncers**, also called **pronunciation guides**, *phonetic tips in news releases to help readers correctly pronounce unfamiliar words such as names of people and places*, such as Drogheda, Ireland (DRAW-heh-deh); and Wauchope, Australia (WAR-hope).

Broadcast style also has special guidelines for abbreviations. For example, the Food and Agriculture Organization of the United Nations is abbreviated to FAO for print releases; broadcast releases would use F-A-O, indicating that each letter should be pronounced separately. But the United Nations' Educational, Scientific and Cultural Organization would use UNESCO for print releases and Unesco (you-NESS-koh) for broadcast releases, indicating that the acronym should be pronounced as a word rather than a series of letters.

Broadcast releases often include **sound bites** (also called **actu-alityies**), *brief, memorable quotes from a news source.* These may be eyewitness reports, explanations by experts, or comments with an organization's viewpoints. A **lead-in** or **throw** is *a transition in a broadcast news release that introduces a sound bite.*

Broadcast releases are sometimes repackaged as ready-to-air packages as **audio news releases**, *news releases written for radio use including an actuality*, or **video news releases**, *news releases produced specifically for television stations with actualities, presented as an edited story package.* Another option is **video B-rolls**, *sound bites, and raw, unedited footage provided to television stations to use in news reports.*

EMAIL AND MULTIMEDIA NEWS RELEASES

A news release can be adapted as an **email release**, *a news release that is briefer and more concise than a printed release, with photos, links, and supplemental text.* Generally the subject line indicates that it is a news release from a particular organization, with the topic part of the subject line, making it easy to locate archived copies.

A **multimedia news release** is *a news release that includes features such as web links, videos, photos, infographics, live social media feeds, social sharing, and call to action buttons.* Such multimedia elements can drive home key messages and paint a visually impactful picture of stories.

Writing for digital and social media also has some unique standards for public relations practitioners. Web writing should be short and concise, generally fit for a single screen. It should be scannable, which means it features short paragraphs, bullets, and boldfaced, or otherwise highlighted, text to make it easy for readers to scan through a piece rather than read every word. It also includes links and navigation tools.

Writing for blogs and other types of social media should be professionally casual; that is, writing that is conversational, friendly, and less formal than other news releases but not chatty. The same kind of writing that produces good news leads can cut to the chase with blog items, online newsletters, web pages, and related media. As with all public relations writing, accurate information as well as correct grammar and spelling are important.

Specialized stylebooks also have tips for writing for blogs and other venues of social media. These include acceptable uses for terms such as "app," "click-through," "LOL," and "unfriend," as well as advice against retweeting without full disclosure and confirming sources found on blogs.

FEATURE RELEASE

Feature releases *emphasize personalities and human-interest angles rather than hard news*, going behind the news with information about people, organizations, and issues that touch on a news peg. As noted in Chapter 3, this category includes **biographical releases**, also called **bios**, *narratives about people significant to an organization*; profiles and interviews about organizational people; histories, profiles, and backgrounders about the organizations themselves; and how-to articles, Q&As, case histories, and information digests dealing with issues related to the organization.

Such releases are lighter in tone than news releases. They may not follow the inverted-pyramid style but instead may read more like a magazine article.

Feature leads seldom summarize the story. Rather, they set up a short anecdote, ask a question or provide description. Some feature leads directly address readers. Others may focus on a pun. The intention of such a lead is to captivate readers, to entice them into continuing with the story.

Feature leads are followed by a **nut graph** (short for **nutshell paragraph**; as in, here's the key point of this story in a nutshell), *a paragraph following the lead in a feature story that presents the key point of the story*. It provides a transition into the heart of the story and tells readers how the story is timely and important.

Because feature writing has fewer of the stylistic conventions associated with news writing, many public relations writers enjoy the flexibility and creativity that this type of writing offers. Increasingly, organizations are finding a ready outlet for such articles in their websites.

MEDIA PITCHES, MEDIA ADVISORIES, AND EVENT LISTINGS

A news release is often included with a **media pitch** or **pitch**, *a targeted, compelling message to journalists so that they decide to cover an organization's news, resulting in media coverage*. Pitches are often done via email but also through social media, telephone, or traditional mail. When pitching, make sure your story is newsworthy, pitch to relevant contacts on a **media list** (*a list of people interested in covering an organization's news story such as journalists, social media personalities and influencers, bloggers, and podcast hosts*), and write a clear and short subject line. Grab attention with the specific person's name and job title, and offer expert sources, relevant links, images, and video. Give a call to action and wrap up your message with a summary of your pitch. Keep it short and sweet, thinking from the recipient's point of view: "What's in it for me?"

A shorter alternative to a news release is a **media advisory** (also known as a **media alert**), *a memo written by a public relations practitioner that notifies reporters about an upcoming activity*.

Organizations can promote their upcoming events through **event listings**, *a writing format that provides basic information for use in calendars on websites of media outlets and the organization's own website.*

OPINION WRITING

It might seem that news releases have little to do with advocacy and opinion writing, but the same principles apply. Information should be newsworthy; opinions should be attributed (either individually to a person, or corporately to an organization). The usual news release issues of audience interest and strategic significance to the organization apply equally to opinion writing. The entire process is informed by an issues-management perspective as outlined in Chapter 3.

Public relations people often have a role in advocating for an organization or for causes and issues associated with it. After careful research and strategic decision-making, organizations often wish to communicate their position to employees, customers, professional colleagues, legislators and government regulators, stockholders and donors, and other publics that they might influence.

Vehicles for this include position statements, letters, and op-ed pieces, as described in Chapter 3, as well as lobbying material, speeches, and organizational advertising. Often a news release announces the release of an important organizational statement on matters of public interest.

A position statement generally has a few standard elements:

- An issue backgrounder identifies the topic, explains its significance to the key publics, provides relevant history and context, indicates the current situation, and projects likely developments.
- The position itself gives a clear statement of the organization's official stance, along with a justification for this policy. The justification usually includes supporting arguments and pre-emptively refutes any arguments that opponents are likely to make.
- The conclusion makes recommendations and sometimes includes formal citations that document information included in the statement.

With the position statement as the foundation, organizations often amplify their opinions and policy recommendations through other vehicles. **Talking points** *encourage consistency among organizational spokespersons and supporters.* **Letters to the editor** allow the organization to present its opinion to newspaper readers. **Op-ed pieces** in newspapers and other publications (both print and digital) offer another venue for organizational policy recommendations.

Proclamations and **petitions** also can emerge from position statements. **Proclamations** are *formal advocacy messages made by some authority.* **Petitions** are *requests for action circulated among supporters and signed by many people, often urging governmental or other officials to act in some way.* Online petitions can generate millions of signatures.

FUNDRAISING AND ADVOCACY APPEALS

Appeals to donors and support for social causes may seem far removed from the standard protocols for writing news releases, but the principles of newsworthiness, audience interest, and organizational strategy are always important. These same principles come into play when organizations ask for financial support, seek new members or volunteers, appeal directly—or through constituents—for government support, or invite political action on behalf of a cause.

Examples include **appeal letters**, *direct-mail pieces sent to potential donors by nonprofits engaged in fundraising campaigns*, and **advocacy letters**, *a format for direct-mail or internet release that promotes a cause or supports an issue.*

Writing such appeals calls for careful planning, especially with research into the interests of would-be recipients of the appeal message. The benefit statement associated with news releases is a key ingredient in such appeals, because the focus always should be on how the requested involvement will help the public rather than what it will do for the organization.

Because people are altruistic, the "what's-in-it-for-me?" question may involve helping others. People may want to prevent animal cruelty, support missionary work, feed the hungry, support a political goal, or other advantages resulting from their positive response to an organization's advocacy campaign.

Like feature writing, practitioners often enjoy the challenge and creativity associated with advocacy writing. When they personally believe in the cause they are promoting, their work can become a true labor of love.

SPEECHWRITING

The basic news release process even informs speechwriting. Good speeches generally present news of some kind, telling audience members something that they didn't know before. They also address audience interests and clearly present a benefit. These qualities stem from research on the audience to find out what its members already know and what they care about.

Writing the draft of a speech pulls together elements that public relations practitioners use for broadcast releases, such as a conversational tone and a professionally casual approach. It also includes the use of pronouncers to help the speaker. Additionally, crafting a speech includes much of the flexibility and creativity of approach that practitioners find in writing feature releases.

Speechwriting also involves making effective use of the strategy that is so much of a public relations practitioner's repertoire. Speeches generally revolve around a **proposition**, *a single main idea.* **A factual proposition** *asserts the existence of something*, such as a plan to change a university's foreign language requirements. **A value proposition** *argues the virtue or merits of something*, such as the joy of writing. **A policy proposition** *identifies a course of action and encourages its adoption*, such as a proposal to make parent-education classes a requirement for a high school diploma.

Propositions are only as good as the arguments that support them. Generally, a proposition should have several subordinate points that are strong and convincing. Effective writers are careful not to weaken the argument with over-generalized statements, drawing unwarranted conclusions, building on false facts, launching personal criticism, or otherwise presenting logical flaws that make it easy for audiences to refute the proposition.

An effective conclusion to the speech often summarizes the proposition and offers recommendations.

Speeches that are followed by a question-answer session sometimes are accompanied by talking points to help the speaker remain on track. Forums for this include news conferences, testimony before government agencies, town meetings, and other face-to-face encounters with journalists or with other publics, such as employees or stockholders.

ONLINE NEWSROOM

Most organizations have online newsrooms that archive news releases and virtually all of the writing produced for public consumption. This includes releases for print and broadcast media, social media releases, and both color and black-and-white photographs as JPEG or GIF files (often presented as thumbnails that can be downloaded in varying levels of resolution).

Online newsrooms also post feature releases, organizational media kits, and information with biographies, organizational histories, and other information about the organization and its products, services, or cause. These sites also highlight audio and video material, both packaged for media use as well as background interviews and video footage that media and other users can edit into their own pieces. Often, these sites post organizational documents such as annual reports, speeches and official statements by organizational executives, and sometimes brochures and other material produced by the public relations team.

Many online newsrooms include information on how journalists and others can sign up for RSS feeds and opt-in email notices, along with subscribe buttons inviting readers to join the organization's Instagram or Facebook pages, blog site, and X feed.

Generally, online newsrooms can be accessed not only by reporters but also by customers, donors, shareholders, industry analysts, and both professional colleagues and competitors. They often include links to social media sites, as well as sharing features so readers can easily pass along the information to their friends.

COMMUNICATION SAVVY: UNDERSTANDING THEORIES

Another "must" for public relations professionals is a solid understanding of **communication theory**, *the field of study that tries to make sense of how people communicate.* Such theories can provide the foundation for strategies chosen for a public relations campaign, which we will discuss in Chapter 6.

Communication theories explain the effects of mass communication, ways to use media effectively, and interpersonal communication, communication that involves how individuals as well as groups and organizations use both words and nonverbal forms of communication. Theories also give insight into how culture and social context support or interfere with effective communication. Let's look at some theories that are useful in the practice of public relations.

PROCESS OF COMMUNICATION THEORIES

As a theory of communication, **information theory** *focuses on the content and channels of communication.* It involves a message sent by a source to a receiver, with ideas encoded and interpreted through symbols (words, images, and gestures) that are transmitted person-to-person or through some technical connection.

Harold Lasswell (1948) offered a simple formula of communication: "Who says what to whom with what effect." Today, we add "how" and perhaps even "why" to this formula.

This model was expanded on by Claude Shannon and Warren Weaver, Norbert Wiener, and later by David Berlo and Wilbur Schramm. Shannon and Weaver developed what they called the **mathematical theory of communication**, *a theory that identifies a model for one-way communication, moving from sender to receiver.* In their linear approach, data was encoded and transmitted through a channel to a receiver. It was a model for monologue with the source person or organization talking at an audience. This is the publicity model of public relations.

Norbert Wiener added to that with his **cybernetic theory of communication**, *a theory that identifies a model for two-way communication, moving from sender to receiver and returning via feedback.* In this communication model, a **sender**, *a person or organization originating communication*, crafts a message using verbal and/or nonverbal symbols. This creation involves **encoding**, *a process in creating a message with a specific meaning that can be interpreted by a receiver with approximately the same meaning.*

This message is carried through a particular **channel**, *the specific vehicle through which a message is communicated from sender to receiver*, such as a blog entry, social media post, news release, speech, or photo. It is sent to a **receiver**, *a person or organization obtaining a message.*

This receiver construes the message by **decoding**, *a process by a message receiver in interpreting the intended message of the sender.* The receiver reacts and responds to the original message by encoding **feedback**, *communication by a message receiver sent back to the sender*, such as a blog comment, a question, a smiley face emoji, and so on.

A communication context potentially involves **noise**, *any interference that limits the ability of the channel to carry a message faithfully from sender to receiver.* Common types of noise include **physical noise** (*communication disruption caused by inefficient communication channels*) such as whispering; **physiological noise** (*disruption caused by physical distractions in the message receiver*) such as poor hearing, stress, or anger; **psychological noise** (*disruption caused by preconceived notions such as bias, assumptions, reputation, or racial/ethnic stereotypes*); **semantic noise** (*disruption caused by use of language not understood or appropriately* *interpreted by the receiver*), such as use of a language with which the sender or receiver is not fluent; **demographic noise** (*communication disruption caused by differences between message sender and receiver based on ethnicity, age, social status*); and **environmental noise** (*sound pollution from the outside including construction, transportation, and loud music*).

As you can see, there are many potential barriers to effective communication, but they can be overcome.

OBJECT OF COMMUNICATION THEORIES

Public relations practitioners should realize that communication is a receiver (object) phenomenon, meaning that communication is controlled not by the <u>sender</u>, but by the <u>receiver</u>. One of the earliest theories to focus on the receiver in communication is the **uses-and-gratifications theory** of researchers Elihu Katz and Jay Blumler, which *suggests that people make choices in selecting media for particular purposes, including information, entertainment, value reassurance, social interaction, and emotional release.* This theory sees audiences as taking a proactive role in the communication process. It helps public relations practitioners to attempt to satisfy the interests of people who are actively seeking an organization's information through such venues as websites or livestreaming. It's helpful for PR professionals to understand if their audiences are seeking information for entertainment, news-surveillance, or other reasons.

A related theory is Martin Fishbein's **expectancy-value theory**, which *observes that people make media choices based on what they want, what they expect from the media, and how they evaluate the ability of the media to meet those expectations.*

Sandra Ball-Rokeach and Melvin DeFleur developed the **dependency theory**, which *states that audiences, the media, and society in general are in a three-way relationship.*

From these theories, we learn that audiences use the media to the extent that the media provide information important to society and people's role in it. The more relevant the information, the more influential the media become.

MEDIA EFFECTS THEORIES

Throughout the latter half of the 20th century and into the 21st century, scholars have been studying how the media affect audiences.

Powerful Effects Model. Early media effects research, an outgrowth of stimulus-response research by Ivan Pavlov to condition dogs to anticipate food when they heard a certain sound, produced the **powerful effects model**, meaning that *the media have direct, immediate, and powerful effects on their audiences*. The basic assumption of this theory is that media audiences are passive and homogeneous. Terms such as **magic bullet theory** and **hypodermic needle theory** are associated with this cause-and-effect relationship between message and response.

But the powerful effects model had many flaws, not the least of which was that further research showed that the media simply do not consistently and single-handedly exert a strong impact on audiences.

Limited-Effects Model. In the mid-1900s, researchers such as Joseph Klapper and Hope Lunin Klapper then shifted their attention to a **limited-effects model** *that saw communication as being a weak influence in affecting people's attitudes, opinions, and behaviors*. More important is the influence of family, friends, and respected experts.

This model is closely associated with the **two-step flow of communication theory**, which found that *instead of directly changing attitudes, the media may influence opinion leaders, who then influence others through interpersonal means*. Paul Lazarsfeld and Elihu Katz created their theory after identifying a predictable communication pattern among voters. Lazarsfeld eventually extended this idea into a **multistep flow of communication theory**, *which identifies several layers in the process*. This concept can be useful to public relations practitioners, especially as they identify opinion leaders among their various publics.

But the limited-effects model also has flaws in that it doesn't explain the observations that, in many situations, the media do seem to play a significant role in what people think, say and do.

Moderate Effects Model. More recently, the focus has centered on a **moderate effects model**, *which acknowledges that, over time, the media have a cumulative effect on people, moderated by other social influences*. Many studies have focused on violence, social tolerance, and sexual issues as they are depicted by the media. While no single media message exerts enough power to control audiences, they do seem to be instrumental over time in affecting audiences on issues such as sex and violence and on topics such as social tolerance and acceptance of racial minorities, gay people, and people of various religious affiliations and ethnic backgrounds in participating in society.

Among the many variables that shape how the media will affect people are sex, age, educational achievement, self-esteem, media-use habits, group involvement, and their own sense of identity as it relates to culture, religion, lifestyle, ethnicity, and race.

Agenda-Setting Theory. This theory by Donald Shaw and Maxwell McCombs (1972) *states that the media don't tell us what to think but rather tell us what to think about.* This observation has important implications for public relations practitioners, who try to link organizational issues with those on the news media's agenda and to interest the media in issues important to the organization. The issue has been studied in many contexts, most often in relation to government and voting. Two assumptions are that the news media don't reflect society but instead help shape it by raising up certain issues as being important. A criticism of this is the **herd mentality** of the media, *whereby a news media organization feels compelled to report on something just because its competitors are focusing on the same topic.* Thus, by concentrating on that topic, the public is left to believe that the issue really is important because news coverage seems to be everywhere.

Associated with agenda-setting theory are the related concepts of **priming**, *how a news topic reminds media audiences of previous information*, and **framing**, *the way news media treat a particular topic*. If agenda setting deals with what people think about, priming reminds them what they already know about the topic, and framing deals with how they think about the topic.

Gatekeeping Theory. Related to agenda-setting theory, Kurt Lewin's **gatekeeping theory** *rests on the notion that even journalists trying to be objective will make reporting choices based on their own biases about the presumed interests of their audiences.* Gatekeeping points to the power of an editor or news director to determine what the media report on or what topics it may avoid. Public relations practitioners have learned to focus on providing information to the media that gatekeepers will judge as being of interest, such as a **news peg**, *a topic currently being reported that overlaps with an organization's mission or interests.*

Cultivation Theory. This theory, proposed by George Gerbner, *suggests that the media (notably television) shapes or cultivates people's conception of social reality.* A large amount of media exposure over time affects not only individuals but also society as a whole. Gerbner argued that television cultivated a middle-of-the-road political perspective, though more recent observers have noted that, with the fragmentation of media and the 24/7 news cycle on politically oriented TV networks, the effect now is more divisive in society. Gerbner also articulated the **mean world effect**, which *observes that people who use the media a lot tend to be more fearful, suspicious of the world, and susceptible to social paranoia and conspiracy theories.*

Spiral of Silence Theory. Elisabeth Noelle-Neumann's theory *suggests that people learn through media reporting what appears to be the majority opinion; those holding minority viewpoints often silence themselves*, preferring not to express their opinion and thus not "rock the boat." The theory was an attempt to explain the formation of public opinion that gave social power to the Nazis. Today's public relations professionals, especially those advocating for what appears to be a minority opinion, can "unsilence" people by showing that other people, too, have opinions that run counter to the majority, or even that the presumed majority opinion isn't as common as it is thought to be.

RHETORIC

Rhetorical Theory. The classical **rhetorical theory** associated with Aristotle, *which observes that effective communication is based on ethos, logos, and pathos*, continues to offer insight into the practice of public relations. Public relations practitioners focus on the message source, selecting a spokesperson on the basis of credibility, charisma, and control or influence over the audience. It deals with the logical aspect of an argument, gathering and presenting facts and sound reasoning. And it looks to the emotional impact of messages and the nonverbal communication used to express messages. Much contemporary research is conducted on these aspects of communication, particularly source credibility.

PERSUASION THEORIES

Consistency Theories. Several related **consistency theories** *describe how people deal with information contrary to existing information, attitudes, and biases.* **Balance theory**, articulated by psychologist Fritz Heider, *observes that unbalanced mental stances create tension and force an individual to try to restore balance.* Charles Osgood and Percy

Tannenbaum's **congruity theory** *added some measurement in attitude.* The lesson of these consistency theories for public relations practitioners is that attitude change can be stimulated by information that causes people to realize that two attitudes are in conflict.

Cognitive Dissonance Theory. Drawn from social psychology, Leon Festinger's **cognitive dissonance theory** *notes that when people realize they hold contradictory attitudes or beliefs, they try to reduce the psychological discomfort, usually by changing one of their attitudes or beliefs.* This theory helps explain why public relations practitioners are sometimes frustrated because our publics don't seem to act on information in the way we think they should. Closely related to cognitive dissonance are several concepts dealing with selectivity. Through **selective exposure** and **selective avoidance**, *people expose themselves to messages they think they will like and avoid what they expect not to like*, choices they make because of personal interest. Using **selective attention**, *people pay attention to information that support their attitudes and ignore information opposed to their attitudes.* **Selective perception** *leads people to interpret information based on how it fits their attitudes.* Similarly, using **selective retention**, *people remember information that is of interest and forget information that doesn't seem to be relevant to them.* Finally, via **selective recall**, *people are more likely to remember what supports their beliefs.*

Social Judgment Theory. Muzafer Sherif and Carl Hovland's **social judgment theory** *observes that individuals accept or reject messages to the extent that they perceive the messages are corresponding to their internal anchors (attitudes and beliefs) and as affecting their self-concept.* From this theory, the public relations professional may find it more useful to focus on presenting a new image about a client or organization rather than trying to change the beliefs and values of members of a key public.

Inoculation Theory. Proposed by William McGuire and Demetrios Papageorgis, **inoculation theory** *suggests that unchallenged beliefs and attitudes can be swayed with persuasive information, while attitudes that have been tested are more resistant to change.* This latter aspect is especially useful to communicators seeking to create resistance to potentially opposing arguments.

Sleeper Effect. Carl Hovland and Walter Weiss identified a **sleeper effect**, *noting that the persuasive impact of communication* *sometimes increases as time elapses*. Information that people initially receive from a low-credibility source may become increasingly credible as the source fades from memory. Conversely, what people initially considered as a highly persuasive message may fade over time.

CRISIS COMMUNICATION THEORIES

Theory of Accounts. Michael Cody and Margaret McLaughlin proposed the **theory of accounts**, *which focuses on using communication to manage relationships in the wake of rebuke or criticism*. An account is the verbal and nonverbal language that explains why a person or organization took a particular action. It is a narrative that is especially important in public relations crisis situations and is useful in conflict resolution, whether interpersonal or organizational.

Apologia. Keith Hearit presents an apologia approach to crisis management. An **apologia** *is a formal defense of an organization's actions (not to be confused with an apology)*. Hearit outlines a threefold approach to persuasive accounts that offers an explanation, and if necessary, a defense; statements of regret; and disassociation tactics to distance the organization from the problem.

Image Restoration Theory. William Benoit introduced the **image restoration theory** *to help organizations understand and emerge from crisis situations*. Benoit's model suggests several options, including denial, evasion of responsibility, reduction of offensiveness, and corrective action. Many lessons of this theory emerge in the Public Relations Planning section of this book in Step 6, where organizations consider various options for dealing with outside criticism.

THEORIES ABOUT INNOVATIONS

Diffusion of Innovations. Everett Rogers studied how innovations are spread (or diffused) throughout society, shedding light on the likelihood that new ideas or products will be adopted. He identified five categories of adopters (innovators, early adopters, early majority, late majority, and laggards). The **diffusion of innovations theory** *identifies the role of opinion leaders as models in the process of mass adoption of new products or ideas*, providing insights on who and how to address in messages about new concepts.

PUBLIC RELATIONS MODELS

Grunig's Models of Public Relations. James Grunig provided a matrix of four different approaches to public relations, each with different purposes and characteristics. These loosely translate as the publicity, public information, advocacy, and relationship models that were presented in Chapter 2 of this book.

THEORIES ABOUT PUBLICS

Situational Theory. James Grunig's **situational theory** *looks at publics as being active or passive*. Active publics are likely to seek out information, whereas passive publics tend to deal with information only when it is placed before them. The theory also observes that some publics are active on all issues, others on only one issue. The value of this insight to public relations practitioners: it avoids a one-size-fits-all approach and, instead, helps them engage their publics in an effective way, drawing on the interests of the publics themselves.

SYSTEMS THEORY

Systems Theory. **Systems theory** *explains an organization's relationships with its publics.*

This interdisciplinary theory is rooted in technology and biology, but it sheds light on some aspects of social psychology, especially the concepts of feedback and mid-course adjustment. Public relations practitioners find it useful to understand how organizations relate with their various publics. The associated concept of **linkages** is especially useful, helping to identify various categories of publics and their relationships with an organization.

WORKS CITED

Lasswell, H.D. (1948). The structure and function of communication in society. In L. Bryson (ed.), *The communication of ideas* (p. 34). New York: Harper.

PART II
PUBLIC RELATIONS PLANNING

Effective public relations calls for a strategic planning process. This section of the book outlines a four-phase, ten-step planning model that can work for every kind of organization—corporate or non-profit, large or small, well resourced or penniless.

Part II is presented as a how-to workshop. This approach presumes that you, the reader, are personally and actively engaged in creating a public relations plan for an organization in which you are involved. Thus the writing style in this section is more direct, more "you" centered. It offers a series of steps that unfold into a comprehensive public relations plan.

Here's an overview of the planning process that will be developed over four chapters.

PHASE 1 FORMATIVE RESEARCH

The first of the four phases focuses on the preliminary work of communication planning, which calls for gathering information and analyzing the situation. In four steps, the planner draws on existing information available to the organization and, at the same time, creates a research program for gaining additional information needed to drive the decisions that will come later in the planning process.

Step 1: Analyzing the Situation. Your analysis of the situation is the crucial beginning to the process. Everyone involved—planner, clients, supervisors, key colleagues and the ultimate decision

DOI: 10.4324/9781003521211-6

makers—should be in solid agreement about the nature of the opportunity or obstacle to be addressed in this program.

Step 2: Choosing Research Methods. In this step, you'll do **secondary research** (*re-analyzing existing information obtained by previous researchers for a new and specific purpose*) followed by **primary research** (*generation and analysis of new information to address a research question or problem*).

Step 3: Analyzing the Organization. This step involves a careful and candid look at three aspects of the organization: (1) its internal environment (mission, performance, and resources), (2) its public perception (visibility and reputation), and (3) its external environment (competitors and opponents, as well as supporters).

Step 4: Analyzing the Publics. In this step you identify and analyze your **key publics**—the various groups of people who interact with your organization on the issue at hand. You also will analyze each public in terms of its wants, interests, needs, and expectations concerning the topic of this plan; each public's relationship to the organization; its involvement in communication and with various media; and a variety of social, economic, political, cultural, and technological trends that may affect it.

PHASE 2 STRATEGY

The second phase of the planning process deals with the heart of planning: making decisions dealing with the hoped-for impact of the communication on the key publics, as well as the nature of the communication itself.

Step 5: Creating Positioning Statements, Goals, and Objectives. In this step, you will focus on the ultimate position and the associated goals sought for the organization and for the product or service. This will help you develop clear, specific, and measurable objectives for each key public.

Step 6: Choosing Proactive and Reactive Strategies. A range of possible actions is available to the organization, and in this step you consider what you might do in various situations. It includes both public relations initiatives (proactive strategies) and responses to outside influences (reactive strategies).

Step 7: Developing the Message Strategy. This step deals with various decisions about the message, such as the spokesperson who will present the message to the key publics, content of the message, its tone and style, verbal and nonverbal cues, and related issues.

PHASE 3 TACTICS

During the third phase, you will consider various communication tools, and you will create the visible elements of the communication plan.

Step 8: Selecting Communication Tactics. This inventory deals with the full range of communication options. Specifically, you will consider the four elements of the PESO model: paid, earned, shared, and owned media.

Step 9: Implementing the Strategic Plan. With this step, you turn the raw ingredients identified in the previous step into a recipe for a successful public relations plan, packaging those tactics into a cohesive communication program. You also will develop budgets, set schedules, and prepare to implement the communication program.

PHASE 4 EVALUATIVE RESEARCH

The final phase of strategic planning deals with evaluation and assessment. This enables you to determine the degree to which the stated objectives have been met. On that basis, you can decide about modifying or continuing the communication activities.

Step 10: Evaluating the Strategic Plan. This is the final planning element, indicating specific methods for measuring the effectiveness of each recommended tactic in meeting the stated objectives.

[For more information on this process, see another book by this author, *Strategic Planning for Public Relations*, 7th edition, 2024, Routledge/Taylor and Francis.]

5

PUBLIC RELATIONS PLANNING

PHASE 1: RESEARCH

This chapter begins a step-by-step approach to planning a public relations campaign. It's the first of four chapters that will walk you through each phase of creating an effective campaign. In these chapters, you also will get advice on public relations careers from national leaders in the field.

Research, *a formal program of information gathering*, provides the foundation for strategic communication planning. Without research, you'd be sending messages of little value to your organization and little interest to your publics (who probably won't be listening anyway). Research keeps you rooted in reality.

This phase of the planning process deals with gathering and analyzing **formative research**, *research that results in data on which a communication program can be built*. Even during crises when reaction time is short, most public relations practitioners make time to do some research to get a quick read on public opinion or to pull from relevant existing research. There are two types of formative research: strategic and tactical.

- **Strategic research** is *the systematic gathering of information about issues and publics that affect an organization*. It guides decisions on what an organization might do to address a situation.

DOI: 10.4324/9781003521211-7

- **Tactical research** is *information that guides the production and dissemination of messages.* Tactical research helps public relations professionals do tasks effectively.

During the formative research phase, you will conduct a **situation analysis**, *the collection of information that managers use to analyze an organization's internal and external environments.* You will conduct research in three key areas: the situation you are facing, your organization or client, and your intended public.

Don't let the idea of research scare you. Research begins with informal and often simple methods of gathering relevant information. You'll learn more about various types of research later in this chapter.

PR PROFILE: DR. FELICIA BLOW, APR, CEO AND CO-FOUNDER, WALKER BLOW CONSULTING

Introduction: Dr. Felicia Blow, APR, is an award-winning public relations leader who has a 30-year career spanning work in manufacturing, waste management and environmental services, telecommunications, and higher education. Currently, she is CEO and co-founder of Walker Blow Consulting, a boutique agency specializing in fundraising, strategic communications, and information technology services.

She served as the 2022 National Chair for the Public Relations Society of America, the world's largest organization of public relations professionals, and previously on PRSA's national board of directors as well on PRSA district and local chapter boards. She earned her bachelor's degree in mass media arts from Hampton University, her master's in business administration degree from Strayer University, and her doctorate in higher education administration from Old Dominion University.

Why did you decide on a public relations career? Public relations had all of the attributes for a career I sought: travel, meeting new people, and writing. However, before I landed on my ultimate career choice, I initially wanted a career in broadcast journalism. When I graduated from college, I began working for a Fortune 100 company in its public affairs office. On the weekends, I also worked as a field assistant for a television station in a small market. My lived experience as a public affairs representative compared to my work at the television station showed me that television was not what I wanted to do.

I enjoyed the diversity of collaborating with myriad stakeholders—both internal and external. I loved the complexity of work in having to learn and understand unfamiliar products and projects to bring life to stories about these assets. Being the extrovert that I am, I also enjoyed meeting and engaging with a wide variety of people in the company.

Finally, I love to write. I found joy in business writing and have come to love creative writing as well. Bringing clarity to complex situations and helping to bring people together is what I believe public relations does. That is a recipe for an illustrious career for someone who wants to make a difference.

What's your favorite part of the job? There are two parts of public relations that I love equally. I enjoy writing. And I love working with a wide variety of people. I gain energy from meeting people, learning from them, and applying that information to the telling of stories.

Where do you see the public relations industry in 10 years? I am not sure where the PR industry will be. AI is changing a great deal about how we communicate, engage with one another, engage with technology, and live. When I served as co-chair of the national PRSA 75th Anniversary Committee, I convened a group of top leaders in public relations to consider this topic. We came up with several "shifts" in the profession as follows:

- — Public relations will shift from being a US-centric discipline to a global necessity.
- — Inclusiveness within public relations will shift from simply recognizing diversity to true inclusion in all its dimensions. And it will be our profession that will help organizations and ideas achieve mutual benefits. Our profession will help democracies succeed.

— Our profession will shift from simply promotions, marketing, media focused to helping corporations be purposeful in their delivery.
— Public relations will shift from being a management function to one where PR representatives are the sought-after leaders of organizations and companies.
— Finally, our profession will shift from a perceived focus on tactics to one where we are able to align tactics to AI implementation, but influenced by leaders like us. These shifts are exciting to look forward to, and I am anxious to be part of the evolution of our work.

What advice to you have for graduating students launching their own PR careers? My advice is to learn, experiment, and try new things, consistently. Learn new cultures. Learn a new language. Get an advanced degree. Study in areas outside of communications and public relations. Do something different every day. These efforts give you depth of understanding as well as empathy and compassion for others. Further, these life experiences will make you a more valuable member of your future teams.

Finally, life is truly short. The average person will see 75 winters, summers, springs, and falls. And while expertise in our chosen fields is critical to gain, living life is even more important. Do not get to your 75th year (or more) with regrets. Live life to the fullest.

STEP 1: ANALYZING THE SITUATION

The first step in public relations planning is to identify the **situation**, *a set of circumstances facing an organization.*

A situation for a football or rugby team might be the loyalty of fans. For an auto manufacturer, the availability of side air bags. For a counseling organization, misunderstanding about mental illness.

Note that situations are presented as nouns—loyalty of fans, availability of air bags, misunderstanding about mental illness. Later, when we discuss organizational goals, we'll add verbs to indicate how we want to impact on these situations—e.g., *nurturing* fan loyalty.

OBSTACLE OR OPPORTUNITY

A situation is similar in meaning to a problem—a question to be considered and answered, something that calls for our attention. A public relations situation can be positive or negative:

- An **opportunity** is *a public relations situation offering a potential advantage to the organization or its publics.* An example is fan loyalty to a football team, a positive situation that can enhance the organization and its publics.
- An **obstacle** is *a public relations situation that limits the organization in realizing its mission.* It is a roadblock to be overcome, for example, lack of fan loyalty if the football team is losing.

Make sure there is agreement within your organization on these, because what one person may call an obstacle, another might see as an opportunity.

The ultimate public relations problem is a **crisis**, *a major, negative, public, sudden, and unpredicted event that can seriously disrupt an organization's activity and potentially hurts its bottom line or mission.* A crisis is a decision point where choices point to consequences.

Here are some real-world examples of good public relations that turn obstacles into opportunities.

ALASKA SEALIFE CENTER

Attendance at the Alaska SeaLife Center, one of Alaska's major tourist attractions, was drastically impacted even after Alaska reopened for business following the COVID-19 lockdown because the cruise ship season was canceled. Center leaders estimated they would lose more than 70 percent of their annual visitor revenues, resulting in the Center's possible permanent closure. To avoid this, the Center embarked on a $2 million (£1.5 million; €1.8 million) fundraising campaign.

It created a campaign video shared on social media, sent an appeal email to its supporters, ran challenge matches, and did successful story pitches to local and national news media. Thanks to the video and news coverage, community members helped, too. Children sold lemonade, breweries sold limited-edition beers, musicians held fundraising concerts, arts held makers' auctions, and the Center's Facebook fans created fundraisers on Facebook. By the campaign's original deadline, the Center had raised more than $4 million (£3 million; €3.5 million)—double its original goal.

THE DOVE SELF-ESTEEM PROJECT

Beauty products are traditionally marketed using idealized (and unrealizable) portrayals of women. Unilever, the British-Dutch consumer goods corporation, commissioned an international study on women's attitudes toward beauty that became the basis for the Dove "Campaign for Real Beauty" and launched the Dove Self-Esteem Project.

Using mainly public relations tactics with advertising support, the campaign focused on "real women with real bodies and real curves," a departure from the supermodel approach taken by most competitors in the beauty products industry. The campaign earned local and international news coverage and attracted millions of visitors to its website.

The Dove Self-Esteem Project has sparked an international discussion about women and beauty. The international project has created videos that focus on the toxic effects of the beauty industry on girls and women. It also addresses the impact of social media on self-esteem, since studies have shown that one in two girls say idealized beauty content on social media causes low self-esteem. To date, the Dove Self-Esteem Project has reached 82 million young people in 150 countries.

Even in crisis situations, obstacles can be approached as opportunities, if the problem has not been self-inflicted. Public attention generated by a crisis can help an organization explain its values and demonstrate its quality.

Whether the issue is viewed as an opportunity, an obstacle, or simply an unrealized potential, the communications team and the leaders of the organization or client need a common understanding of the issue before it can be adequately addressed. Ideally, it means trying to turn an obstacle into an opportunity.

For example, fast-food chains such as McDonald's, Arby's, and Burger King could have ignored growing international concerns about obesity, particularly long-term effects on young people. Instead these companies anticipated a growing concern and introduced healthier low-calorie menu items.

Public relations practitioners call this **issues management**, *a process by which an organization tries to anticipate emerging issues and respond to them before they get out of hand.* This involves monitoring and evaluating information, potentially leading to change. The name for this is **adaptation**, *the ability of an organization to make changes on the basis of what its publics want and need.*

Early identification of important issues can give an organization time to study them, to develop an appropriate response, and to act as circumstances change. This is one reason that research skills are so important for public relations practitioners.

Some organizations use a best practice approach by studying and potentially imitating a leader in the field. For example, a hospital wishing to site an off-campus methadone clinic might see how a hospital in another city fared with a similar project. The hospital might even look to the failure of similar efforts in other cities, learning from their mistakes.

Issues management helps the organization interact with its publics. It may help an organization settle the issue early or divert it, or perhaps even prevent its emergence in the first place. More likely, however, the organization will have to adjust itself to the issue in some way, trying to maximize the benefits or at least minimize the negative impact. Public relations often drives this early-warning system within an organization.

Closely related to issues management is **risk management**—*the process of identifying, controlling, and minimizing the impact of uncertain events on an organization.* Public relations people often have early access to criticism from various publics, which is especially important if others inside the organization fail to observe signs of unrest.

NESTLÉ INTERNATIONAL

A company that failed to recognize warning signs of a potential problem is Nestlé International, a Swiss-based multinational food and drink processing corporation. It began aggressively marketing its infant formula worldwide as a substitute for breast milk in the 1960s. Groups such as the International Baby Food Action Network (IBFAN) argue that promoting infant formula over breastfeeding has resulted in health problems and deaths among infants, especially in underdeveloped countries, for several reasons:

— Sanitation. The formula must be mixed with water, which is often impure or not potable, leading to disease among infants.
— Nutritional value. Mothers may use less formula and more water than recommended in order to make a container of formula last longer. Also, breast milk has nutrients and antibodies that are lacking in formula.
— Preserving milk supply. Mothers who rely on free infant formula in hospital maternity wards lose the ability to make their own milk and must buy formula.

Concerns about Nestlé's marketing led to a US boycott in 1977 that spread into Canada, Europe, Australia, and New Zealand in the early 1980s. The boycott temporarily stopped in 1984 when Nestlé signed an agreement to implement the International Code of Marketing of Breastmilk Substitutes, but the boycott resumed a few years later when IBFAN alleged that Nestlé and other formula companies were flooding health facilities in underdeveloped countries with free and low-cost supplies. The boycott continues today.

Although Nestlé is the world's largest food and beverage company, worth about $287 billion (£211.9 billion, €250.8 billion), the opposition and negative publicity from the boycott has cost Nestlé millions of dollars in bad publicity, lost customers, legal fees, and a weakened reputation.

EXXON

This oil giant was another company that refused to take critics seriously, apparently having little interest in risk management. As a result, the company suffered in the long term for mishandling the Alaska oil spill caused by its tanker *Valdez* in 1989, which dispersed nearly 11 million gallons of crude oil along the Alaska coastline. It was the worst oil spill in US history at that time.

Multiple government and private lawsuits resulted, dragging on for years and costing Exxon (now ExxonMobil) millions in legal fees. In 1991, a federal judge approved a criminal plea agreement for Exxon's environmental violations and a civil settlement between Exxon and the Alaska state and US federal governments. Exxon paid $125 million (£92.3 million, €109.3 million) for a criminal fine and agreed to pay the two governments $900 million (£664.4 million, €786.6 million) over 10 years under the civil settlement.

The 1991 settlement included a "reopener" provision that allowed the governments to ask for another $100 million (£73.8 million, €87.4 million) if they learned of environmental problems after the settlement. In 2006, Alaska filed for that money, citing impacts on harlequin ducks and sea otters from the oil spill. However, in 2015, Alaska and the US government decided not to pursue the funds after positive environmental study results, thus ending 26 years of litigation over the oil spill.

Private lawsuits on behalf of fishermen and Alaska residents also took years to resolve. In 2008, the US Supreme Court approved a $507.5 million (£374.7 million, €443.6 million) settlement on behalf of fishermen and Alaska residents—one-tenth of the $5 billion (£3.7 billion, €4.4 billion) that a jury originally awarded. Not surprisingly, there was anger over that verdict, with some calling it "an unconscionable betrayal of public trust."

The purpose of issues management is to deal with issues before they get out of hand. When that happens, the issue becomes a crisis. **Crisis management** is *the process by which an organization deals with out-of-control issues.*

Issues management deals with preparation for dealing with potential events; risk management is about implied threats; and crisis management focuses on reactive responses to actual occurrences.

Organizations that are committed to the concept of strategic communication are probably engaged in an ongoing issues management program that identifies crises in their early stages. Less nimble organizations may be caught off guard by a crisis.

Sometimes, reality slaps you in the face and forces you to think the unthinkable. It happened in shootings at elementary schools in Texas, Connecticut, Florida, and Pennsylvania, university campuses, grocery stores, churches, synagogues, mosques, and temples.

It was inconceivable what happened at the World Trade Center, Oklahoma City, the Boston Marathon, and in theaters and nightclubs around the world, as well as train bombings in Spain, pedestrian attacks in France, and white nationalist terrorism across the US It was unimaginable what happened in an attack on the Canadian Parliament and in police headquarters in New York City, Paris, and Indonesia. Forward-thinking organizations prepare for the unthinkable and plan for unexpected disasters.

TYLENOL

What happened in Chicago in 1982 remains an example of how companies should face an unthinkable tragedy. Pharmaceutical giant Johnson & Johnson woke up in crisis when somebody laced Tylenol capsules with cyanide, killing seven Chicago-area residents.

As the country panicked, Johnson & Johnson pulled 31 million bottles of Tylenol from store shelves. The company used satellite news conferences to reintroduce Tylenol as an over-the-counter medicine with a triple-seal, tamper-resistant package that soon became an industry standard. Johnson & Johnson also offered customer incentives such as free replacements and discount coupons.

The company saw a quick recovery of its 35 percent market share and in the process fostered an ongoing customer loyalty. Because of its good reputation and its responsible handling of the still-unsolved murders, the company emerged from the crisis with even more consumer respect and confidence.

Today, the legacy of Johnson & Johnson is a case study in good crisis communication and solid public relations, a morality tale that shows the value of a corporate conscientiousness that places its customers first and keeps its promise of safety.

Considering subsequent corporate scandals, obviously some companies didn't get the point. But those that did noted the value of proactive management and quick communication in crisis situations. Forward-looking companies realized that preparedness is the key to effective issues management, particularly in crisis situations.

Crises may be sudden and unpredicted, but they seldom are unpredictable. Crises are more like volcanoes that smolder for a while before they erupt. Warning signs abound, if a trained eye is watching.

Studies by the Institute for Crisis Management (https://crisisconsultant.com/) consistently find that only about 33 percent of companies' crises burst suddenly onto the scene, while 67 percent have been smoldering situations that eventually ignited. The biggest crisis categories involve whistleblowers, followed by catastrophes (such as storms, floods, earthquakes, and hurricanes), consumer activism, class action lawsuits, and mismanagement.

Crises are inevitable for every organization. You can't prevent them entirely, but you should aim to control how you communicate during a crisis. As we saw in Chapter 3, there are several ways to do that: communicate with existing key publics, treat the media as allies, focus on the organization's reputation after safety issues are addressed, respond quickly, speak with one voice, disclose as much as possible, and frame the message by providing information early in a crisis that sets the tone for subsequent reporting.

Some experts have banded together as a kind of self-help group to guide each other in risk and crisis situations. One such coalition is the British-based CIPR Crisis Communications Network (https://ciprcrisiscommsnetwork.com/), a network of public relations and communication professionals with experience in managing crises that is part of the Chartered Institute of Public Relations.

BP-DEEPWATER HORIZON

The 2010 BP-Deepwater Horizon oil spill in the Gulf of Mexico has been called the worst environmental disaster in North American history. It also was a public relations catastrophe for the once-named British Petroleum (BP), raising questions about the capabilities of international corporations in crisis management.

The crisis began when a deep-sea explosion off the Louisiana coast killed 11 oil-rig workers and led to the release of nearly 210 million gallons of oil that polluted an area of 3,900 square miles.

The out-of-control spill and efforts to cap the well led the news for weeks. The economic impact was severe: $2.5 billion (£1.8 billion, € 2.2 billion) in immediate damages to the fishing industry and $24 billion (£17.7 billion, €21 billion) to tourism, with predictions of decades-long effects. BP estimated the cleanup costs would mount to nearly $40 billion (£29.5 billion, €35 billion).

BP, once considered the greenest oil company in America, was blamed for the disaster and criticized for how it handled the tragedy. When the crisis began, its British CEO, Tony Hayward, was the face of BP. He had a reputation in Britain as being a knowledgeable and trusted corporate leader. But the crisis wore on him. He was photographed sailing in a yacht race at the height of the crisis, followed by an outburst about "wanting his life back." Hayward resigned several weeks after the explosion.

How did BP handle its crisis communications? First it tried to blame others: drillers it had hired, owners of the rig, and government regulators. This violated one of the tenets of good crisis communication: accept responsibility for fixing the problem, and don't lay blame.

Rather quickly, BP's public relations strategy turned toward the future: how the company would contain the spill and compensate the victims. BP set up a $20 billion (£14.8 billion, €17.5 billion) fund to reimburse victims for their economic loss. It was a good move, though one later threatened by charges that BP mismanaged the fund.

Critics observed that BP lost public confidence by ceding to the media the task of providing public education about deep-water drilling. It let others tell its story. BP eventually created an educational component to its website, but the details were too technical and confusing for most visitors.

A year and a half after the spill, BP engaged in some heavy-duty image repair with advertisements reporting that the gulf ecology had not been as severely damaged as it originally seemed to be and that the fishing industry was then showing signs of economic recovery. BP hired chefs Emeril Lagasse and John Besh to promote gulf seafood, and it gave away fish tacos and seafood jambalaya at Sugar Bowl parties in New Orleans.

Inevitably, the BP-Deepwater Horizon spill has been compared with the Exxon *Valdez* oil spill 21 years earlier. Both companies made public relations mistakes in appearing to emphasize technology over people, minimizing environmental consequences and the emotional reaction to oil-slicked birds and oil-drenched shorelines. But BP was quicker to compensate fishermen and other victims, and it cooperated with government regulators more than Exxon did.

Another difference concerns fault. The Exxon *Valdez* spill happened because the ship's captain was not at the helm, and cleanup was delayed because Exxon had removed cleanup equipment from the area prior to the accident as part of a corporate strategy to de-emphasize the risk of such a spill. The public concluded that Exxon was to blame. On the other hand, the BP explosion resulted from the failure of safety equipment on a rig owned and operated by another company.

Neither company appeared to have had a workable crisis communication plan, and the companies seemed not to know how to act once the crises occurred.

But there are significant differences that lead to the conclusion that BP handled the situation better than Exxon did. For the most part, BP's leaders were seen as part of the solution, rather than as avoiding responsibility and ducking public exposure as in the *Valdez* spill.

WORKSHEET FOR STEP 1: ANALYZING THE PUBLIC RELATIONS SITUATION

In Step 1, the focus has been on identifying and analyzing the nature of the issue you are addressing. It may be a routine activity in the life of an organization or it may be a crisis situation. Your purpose in Step 1 is to make strategic decisions about the issue that later will guide you in addressing it.

Specifically, answer these four basic questions:

1. What is the situation facing the organization?
2. Do you consider this situation an obstacle or an opportunity?
3. What is the significance or importance of the situation?
4. How might the situation be resolved for the mutual benefit of everyone involved?

You may also flesh out these basic questions by considering whether the situation is new or ongoing, how it is linked to the organization's mission, what trends may be associated with it, and the extent to which it is a priority for the organization.

PLANNING EXAMPLE FOR STEP 1

This is the first of an evolving example of the planning steps in action. It focuses on the hypothetical University Exchange (UE), a nonprofit organization that supports a variety of international engagements between young adults in professional environments. The organization works with professional organizations, colleges, and universities to support international internship opportunities and higher education exchange programs. To make this scenario easier to understand, we'll focus on a local chapter of this organization in a mid-sized city.

The situation that University Exchange is dealing with involves creating greater awareness about the value of international engagement among young professionals. Overall, UE considers this to be an *opportunity*, though it also involves some *obstacles* to be overcome.

UE realizes that there are advantages as well as impediments to international engagement for young professionals; the organization will need to do research as the next step in its campaign.

The significance of the issue is that valuing international engagement is central to the mission and vision of success for UE.

Ideally, the situation will be handled in such as a way as to address the benefits of international professional engagement as well as to deal realistically with the obstacles.

STEP 2: CHOOSING RESEARCH METHODS

Research is like the foundation of a house. You might have innovative communication tactics, but without adequate research, your tactics risk being ineffective.

There are two types of research, primary research and secondary research. **Primary research** *is the generation and analysis of new information to address a research question or problem.* **Secondary research** *re-analyzes existing information obtained by previous researchers for a new, specific purpose.*

You should start with secondary research. It helps you to refine your research topic, it's less expensive than gathering new data, it helps you to keep current with new developments in the field, and most importantly, it provides a launching point for your own primary research that follows.

Sources of secondary information include organizational files, trade and professional associations, libraries, government agencies, commercial information services, and online research databases.

After you complete your secondary research, it's time to do primary research—gathering original information by conducting your own research—such as surveys, focus groups, interviews, and content analysis.

SURVEYS

A **survey** is *a quantitative research technique based on a standard series of questions, which yields statistical results and conclusions.* Related to the survey is the **poll**, *a very short, survey-like method that focuses more on immediate behavior than attitudes and asks only short, closed-ended questions.*

Surveys and polls are appropriate for description, analysis, and prediction—three major research needs. They are among the least expensive and quickest types of research, and can be applied to both large and small groups of people. They can be very accurate, and their findings are easy to compare. However, they are subject to both the bias and limitations of the researcher, especially through inadequate samples or poorly worded questions.

Surveys can be administered via telephone, online, mail, interviews, or with groups of people. Response rates vary considerably, with higher response rates regarded as more reliable. The more involved survey respondents are with the organization sponsoring the survey, the higher the response rate. Researchers often use incentives to increase the response rate, such as gift cards or a small amount of cash. Follow-up mailings also can greatly improve the response rate.

Here are a few aspects of surveys:

- **Sampling** involves *selecting relatively few respondents to stand in for the wider population.* The key to effective sampling is **probability**, meaning that *each element within the population has an equal chance of being selected for the sample.* A **nonprobability sample**, *a series of techniques for selecting samples of a population* <u>*not*</u> *based on the principle of probability*, is one that is haphazard: a **convenience sample**, *a type of nonprobability sample in which respondents are selected mainly on their availability*, such as shoppers in a mall or students in one class, or a **volunteer sample** *that invites people to participate if they feel strongly about an issue.* A better approach is the **probability sample**, *a series of techniques for selecting samples of a population based on the principle of probability.* These include a true lottery-style **random sample**, *in which everyone has an equal opportunity to be selected*, or a **systematic sample** that *involves selecting, say, every 10th name on a list.*
- Some more sophisticated techniques are a **weighted sample**, *an approach to sampling in which each demographic group is sized according to its proportion in the population to compensate for its being a small proportion*; **stratified sample**, *a sophisticated approach to sampling that ranks elements according to demographic factors, then draws elements from each factor to be part of the sample*; and **cluster sample**, a *sophisticated approach to sampling that subdivides a complex population, drawing elements from each demographic subsection for the final sampling.*

- **Sampling error** is *a measurement of the extent to which the sample does not perfectly correspond with the target population*. Basically, the larger the sample, the smaller the margin of error. Many researchers are comfortable with 3–6 percent sample error.
- The ideal **sample size**, *the optimum minimum size for a sample to be considered representative of the population*, is not a specific percentage of the population. Many researchers use 384 as the ideal sample size for a 5 percent margin of error for any size of population of 50,000 or larger. Most polling aims for a sample of 2,000-3,000 to allow for analysis of subcategories (such as by geographic area, race, age, political affiliation, and so on).

Beyond careful selection of a proportional sample, the main ingredient for a quality survey is a good questionnaire. This is the list of items given to respondents. Here are some guidelines for creating effective questionnaires.

- Keep items short and clear.
- Be specific and avoid ambiguous words that could be open to different interpretations.
- Ask only questions relevant to the research topic.
- Use positive constructions. For example, ask "Do you participate in a fitness program?" rather than "Do you avoid fitness programs?"
- Avoid "double-barreled" items that ask two questions but provide only one answer.
- Use neutral, nonpartisan words. And don't signal a bias with a question such as "Do you prefer reading good literature or just popular novels?"
- Avoid a prestige bias by associating a statement with an authority figure. "Do you agree with the mayor that property taxes are too high?"
- Don't ask for an opinion on something that is a matter of fact.
- Avoid hypothetical questions. "Would you prefer to move to a colony under the sea or in outer space?"
- Make sure questions can be reasonably answered. Don't ask how many hours of television a person watched in the last six months. Rather, ask how many hours of TV watching they do in an average weekday.

There also are some suggestions for presenting response categories.

- Give ranges for responses dealing with income and age.
- Allow "other" categories when these might reasonably occur, such as when asking a person's racial or ethnic background.
- Make sure that multiple-choice responses are both comprehensive (offering every possible response) and mutually exclusive (only one possible response for each respondent).
- Use checklist items to allow for more than one response, such as types of music or food that a respondent likes.
- Use forced-choice items to lead a respondent to indicate agreement with one of two or three statements.
- Rather than a simple yes/no, use a rating scale such as 1–5 to learn about the intensity of a respondent's feelings. Or use the Likert scale with four or five points between agree and disagree.

FOCUS GROUPS

A type of small-group discussion is a **focus group**, *a qualitative research technique involving conversation among several participants, guided by a monitor and recorded for later analysis*. In a focus group, the researcher guides a conversation about a particular issue and thus stimulates comments among group members. The result: a more interactive, robust, and complete discussion than would be possible through individual interviews.

Focus groups are quick, inexpensive, flexible, and practical. On the other hand, they can become expensive and more complex if the public relations client requires recording and a special viewing room with one-way mirrors.

Focus groups can be held in-person or online, which is typically cheaper than in-person focus groups and can include participants from multiple geographic areas. The group typically consists of between eight and 12 people. A focus group session generally lasts 60 to 90 minutes.

Focus groups generate ideas, comments, and anecdotes that can help you gain insight into an issue. They are not appropriate, however, if you need statistical data; in that case, conduct a survey.

In some cases, focus groups are the main research technique used. Other times, researchers use them to complement surveys, either as preliminary tools to gain understanding of the issue or as follow-ups to shed light on survey findings.

INTERVIEWS

Interviews are a commonly used form of primary research. Researchers can obtain information in person, by phone, email, or videoconferencing such as Zoom or Microsoft Teams. In-person interviews and videoconferencing interviews generally are the best because they allow the interviewer to "read" the body language of the person providing the information.

Interviews can be either **structured interviews**, *meaning that standardized questions are asked in a certain order*, or **unstructured interviews**, *meaning that the interviewer has the freedom to determine what additional questions to ask.*

There are two types of interviews: **one-on-one interviews**, *in which people are interviewed at their home, office, a research office, or field service location*; and **in-depth interviews**, *a qualitative research technique involving lengthy, detailed, and systematic interviews conducted individually with several respondents.*

The one-on-one interview allows the researcher to easily obtain information in a face-to-face setting and to develop a rapport with the interviewee that might elicit replies to sensitive question. Disadvantages include time, cost, and the potential for interviewer bias based on physical appearance and comments of the interviewer.

The in-depth interview presents the same questions for each respondent, so information more easily can be compared, and provides a wealth of detail. However, generalizability can be a problem because the in-depth interview is typically done with a non-random sample.

CONTENT ANALYSIS

Content analysis is *a quantitative research technique based on unobtrusive, after-the-fact analysis of a set of media artifacts, such as a newscast,* *editorials, tweets, blogs, or articles on a particular topic*. Is has been used for years to study mass media. It can shed light on the messages of communication, assess the image of an organization, and make comparisons between media and reality.

Content analysis can be used in tandem with results obtained from surveys or focus groups. For example, if you are evaluating the effectiveness of an online newsletter for employees, you might begin with a content analysis of the last three years' issues to identify topics previously covered. Then you could conduct a focus group or readership survey to identify topics that your employees want to read about. Finally, you could compare the results of the content analysis with the focus group or survey results, then create a more popular employee publication.

Content analysis has several advantages, including a low investment of time and money. It can be done by a person working alone with little equipment beyond a simple calculator or computer with standard software. It also allows you to go back in time to examine past messages. It can be used to compare an organization with industry norms or with wider trends. Finally, it helps the researcher separate the routine from the unusual.

The disadvantages of content analysis include its limitation to recorded (or recordable) information and its susceptibility to coder influence and bias.

Another aspect of content analysis—not necessarily a negative but certainly a concern—is **intercoder reliability**, *the degree to which various coders in content analysis agree on their interpretation of a unit of analysis*. The more consistency among various coders, the stronger the reliability of the study. Researchers foster high intercoder reliability by training coders to follow common rubrics when they are reviewing content in a media artifact.

WALMART'S JUNETEENTH-THEMED ICE CREAM

Formative research is critical before a brand launches a new product, as this case illustrates.

In 2022, Walmart faced backlash after releasing a new Juneteenth-themed product featuring swirled red velvet and cheesecake flavored Great Value ice cream.

The ice cream flavor was apparently intended to demonstrate Walmart's support for the Black community by commemorating the June 19th holiday. Juneteenth originated in 1865 in response to the abolition of slavery in the United States and became a federal holiday in 2021. The ice cream container's label read, "Share and celebrate African-American culture, emancipation and enduring hope."

Social media users accused Walmart of trying to profit off the holiday. One Twitter user said, "It's problematic when White-owned brands and companies treat Juneteenth as another commercialized opportunity void of any commitments to the [African-American] community, change or simple understanding of what Juneteenth is."

In response to the backlash, Walmart issued an apology. "The Juneteenth holiday marks a celebration of freedom and independence," a Walmart spokesperson acknowledged in the company's official statement. "However, we received feedback that a few items caused concern for some of our customers and we sincerely apologize. We are reviewing our assortment and will remove items as appropriate."

Walmart pulled the ice cream from store shelves.

WORKSHEET FOR STEP 2: CHOOSING RESEARCH METHODS

In Step 2, you have considered various research methods to provide you with data for your public relations campaign.

Here are some questions to guide you:

1. What type(s) of secondary research will you use?
   —Organizational files (e.g., annual reports, news releases, internal documents)
   —Files from trade and professional associations
   —Libraries
   —Government agencies
   —Commercial information services (e.g., polling firms and polling centers)
   —Online sources

2. What type(s) of primary research will you use?
   —Surveys
   —Focus groups
   —In-depth interviews
   —Content analysis

PLANNING EXAMPLE FOR STEP 2

University Exchange's *secondary research* included a review of academic journal articles and public relations case studies about student exchange programs and international internship programs. UE also examined reports and brochures of other student exchange programs, international business internship programs, and international service organizations. In addition, UE investigated several discipline-specific programs involving journalists in Canada, Mexico, and the US; engineers in the UK and Australia; British, French and American chefs; and other global exchange programs for accountants, lawyers, nurses, teachers and business executives.

Based on the findings of its secondary research, UE conducted *primary research*, including *surveys* and *focus groups* of past and current university students enrolled in student exchange programs and international internship programs. UE also did *in-depth interviews* with several of its local leaders, businesses, and nonprofit organizations, as well as *content analysis* of the websites and social media of its own and several competitor organizations.

The research found that university students believe that there are several advantages to global engagement for young professionals. Among these are practical enhancements for an individual's career, networking opportunities, expansion of job skills, strengthened communication and interpersonal skills, and personal development. Interviews with UE, business, and nonprofit leaders found that opportunities are present for businesses and nonprofit organizations, which benefit from employees with these qualities, as well as potential business connections that can result from international engagement.

UE's surveys and focus groups with university students also revealed some impediments to enrollment in its programs, including the cost in time and money, ignorance of the professional benefits of this engagement, a feeling of being insufficiently prepared, and a sense of cultural superiority. Content analysis of the websites and social media of UE and several competitors revealed that although the UE website's content overall was good, its social media efforts on specific platforms used by its key publics were lagging both in terms of content and frequency of posting.

STEP 3: ANALYZING THE ORGANIZATION

Effective communication involves self-awareness. This calls for a close look at the organization—its performance, visibility and reputation, and structure—as well as the organization's external environment. This review is called a **communication audit**, *an analysis of the strengths and weaknesses of the public relations concerns of an organization.* The process is the same for all types of organizations: large multinational corporations, small family businesses, nonprofit organizations, hospitals, schools and universities, government, cultural organizations, and more.

Public relations professionals generally start this audit with a situation analysis that can provide a comprehensive overview of the organization's resources and important concerns. The situation analysis is sometimes conducted through a **SWOT analysis**, *a strategic planning tool that analyzes an organization's strengths, weaknesses, opportunities, and threats* as follows:

- **Strength** is an advantage or resource that can help advance the organization.
- **Weakness** is a deficiency such as a product defect, a service shortcoming, or some other challenge the organization might seek to overcome.
- **Opportunity** is a situation offering potential advantage to an organization.
- **Threat** is a situation that can negatively impact an organization.

The information gathered from the SWOT analysis can be incorporated into the audit in three areas: the organization's internal environment, public perception, and external environment.

INTERNAL ENVIRONMENT

Public relations involves more than words, and an audit of an organization's strengths and limitations begins with a candid understanding of what the organization is and does. Here are some areas you will need to assess as you enter Step 3 of the strategic planning process.

- **Performance**. This is the most important aspect of an organization's internal environment. It involves the quality of the goods and services provided by the organization, as well as the causes and ideas it espouses.
- **Niche**. This focuses on the organization's specialty, the function or role that makes it different from other organizations.
- **Structure**. The audit considers how the public relations operation functions within the organization. This includes both the mission of public relations (for example, whether it sits at the management table where decisions are made) and the financial, equipment, and personnel resources it has for conducting public relations.
- **Ethical Base**. Public relations has been called the conscience of an organization, giving it moral grounding. In analyzing the internal environment, give thought to this ethical base, and identify the values and operating principles that are important to the organization.
- **Internal Impediments**. End your analysis of the internal environment with a look at the **internal impediments**, *obstacles within the organization that might impede the public relations program.* Remember that impediments are merely temporary roadblocks to be circumvented, rather than permanent blockages.

PUBLIC PERCEPTION

The next task in preparing your communication audit is to consider what people know and think about the organization.

- **Visibility**. Examine the extent to which the organization is known, and the accuracy of the information people have.
- **Reputation**. This deals with perception, what people think about the organization based on what they know. Reputation is part of

the social capital of an organization; arguably it's the most important public relations asset. Reputation is based on what the organization says but more so on what it does, and on what others (including the media) say about it.

EXTERNAL ENVIRONMENT

This part of the analysis looks at how outsiders might impact an organization.

- **Supporters**. Every organization has a group of people who currently or potentially can help the organization achieve its objectives. Make sure you know whom they are.
- **Competitors**. Likewise, most organizations have people or groups who are producing similar goods, performing similar services, or espousing similar ideals. In highly competitive environments, it is important for public relations to understand the role of others in the field.
- **Opponents**. Many organizations also have groups who act in some way to counter the organization. These groups may be advocates of an opposing cause, dissidents who oppose you because of your stance, activists organized to foster change at odds with your organization's products or services, or any number of other types of opponents.
- **External Impediments**. Other political, social, or economic factors may limit the effectiveness of an organization.

WORKSHEET FOR STEP 3: ANALYZING THE ORGANIZATION

Step 3 has focused your attention on the organization itself.

Here are some questions dealing with the organization's internal environment:

1. What is the quality of the organization's performance?
2. What communication resources exist?
3. How supportive is the organization of public relations activity?

Here are questions about the public perception of the organization:

4. How well known is the organization?
5. What is its reputation?

Finally, some questions on the external environment:

6. What is the major competition?
7. Does any significant opposition exist?
8. Is anything happening in the external environment that can limit the effectiveness of the organization?

PLANNING EXAMPLE FOR STEP 3

The *internal environment* of University Exchange is strong and open. It has strong support with a small number of organizations, particularly environmental nonprofit organizations and businesses with engineering and technological focuses. UE leaders are on record as seeing a potential for expanding into other sectors.

The *quality* of UE services is high; the cost of those services is relatively low, due in part to some past grants by the state Business Development Council, though there is no certainty of receiving future grants from this agency.

Communication resources for UE include a part-time staff member with experience in media relations and several volunteers with interest and skills in social media. In the past, the organization often worked directly with business associates and did not have a media plan. New board direction is pushing the need for a more proactive strategic approach to communication.

In terms of its *public perception*, UE is known by some organizational executives, but it has low *visibility* among rank-and-file employees and in the community. Where it is known, its *reputation* is generally positive. Past partner companies have described UE as being well organized, reliable, and cost-effective.

The *external environment* seems not to involve any organized opposition, nor are there other organizations with a parallel mission. Some service clubs do small projects involving international business exchange, and the state Economic Development Council occasionally organizes short-term discipline-specific visits to other countries.

Overall, UE has been hurt by a weak economy, but this is changing as local companies emerge from the economic slump and once again are looking toward long-term interests of building a productive workforce in increasingly competitive circumstances. Financial belt-tightening has caused the largest local university to cut staff in its international exchange program, creating a potential void that UE might fill.

STEP 4: ANALYZING THE PUBLICS

A **public** is *a group of people that shares a common interest vis-à-vis an organization, recognizes its significance, and sets out to do something about it.* Members of publics are homogeneous in that they are similar in their interests and characteristics. They usually are aware of the public relations situation and their relationship with the organization. They think the issue is relevant, and they are at least potentially organized or energized to act on the issue.

A public is like your family. You don't pick them; they just are—like generous Cousin Freddie and crazy Aunt Bertha. Publics may be helpful or annoying, friendly or not, but an organization must deal with them regardless. They exist because they share an environment and interact with the organization. Note that there is no such thing as a "general public" because, by definition, a public has a specific relationship with an organization.

There are some important differences among publics and related groupings. If a public is like your family, a market is more like your friends. You pick them; they pick you. A **market** is *a segment of a population including people with characteristics (e.g., age, income, lifestyle) that can help an organization achieve its consumer-oriented goals.* Organizations identify markets by determining those that might be interested in buying their products or using their services.

An **audience**, meanwhile, is merely *a group of people who pay attention to a particular medium of communication*—people who read the same blog, watch the same TV program, or follow the same person on Instagram. Audiences are important for public relations only to the extent that they include members of an organization's public.

A final category is a **stakeholder**, *a person or group that relates to an organization through its potential impact on the organization's mission and objectives.* "Stakeholder" is a bit fuzzy because it has different meanings.

Some see stakeholders as groups of people relating to an organization on the basis of its mission and objectives, as compared to publics that relate on the basis of the organization's message on a particular topic. Others suggest that stakeholders care about an organization, whereas publics may or may not care. This book treats stakeholders as synonymous with publics.

CHARACTERISTICS OF PUBLICS

When you identify publics, you can look for five distinguishing characteristics.

- **Distinguishable**. A public is a recognizable grouping of individuals, though not necessarily a formal group. For example, a public for a jewelry company might include people getting engaged or people celebrating significant birthdays or anniversaries. Not formal groups, but groupings of people with common interests with whom you can communicate.
- **Homogeneous**. A public's members share common traits and features. They may not know each other, but they have enough in common for you to treat them as a group.
- **Important**. Not every identifiable group is worth your attention. A public has a potentially significant impact on the organization, and vice versa.
- **Large Enough**. A public should be large enough to warrant the organization's time and resources. Generally, a handful of people would not be considered a public but rather could be dealt with in personal ways.
- **Accessible**. A public is a group with which you can interact and communicate. A community college might find it relatively easy to interact with potential students because they all live in a small geographic area. But an internationally renowned university would have a much harder time connecting with potential students thinly scattered throughout the world. The difference might mean that the community college could push messages out, but the university would have to more passively respond to inquiring potential students.

CATEGORIES OF PUBLICS

It becomes a bit easier to identify publics if they are subdivided into four categories. This is based on the concept of linkages, the study of how organizations and groups are interrelated.

- **Customer. Customers** are *publics who receive the products or services of an organization,* such as purchasers, clients, members, students, fans, patients, or patrons. They may be current, past, or potential customers.
- **Producer. Producers** are *the publics that provide input to the organization.* They include employees and volunteers, unions and management, vendors and suppliers, and donors and investors.
- **Enabler. Enablers** are *groups that help organizations exist and prosper.* These include regulators, opinion leaders, allies, and the media.
- **Limiter.** On the other hand, there may be **limiters**, *groups that inhibit the success of an organization.* These include competitors, opponents, unfriendly media, opinion leaders who hold negative views of the organization, and watchdog organizations.

Publics in these categories generally are in direct relationships with the organization. However, there are some other publics that are more distantly linked.

Public relations identifies a **secondary customer** as *the customer of your customers.* Examples are businesses that might hire a university's graduates or a graduate school that might attract applicants to them for advanced education.

An **intercessory public** is *a public that bridges the organization and its publics.* In everyday life, we often ask a friend or colleague to intercede for us, put in a good word as we look for a job, go for a loan, or seek a date with the new staffer who works in another department. In professional terms, organizations may direct attention to groups that are already in contact with a key public. For example, a university might communicate with high school guidance counselors, asking them to mention the university to their students. In this step of the planning process, identify such potential associates for networking possibilities later on.

In addition to intercessory publics, we sometimes deal with intercessory individuals. An **opinion leader** is *a person with a particular influence on an organization's publics.* Research shows that the media often influence opinion leaders such as business leaders, political figures, teachers, clergy, celebrities, media commentators, and others who, in turn, influence an organization's publics. Opinion leaders often generate word-of-mouth support for an organization or its products, services, or causes.

Where are opinion leaders located? Everywhere, it seems, depending on the issue involved. A study at Shih Tsin University in Taiwan asked more than 2,000 people around the world where they get information on energy and technology. The study found that 68 percent of respondents get their day-to-day information online (from personal, professional, organizational, and media sites), 11 percent from magazines, 6 percent from television, 6 percent from newspapers, 2 percent from radio, and 7 percent from other sources.

COCA-COLA IN EGYPT

Opinion leaders can be especially important when practicing public relations in an international context.

Pepsi has always been the soft-drink standard in Egypt and in most other Arab countries. To its cultural detriment, Coca-Cola has been linked with non-Arab Western interests and with American consumerism. An old saying in Egypt, laden with cultural implications, is that Pepsi is for Arabs and Coke is for Jews.

A rumor circulated in 2000 that Coca-Cola was anti-Islam, "proof" of which was that when the Coke logo was viewed upside-down in a mirror, it read as "No Mohammed. No Mecca." Or not. Regardless, Coke sales plummeted 20 percent. Protests erupted. Some areas of the country banned Coke advertising and signage.

Coca-Cola Egypt decided to move quickly, with a particular emphasis on the concept of opinion leader. The company requested a meeting with the grand mufti, the country's top religious leader, asking his advice. It also asked a panel of Islamic scholars to consider the matter. Both the grand mufti and the scholarly panel ruled that the rumor was unsubstantiated.

In a public statement, the religious leader scolded those who disseminated the false rumor for risking the jobs of thousands of fellow Muslims employed by Coca-Cola. He also later said in interviews that he himself enjoyed a daily Coke.

Besides relying on news coverage of the intervention, the company highly advertised the grand mufti's statement and gave copies to its drivers, distributors, and sales people. Within weeks, sales returned to pre-crisis levels where Coke, though still a distant second in the cola wars, was playing in a more even cultural environment.

Today, marketing reports suggest that Coca-Cola accounts for about 40 percent of the market in Egypt, but still trailing Pepsi, which remains the No. 1 soft drink throughout most of the Middle East.

KEY PUBLIC

Every organization has many publics that it communicates with on a regular basis, but no public relations plan will be successful if it tries to engage everyone. Instead, practitioners prioritize the various publics and select a few **key publics**, *specific publics that are identified as being most important to an organization's public relations activity*. These are also called **strategic publics**. (Note that some sources call these "target publics," though that term implies one-way communication that fails to focus on mutual engagement.)

Once the key publics are identified, the planning process focuses on analyzing each. Some of the needed information might come from brainstorming with colleagues, but you also may need to conduct interviews, focus groups, or surveys. Here are some things to consider when analyzing each key public.

- **Public Relations Situation**. Assess the public's wants, interests, needs, and expectations related to the issue, as well as what it does not want or need. Consider relevant attitudes of the public.
- **Organization**. Consider each key public's relationship with the organization—how your organization impacts the public and vice versa. Consider the extent to which the public understands this relationship and knows about the issue at hand. Also consider the visibility and reputation of your organization with this public.

- **Communication Behavior**. Study the public's communication habits, such as the media or communication channels it uses. Identify opinion leaders and others who might be credible message sources. Indicate whether the public is seeking information on the issue. (This assessment will have a major impact later when you choose your communication tactics; you should choose tactics that your key publics are already using.)
- **Demographics**. Identify demographic traits such as age, income, gender, socioeconomic status, or other relevant information about this public.

Conclude your analysis of the key publics with a **benefit statement**, *a statement that clearly articulates a benefit or advantage that a product or service offers to a public.*

For example, the benefit an online bookstore might offer college and university students could be written as this: "Cyber Booksellers can assure university students that it can provide class textbooks at discount prices with immediate delivery."

CULTURAL CONTEXT

Publics don't exist in a vacuum. Understanding their cultural context is crucial in this research phase of the strategic planning process. Public relations practitioners who give a priority to learning the nuances of the culture in which the publics exist are likely to develop campaigns that can be successful.

This is particularly important in the international arena. What works in one culture may not be appropriate for another.

Even basic communication can be hampered in international contexts. Language itself can be a barrier to communication. This is particularly true in Africa. South Africa, for example, has 11 different national languages. Nigeria has more than 500 languages and dialects, with English as the official language used mainly in cities, making it very difficult to mount any countrywide communication program.

Technological differences can add to the problem. Social media and mobile media, so common in Western societies, are not present enough in some parts of the world to make them useful tools for public relations, though this is changing rapidly as many countries are experiencing sustained growth in cellular technology. Social media may be banned or censored in some countries.

Outsiders do themselves and their public relations interests a disservice when they fail to understand the diversity that exists within a culture. In the United States, for example, public relations practitioners should understand that there are major differences within the Hispanic community. For example, mistakenly thinking that Puerto Ricans, Cuban-Americans, and Hispanics from the Dominican Republic all have the same cultural perspectives can create embarrassment for organizations and counterproductive responses from publics. Likewise Mexican, Panamanian, Colombian, and other Latin American cultures may share a common language base, but from a public relations perspective they may have more differences than similarities.

Asian Americans can also have very different national and cultural backgrounds. About the only thing they have in common is that non-Asian Americans tend to see them as all being the same.

Situations can get even more complicated when applied to other countries. Some nations such as Mexico, Canada, Australia, and Japan—as well as the United States—have historic tensions between indigenous peoples and the dominant culture. Others experience significant differences, even hostility, based on language (such as Canada and Ukraine), religion (Uganda, India, and sporadically, Northern Ireland), race (South Africa), or tribal background (Rwanda).

Gender roles and socially acceptable relations among men and women also vary greatly, as do social attitudes toward people who are gay, aged, disabled, or otherwise different from the social norm.

WORKSHEET FOR STEP 4: ANALYZING KEY PUBLICS

In Step 4 you have focused on your key publics—who they are, what they are like. Most importantly, you have looked at ways to identify the interests and aspirations of each key public, which is the needed foundation for eventually formulating an appeal to each.

Here are four basic questions to be addressed in Step 4:

1. What are the key publics for your organization on this issue?
2. What is the nature of each key public?
3. What are the major wants, interests, needs, and expectations of each key public?
4. What benefits can you offer each public?

You can build on these questions with more probing information about the awareness of each public toward these potential interests, whether the public is seeking information on the topic, and who might be influential opinion leaders.

PLANNING EXAMPLE FOR STEP 4

Here is a listing of major publics that University Exchange communicates with on a regular basis.

- *Customers* include local organizations with international counterparts and young professionals (up to age 35). Potential customers include university seniors and graduate students in professional programs.
- *Producers* include University Exchange staff (two full-time, three part-time); volunteer workshop presenters (approximately 14); and the nine-person board of directors of the local chapter. Producers also consist of donors including individuals, foundations, corporations, and grant-giving agencies and organizations.
- *Enablers* include the news media (general, business-oriented, cultural, and university-based); social media with professional or global interests; professional and business organizations with an international perspective; and cultural organizations with a global/intercultural agenda. Opinion leaders include university faculty in professional programs. Enablers also include approximately 35 current and past participants in the UE international programs, as well as their employers and professional mentors/colleagues. Another category of enablers includes groups and individuals associated with trade organizations, foreign consulates, and (at a greater distance) foreign embassies.
- *Limiters* include banks that are cutting back on loans. There are no apparent opponent groups.

These major publics were narrowed down for this campaign to three key publics:

1. Young business professionals, and university seniors, and graduate students in professional programs.

2. Companies, nonprofit groups, and professional organizations with a global perspective.
3. News media (particularly business-oriented media) and associated social media.

Here is an analysis of each key public:

1. Young business professionals and university students want an opportunity to be successful in their careers, especially by pulling ahead of others competing for the same jobs. They use various media, particularly websites, podcasts, social media such as Instagram, LinkedIn, YouTube, and TikTok, and news media, such as business-oriented newspapers, that address their career interests. By definition, this public is young. It has better-than-average education and reflects the general ethnic, racial, lifestyle, and religious demographics of university graduates living in this area. This public is likely to be open to mobility, travel, and intercultural/international engagement. Collectively these are wants and interests, though perhaps this public would not identify them as needs.
2. Businesses, nonprofits, and professional organizations want and need opportunities to be more competitive and more effective in their work. An interest is to have a workforce of people who are open, creative, resourceful, motivated, and committed to both customers and the company. Leaders in these organizations read business-oriented newspapers, the business section of their local daily newspaper, listen to podcasts on business topics, watch or listen to business-oriented programs and business segments on newscasts on radio and television, and are active on LinkedIn, Facebook, and YouTube.
3. News media want and need information that is newsworthy, available, and relevant to their audiences. Journalists seek information from many sources, including public relations professionals and organization leaders, organization websites, and social media.

Here is the benefit statement: University Exchange can provide information to each of these key publics that will interest them and will satisfy their wants and needs.

6

PUBLIC RELATIONS PLANNING

PHASE 2: STRATEGY

> Strategy deals with planning that focuses on the desired outcomes and the conceptual ways of achieving them. It's not about specific tools of communication, but rather, the big picture from the 10,000-foot level.

Strategy is *an organization's overall plan.* Building on the research from Phase 1, the strategy section determines what the organization wants to achieve and how it wants to achieve it. Strategy focuses on being both proactive and reactive, according to the organization's needs. It also deals with the presentation of the organization's messages (theme, source, content, and tone).

This phase is interrelated and interdependent. Goals guide the development of objectives. These, in turn, help drive decisions about what persuasive approaches to use and who can best present the message.

Later, in the next phase, strategy will guide your selection of tactics that will present the organization's message to its publics.

DOI: 10.4324/9781003521211-8

PR PROFILE: C. DEL GALLOWAY, APR, FELLOW PRSA

Introduction: Del is a public relations executive with proven success building brands, strengthening reputations, and driving results for Fortune 500 companies and other global organizations—from AT&T and United Way to Wells Fargo. He has a gift for "connecting the dots" between organizations and stakeholders, brands and consumers, and key influentials and communities. It's Del's understanding of relationships, his focus on reputations, and his ability to convey the right message at the right time—when to push, pull, or pause—that have made him a trusted advisor to clients worldwide.

Del is a former President of ACEJMC (Accrediting Council on Education in Journalism and Mass Communications), the governing body that accredits colleges of journalism and communications in the US and countries worldwide. In 2004, Del served as President and CEO of the Public Relations Society of America, a leading global public relations association.

In 2018, PRSA recognized Del with its Gold Anvil Award—the Society's highest individual honor—for lifetime achievement in public relations. In 1990, Del led the Florida Public Relations Association, and in 2002, he received FPRA's Dillon Award for lifetime achievement.

He is accredited in public relations (APR) and is a PRSA Fellow, recognizing public relations leadership and excellence.

Del holds a master's degree in communications and a bachelor's degree in public relations from the University of Florida, which has honored him with its Alumni of Distinction Award.

Why did you decide on a public relations career? My interests and skills lend themselves beautifully to public relations and the important role of strategic communications. Like a journalist, I'm curious—I want to know more. I'm well organized, and I find reward in helping individuals and organizations recognize and achieve their potential.

What's your favorite part of the job? Reputation management. Public relations is the bridge between a problem and a solution. We're the glue—the conscience of an organization. We anticipate and prepare for what's coming (issues management) and help create solutions that protect and advance reputations.

Where do you see the public relations industry in 10 years? Public relations will continue its evolution and rise as a vital societal function—be it in business, politics, or civil society writ large. The advancement of AI will create opportunities for strong, ethics-based communications strategists.

What advice to you have for graduating students launching their own PR careers? Be curious. It's much more important to be *interested* than interesting.

STEP 5: CREATING POSITIONING STATEMENTS, GOALS, AND OBJECTIVES

The purpose of this step is to clearly indicate the direction you are heading toward addressing the key publics about the situation. This involves articulating both the general direction and the specific marks of success. Here are short definitions of key concepts used in this step.

- A **positioning statement** is *a general expression of how an organization wants its publics to distinguish it vis-à-vis its competition.*
- A **goal** is *a statement rooted in an organization's mission or vision, sketching out how the organization hopes to see an issue settled.*
- An **objective** is *a statement emerging from an organization's goal, presented in clear and measurable terms with a deadline.*

POSITIONING STATEMENT

As you spell out the desired interaction with your publics, focus first on positioning. This means asking yourself a simple question: What do we want the key public to think about us?

Positioning is *the process of managing how an organization distinguishes itself with a unique meaning in the mind of its publics*—that is, how it wants to be seen and known by its publics. This usually means an implicit comparison with the organization's competitors.

Most organizations are known for their distinctiveness: the large public university, the small church-affiliated college, the high-priced two-year private school, the community college with open access, the mid-sized public institution that began as a teachers college, and so on.

Make sure your desired position is realistic. Who wouldn't want to be known as "the best in (whatever)"? But there can be only one best, and public relations is not about pretense or stretching beyond possibility. Here are some reasonable positioning statements:

- Great value, reflecting low cost and high quality.
- The most economical.
- The hospital preferred by women.
- The family-friendly restaurant.
- The eco-friendly garden center.

GOAL

With the positioning statement as a guidepost, turn your attention to the goal. It is stated in general terms, lacking measures (these will come later in the objectives).

Think in terms of three types of goals focused on reputation, relationships, and tasks.

1. **Reputation management goals** *deal with the identity and perception of the organization.* Here are some examples:
   - Improve the university's reputation for science education.
   - Reinforce the museum's image with potential donors.
   - Enhance the hospital's reputation for cancer treatment.
2. **Relationship management goals** *focus on how the organization connects with its publics.*
   - Reduce opposition to the building of a wind farm near an affluent community.
   - Enhance the relationship between the store and its customers.
   - Maintain a favorable relationship with season-ticket holders.
3. **Task management goals** are *concerned with getting certain things done.*
   - Influence motorists to refrain from texting while driving.
   - Attract a sell-out crowd for the concert.
   - Foster continued growth in the number of new customers.

OBJECTIVE

A public relations objective, which emerges from a goal, is measurable with a deadline. Here are some elements of an objective:

- **Goal rooted**—growing from and giving detail to the goals.
- **Public focused**—linked firmly to a specific key public.
- **Impact oriented**—defining the effect you hope to make on the public by focusing on intended achievements rather than tools to reach these.
- **Research based**—consistent with the data obtained in the first phase of the strategic planning process.
- **Explicit**—offering a concrete and precise indication of the intended outcome.
- **Measurable**—with metrics indicating quantifiable performance indicators.
- **Time definite**—with a clear timeframe for achieving the results.
- **Singular**—focusing on only one desired response for each objective.
- **Challenging**—offering the organization something to stretch toward.
- **Attainable**—yet also able to be achieved.
- **Acceptable**—earning the buy-in of the organization's managers.

Objectives are presented in a logical progression through three stages of persuasion: awareness, acceptance, and action.

Awareness objectives *deal with what people know about the organization.* This is the cognitive (informational) component of a message. It deals both with visibility and reputation, allowing an organization to build on accurate and positive awareness or to attempt to counter misinformation.

These awareness objectives often are used for transmitting functional information, for communicating on noncontroversial issues, and for the early stages of any communication campaign.

Acceptance objectives *focus on the interest in and attitudes of the publics based on what they know.* These objectives deal with the affective (feeling) part of the message. They indicate the level of interest or the kind of attitude an organization hopes to generate in its publics.

These objectives are useful in forming interests and attitudes where none existed before, reinforcing existing interests and attitudes, and changing existing positive or negative attitudes.

Action objectives *articulate how we want the publics to act, based on what they think or feel about what they know.* They offer two types of action: opinion (verbal action) and behavior (physical action).

These action objectives may attempt to create new behaviors or change existing ones, positively or negatively.

Generally, a goal should have at least one of each of these three types of objectives. Here is a scenario to help you understand how these fit together. Let's say they are for a task management goal of obtaining volunteers among university students for a program called MMS, Mentors in Math and Science.

- To *create awareness* of the MMS program among students, specifically to have 40 percent of the 25,000 students (10,000) at three area colleges and universities understand the program and the benefits of volunteering, within six months.
- To *create acceptance* among these students, specifically generating interest among 5 percent of the student population (1,250 students), within six months.
- To *generate action* among the students, specifically to achieve an action rate of 1 percent, achieving 250 volunteers after a six-month campaign.

Notice how each level grows from the previous one. Notice also that there will be no guessing about whether success is achieved. The outcomes of measures and timeframes are identified clearly.

ADIDAS

Reputation management goals are especially significant in crisis situations, as illustrated by this case involving Adidas, the German multinational retailer.[1]

The company had a longstanding partnership with rapper and entrepreneur Ye (formerly Kanye West), resulting in Yeezy-branded products. In 2022, following a series of antisemitic remarks by

Ye on social media, Adidas faced public pressure to denounce his remarks after many other companies—including his talent agency—dropped him.

Adidas terminated its partnership with Ye, noting in a statement that it doesn't tolerate antisemitism or hate speech and that "Ye's recent comments and actions have been unacceptable, hateful, and dangerous, and they violate the company's values of diversity and inclusion, mutual respect, and fairness."

Adidas ceased production of Yeezy-branded products, resulting in a loss in revenue of $283.9 million (£209.5 million; €248.2 million) and a decline in its ethics score. Since then, Adidas has worked to rebuild its reputation by selling off remaining Yeezy products and donating the proceeds to the Anti-Defamation League.

WORKSHEET FOR STEP 5: CREATING POSITIONING STATEMENTS, GOALS, AND OBJECTIVES

Step 5 is all about what the organization wants people to know and feel and how it expects them to act on these factors.

Here are the basic questions for this step:

1. What position do you seek?
2. What are the goals to achieve this positioning?
3. What are the specific objectives (awareness, acceptance, and action) for each public and each goal?

As necessary, flesh out these questions with additional information about the viability and practicality of the position and goals, the level of support for the position and goals, and the consistency of each objective with previous decisions about the organization's publics.

CONSENSUS CHECK

At this point, meet with your planning colleagues and with your boss or client. Make sure that agreement and harmony exists within the organization about the recommended objectives, because what is formulated here will be the basis for subsequent strategies and tactics.

If there is agreement and buy-in, proceed to Step 6. If not, consider the value and/or possibility of achieving consensus before proceeding.

PLANNING EXAMPLE FOR STEP 5

University Exchange's *positioning statement*: University Exchange wants to be the go-to source for international professional engagements.

Two *goals* are associated with this:

- A *reputation management goal* to promote the visibility and reputation of University Exchange among young business professionals and the companies or organizations that employ them.
- A *task management goal* of increasing the number of participants in its engagement and exchange programs.

Objectives for Public #1 (individual professionals):

1. To have an effect on the *awareness* of young professionals about University Exchange, specifically to increase their understanding of the advantages that University Exchange offers by 50 percent within one year.
2. To have an effect on their *acceptance*, specifically to increase their interest in the engagement/exchange programs by 25 percent within one year.
3. To have an effect on their *action*, specifically to generate ten applicants for long-term exchange programs and 40 for short-term engagement programs within one year.

Objectives for Public #2 (organizations):

1. To have an effect on *acceptance*, specifically to increase the awareness of corporate executives and human resources staff about the University Exchange program opportunities (50 percent of identified organizations within one year).
2. To have an effect on their *acceptance*, specifically to generate feedback and inquiries from these organizations (15 percent within one year).

3. To have an effect on their *action*, specifically to generate invitations for University Exchange to meet with organizational leaders (25 organizations within one year).

Objectives for Public #3 (news media):

1. To have an effect on their *awareness*, specifically to increase their knowledge about the University Exchange programs (journalists at 50 percent of identified news media and news blogs within one year).
2. To have an effect on their *acceptance*, specifically to generate inquiries from these journalists (25 percent of identified news venues within one year).
3. To have an effect on their *action*, specifically to see publication/broadcast of positive/neutral pieces by 10 percent of identified news venues within one year.

STEP 6: CHOOSING PROACTIVE AND REACTIVE STRATEGIES

Strategy is an organization's overall plan, as noted earlier. Strategies provide the framework for specific communication tactics that will follow (tactics are described in Step 8). Ideally, public relations strategies involve actions as well as words, complementing each other as an organization interacts with its publics. This step in the planning process will focus on strategies for achieving objectives created in the previous step. Public relations strategies fit into one of two categories: proactive or reactive.

Proactive strategies *enable an organization to take the initiative by launching a campaign under conditions and according to a timeline that best fits the organization's interests*, such as when it launches a campaign to publicize a new product or service. There are two types of proactive strategies, action and communication.

Reactive strategies are *strategies through which an organization responds to influences and opportunities from its environment*, including hostile pressures from the outside. Types of reactive strategies include pre-emptive action, offensive response, defensive response, diversionary response, vocal commiseration, rectifying behavior, and deliberate inaction.

PROACTIVE STRATEGY 1: ACTION

The first category of proactive public relations involves tangible deeds undertaken by the organization to achieve its objectives.

Organizational performance, a key type of proactive action, *involves assessing and, when necessary, changing the output of an organization.* This process is known as **adaptation**, *the ability of an organization to make changes on the basis of what its publics want and need.*

A publicity campaign on behalf of a restaurant that serves mediocre food won't be very successful until the food improves. A politician who fails to address the interests of voters isn't going to attract much support.

Review Steps 3 and 4 of this strategic planning process. Compare the output of the organization with the wants, interests, needs, and expectations of the publics. Then address any differences between the two.

Audience engagement, *a strategy involving two-way communication between an organization and its publics*, is another important proactive strategy. If possible, build in opportunities for your publics to participate in the program.

For example, Bosque de Chapultepec in Mexico City, the hemisphere's oldest urban park, invited thousands of volunteers to pick up trash as part of a wider effort to encourage its 15 million visitors to use sanitary facilities. The involvement of these volunteers spurred the campaign and created thousands of environmental ambassadors who continued to look after park sanitation and cleanliness long after their volunteer cleanup ended. Audience engagement also involves creating feedback opportunities, such as online surveys and interactive websites.

To generate audience participation, organizations sometimes sponsor a **staged event**, *an activity created by the organization as a focal point for public involvement and potential media attention.* Staged events can involve positive activities such as tree-planting ceremonies, recitals, competitions such as sporting events or essay contests, parades, and anniversary events. They also could feature more confrontational approaches such as rallies, demonstrations, and other activist events.

Organizations with a common goal sometimes join together in **alliances**, *informal relationships among organizations that compound their influence and often generate media attention as the organizations work toward a goal.* **Coalitions** are *formal, structured relationships among organizations.*

Related to alliances and coalitions are **sponsorships**, *through which an organization provides financial, personnel, and other resources to support a community project.* The relationship should be a strategic one with mutual benefits. For example, a technology company might sponsor a science fair.

Some sponsorships are based on existing marketing relationships. For example, Lexus sponsors polo championships because enthusiasts of that sport reflect the luxury car's customer base.

Activism is *a confrontational proactive strategy focused on persuasive communication and advocacy.* It's a strong strategy with pros and cons, and because it can generate opposition as well as support, organizations are cautious about engaging in activism. But this strategy can be very successful, especially for cause-related organizations and movements dealing with social issues, environmental matters, and political concerns.

Some of the tactics associated with this strategy include boycotts, marches, petitions, pickets, rallies, sit-ins, strikes, vigils, and outright civil disobedience.

Sometimes activism takes the form of street theater, such as when Amnesty International coordinated a protest in 83 cities around the world, mostly near military bases or embassies. Protestors dressed in orange jumpsuits and black hoods, courting media attention to protest the lack of due process for suspected terrorists detained for years by the US military at Guantanamo Bay.

Some activism is in-your-face, literally, as pie-throwing became a publicity tactic to protest designer use of fur (pieing Oscar de la Renta), euro currency (Dutch finance minister Gerrit Zalm), endangered sea turtles (Renato Ruggiero, director general of the World Trade Organization), seal hunting (Canadian Fisheries and Oceans Minister Gail Shea), and the faces associated with many other causes.

ONLINE ACTIVISM

Many organizations around the world have embraced **online activism**, *a proactive strategy that uses digital and social media for social engagement*. Also called **digital activism**, **cyberactivism**, or **hashtag activism**, it erases geographical boundaries, circumvents local media interests, and allows organizations to engage their publics directly and frequently.

Hashtags related to social causes have trended globally on social media platforms such as Facebook, X (formerly Twitter), Instagram, and YouTube, sparking discussions and mobilizing actions on a massive scale. Social media platforms are making e-activist tools available to their users, making it easy for supporters to volunteer, donate, and share the organization's message to their own list of online friends.

Cyberactivism has been a catalyst for social protests such as Black Lives Matter, Me Too, MAGA (Make America Great Again), America's Hands Off!, Climate Change, the UK's Stop Funding Hate, Nigeria's Bring Back Our Girls, the Arab Spring uprisings in the Middle East, the Greek economic protests, and the Occupy movement. As a tool of social engagement for public relations purposes, cyberactivism can involve advocacy, mobilization, and action/reaction, making it useful in fundraising, lobbying, and community building.

Groups such as Amnesty International and Greenpeace have embraced online activism in a big way. Such organizations long have encouraged volunteers to sign petitions and contact government leaders and corporate executives on behalf of various causes. Now visitors can go to the organizations' websites to learn about current campaigns and to sign up to receive information on topics of particular interest.

Greenpeace uses its website (greenpeace.org) to update visitors on various environmental issues and campaigns around the world. With a simple mouse click, visitors to the website can add their name to petitions and mail campaigns on issues such as global warming, forests and oceans, endangered animals, green energy production, and sustainable fishing.

Friends of the Earth (foe.co.uk) offers online petitions and social media support for clean air, bees, sanitation, biodiversity, and support for a green economy. People for the Ethical Treatment of Animals (peta.org) invites online visitors to contact lawmakers and advertisers and to spread the word via their own social media networks.

PROACTIVE STRATEGY 2: COMMUNICATION

Another category of proactive public relations strategies deals with communication, specifically, the various options an organization has to communicate with its publics.

At some time, every organization seeks **publicity**, *attention given by the news media to an organization, person, event, product, or idea.* The value of this is that information reported by the news media and blogs has both credibility and potentially a wide audience. A limitation is that the information must be considered **newsworthy**, a decision that is made by media **gatekeepers**, *editors, reporters, and news directors who determine what gets reported.*

So what is "news"? In Chapter 4, we defined **news** as *significant information relevant to a local media audience, presented with balance and objectivity and in a timely manner.* Balance and objectivity are key considerations; ethical public relations practitioners strive to avoid presenting fake news to their key publics, as noted in Chapter 2. Honesty and accuracy in communication are vital to maintaining the trust of an organization's key publics, concepts articulated in the codes of ethics of many professional organizations, such as the Public Relations Society of America.

A lot of information is important to an organization but not "news" as media gatekeepers would see it. For example, an organization might be planning a major fundraising dinner and needs advance reservations, but the news media are not going to report it three weeks early just so the caterer can get a head count. The organization would have to find other ways of reaching its key publics.

To attract media interest, news and publicity also should have a strong **visual element**. Stand-up commentators or talking heads just don't make it on most TV news reports—visuals are a "must"! For example, an early morning TV newscast that has a news story about an ice-skating show that evening might feature a brief performance and interview with the ice skaters.

For publicity efforts to be successful, organizations must have newsworthy information. Sometimes this is unexpected news (possibly bad news) such as an accident in the workplace. But public relations professionals know how to generate news that can be more favorable for their organizations. Here's a short list of some ways to create news.

1. Give an award to draw attention to values and issues.
2. Hold a contest to involve others in your values and issues.
3. Select personnel to head a new program or begin a new project.
4. Comment on a local need or problem.
5. Conduct research and issue a report about a local need or problem.
6. Launch a campaign to accomplish something.
7. Give a speech to a significant audience and tell the media about it.
8. Involve a celebrity visiting and/or addressing your organization on a topic of concern to you.
9. Tie into an issue already high on the public or media agenda or link your organization to the top news of the day.
10. Localize a general report.

Public relations professionals try to find topics that are associated with all three groups involved in the dissemination of newsworthy information: the news media, the organization, and its key publics. At the intersection of these three groups is a **news peg**—*linking an organization's message to something already in the news.*

For example, if a high-profile celebrity goes public with a diagnosis of breast cancer, a cancer research center might move quickly to offer media interviews on how to identify and deal with the illness.

Here are two real-world examples of effective public relations use of news pegs.

DAWN DETERGENT

Every time there is an environmental disaster involving oil-covered birds, Proctor and Gamble gets the opportunity to note that its Dawn detergent is THE cleaning agent of choice for groups such as the International Bird Rescue Research Center and the US Fish and Wildlife Service.

The company generates news releases, promotes interviews, and uses internal and social media to communicate directly with its consumers—all ways to enhance Dawn's positioning as a skin-friendly but high-powered cleaner.

OAKLEY SUNGLASSES

When the world watched as 35 miners were rescued in Chile after being trapped underground for 69 days, Oakley donated sunglasses to help the miners' eyes return to normal after so much time without sunlight.

At a retail cost of $180 (£133, €157) for each pair of sunglasses, the company turned an investment of $6,400 (£4,723, €5,597) into international media exposure estimated to be worth $41 million (£30.3 million, €35.9 million).

Proactive public relations also calls for **transparent communication**—*proactive, open, and observable activity that helps publics understand the organization and support its actions*. Transparent communication enhances trust, accountability, and engagement with key publics.

For example, ice cream manufacturer Ben & Jerry's openly communicates its stance on social justice issues and how its business aligns with those values. Outdoor clothing giant Patagonia, renowned for its commitment to environmental and social responsibility, shares information about its supply chains. Netflix's "sun-shining" policy encourages executives to publicly explain decisions, especially significant actions such as employee firings. Whole Foods Markets requires all non-GMO (genetically modified organism) label claims to be third-party verified or certified.

Organizations engage in transparent communication when they lay out for their publics the issues, background, influences, and options. If financial pressures are pushing your organization to curtail services, let your publics know about the financial problems and the various options before announcing a service cutback. Nobody likes bad surprises, especially when it suggests that the organization has been hiding information from key publics.

REACTIVE STRATEGY 1: PRE-EMPTIVE ACTION

A pre-emptive strike is one taken before an opponent launches its first charge against the organization. From a public relations perspective, it's a **prebuttal**, a play on the word "rebuttal," *presenting advance information defending an organization when bad news is inevitable.* The concept underlying a prebuttal—its benefit—is the idea that the first person to tell the story sets the tone, against which all alternative versions must compete.

CBS late night talk-show host David Letterman effectively used a prebuttal in 2009 when a CBS producer attempted to blackmail Letterman by threatening to tell the public that Letterman had had affairs with female staff members. The producer demanded a large sum of money. Letterman went to court, then went public with his side of the story that same day on his own television show. Media coverage resulted, but Letterman apologized on air to his family, and the media coverage died down. The producer was found guilty of extortion.

REACTIVE STRATEGY 2: OFFENSIVE RESPONSE

Public relations planners sometimes try to operate from a position of strength in the face of opposition. For example, they may use the **attack** strategy, *claiming that an accusation of wrongdoing is motivated by an accuser who is negligent or malicious.*

Another offensive strategy is **embarrassment**, *in which an organization tries to lessen an opponent's influence by using shame or humiliation.* It is often used by political candidates. For example, Donald Trump has frequently employed mocking nicknames to belittle his political adversaries and shape public perceptions, labeling Hillary Clinton as "Crooked Hillary" and Elizabeth Warren as "Pocahontas" in the 2016 presidential campaign, and Joe Biden as "Sleepy Joe" Biden in the 2020 race. During the 2016 campaign, Hillary Clinton characterized half of Trump's supporters as a "basket of deplorables," labeling them as racist, sexist, homophobic, xenophobic, or Islamophobic. That remark, widely criticized, is believed to have contributed to Clinton's loss by alienating undecided and moderate voters.

One step beyond embarrassment as an offensive response strategy is **shock**, *deliberately agitating publics by presenting information that surprises, causes fear, or disgusts them*. Certain fashion and cosmetics companies, such as Calvin Klein, Dolce & Gabbana, Sisley, and Benetton, have produced many shock ads over the years. But the most consistent shocker is People for the Ethical Treatment of Animals (see box below).

Sometimes organizations use **threat**, *an offensive response strategy that promises that harm will come to the accuser or the purveyor of bad news*. The threatened harm may be a lawsuit for defamation, for example. Public relations practitioners have learned to use threats only if the information cannot be disputed in another way.

Another strategy is **doubledown**, *an offensive response strategy in which an organization reiterates its action or position as a matter of principle and stands firm*. For example, critics blasted Starbucks for its supposed war on Christmas because one holiday season, it featured a plain red cup with a green corporate logo rather than a traditional holiday scene. The company stood firm and largely ignored its critics.

PETA

People for the Ethical Treatment of Animals has built a reputation for outrageous strategies in its animal-rights campaigns. To protest the use of leather, PETA activists have disrupted fashion events, such as the Coach runway show at New York Fashion Week. PETA used shock strategy to force McDonald's to agree to more humane practices in chicken coops and slaughterhouses. The organization also has produced graphic advertisements featuring disturbing imagery, such as models holding skinned animal carcasses, to show the realities of the fur industry.

Although PETA's tactics often attract criticism, the organization maintains they are effective in raising awareness about animal rights and prompting change.

REACTIVE STRATEGY 3: DEFENSIVE RESPONSE

Another set of strategies involves a more overt defensive approach by the organization. One such strategy is **denial**, where *an organization refuses to accept blame by claiming innocence ("We didn't do it"), mistaken identity ("You've confused us with someone else"), or by shifting blame ("So-and-so did it").*

Another common defensive strategy is **excuse**, through which *the organization tries to mitigate wrongdoing.* This may be based on provocation ("We didn't have a choice"), lack of control ("The problem was caused at a higher level"), accident ("We were at the whim of natural causes beyond our control"), victimization ("A culprit outside our organization caused this"), or mere association ("We inherited this problem").

Justification is a related *defensive response strategy in which the organization admitting to the deed but explaining that it did so for a good reason.* One type of justification is based on good intention ("We were trying to avoid worse harm"), context ("Look at this from our side"), idealism ("We are following higher principles"), or mitigation ("We did this, but it was the result of impairment/illness/coercion/etc.").

Another defensive response strategy is **reversal**, *in which an organization under criticism tries to gain the upper hand.*

PEPSI

The cola giant faced an accusation in 1993 that medical syringes had been found in cans of diet soft drink. After the news media reported the first case in Tacoma, Washington, similar claims popped up throughout the US.

Pepsi used defensive strategies by saying that it was an innocent victim and by denying that any crisis even existed. It supported this denial with video news releases showing how its production process made it impossible to contaminate the product before it left the plant.

The company also used offensive strategies by claiming that the accusers had planted the objects and by vowing to pursue legal action against people making false claims. Pepsi later produced video news releases showing the arrest of a tamperer, and the circulated convenience store surveillance videos of the tampering incident.

It quickly became clear that there was no basis to the claims, and thus no continuing crisis. Pepsi concluded with a campaign to thank loyal customers, with advertising headlines that read: "Pepsi is pleased to announce ... nothing."

REACTIVE STRATEGY 4: DIVERSIONARY RESPONSE

Sometimes an organization uses a **diversionary response strategy**—*trying to divert attention away from itself and the problem it is associated with*. One way to do this is through **concession**, *where an organization tries to rebuild its relationship with aggrieved publics by giving them something they want, drawing attention away from the problem that remains*.

Related to this is **ingratiation** ("Let's try to divert them by tossing a bone"). This *approach, which raises ethical questions, involves giving a public something insignificant under the pretense that it has value*.

Disassociation ("We've just fired the people who caused this problem") is another *diversionary response strategy in which an organization tries to distance itself from the wrongdoing associated with it*. Sometimes this involves firing employees who violated organizational policy, for example, when schools or youth organizations move quickly to get rid of employees or volunteers accused of abusing children.

An associated diversionary response strategy is **relabeling**, *offering an agreeable name to replace a name with negative connotations*. This has led Al Qaeda in Yemen to change its name to Ansar al Sharia, Philip Morris tobacco corporation calling itself Altria Group, and Exxon successively changing the name of the notorious tanker *Valdez* to *Sea River Mediterranean*, later sold and renamed *Dong Fang Ocean* and most recently *Oriental Nicety*. Relabeling takes place in the food industry, too. Which would you rather eat: Chinese gooseberry or kiwi? Dolphin fish or mahi mahi? Rapeseed oil or canola oil? Toothfish or Chilean sea bass? Slimehead or orange roughy? You get the idea: labels matter.

PAPA JOHN'S PIZZA

When a franchise causes problems for a global corporation, the home office should be quick to respond. That's what happened when one of Papa John's franchise owners, a fan of Washington Wizards basketball, tried to distract an opposing team's star player during an NBA play-off game.

The franchise distributed "Cry Baby" T-shirts ridiculing LeBron James of the Cleveland Cavaliers, known for complaining about being fouled. One photo of the provocative T-shirt was posted on the SoGood.com food blog, and 12 hours later Cav fans had started a nationwide boycott of Papa John's.

Papa John's acted quickly with a Sunday afternoon emergency strategy session with its Fleishman-Hillard agency. The client first considered an advertising response, but public relations planners successfully argued the merits of a proactive media response.

First, the corporation distanced itself from the franchise with an apology to James, his fans, and the city of Cleveland. Such distancing is standard with a diversionary response.

Then Papa John's maneuvered another diversionary response by offering fans two concessions. It donated $10,000 to the Cavalier's Youth Fund and an additional $10,000 to James' own foundation for kids. The corporation also prepared its 115 franchises in and around Northeast Ohio for a special promotion four days later, when it sold 66,000 pizzas for 23 cents each (reflecting James' jersey number).

The result was positive international news coverage of corporate philanthropy, thousands of happy customers, online chat rooms, and blogs gushing with praise for the way Papa John's made up for one franchise's mistake, and in Cleveland a 15 percent increase in pizza sales that lasted several months.

REACTIVE STRATEGY 5: VOCAL COMMISERATION

Another family of strategies is **vocal commiseration**, *ways in which an organization expresses empathy and understanding about a misfortune.* The least apologetic of these is **concern** ("This is a serious and troubling situation") *with the organization expressing distress but not admitting any culpability.*

Condolence ("We are deeply sorry that this happened") is the next level, *with the organization expressing grief over someone's loss or misfortune, again without admitting guilt.*

Next comes **regret** ("Words cannot express how sorry we are for our role in this accident"), *in which the organization admits its role but doesn't necessarily accept responsibility or admit wrongdoing.* This often is a crisis response endorsed by public relations practitioners who understand that publics generally need to see and hear that the organization is not minimizing its role in problem situations.

Occasionally organizations express regret for the actions of others. Congress incurred the wrath of the Turkish government when one of its committees passed a nonbinding resolution labeling as "genocide" the Turkish massacre of 1.5 million Armenians during World War I. Formal consideration of the resolution, which threatened US security interests in the Middle East, was stalled. The irony is that the US Congress had yet to apologize to its own people for Black slavery in the American South, the forced relocation of Japanese-Americans during World War II, or relocation and ethnic cleansing campaigns against American Indians.

The highest level of vocal commiseration is the **apology** ("We are sorry we did this; please forgive us"), *where an organization publicly accepts responsibility and asks pardon.* Particularly in crisis situations, public relations strategists point out that an apology often can shorten the lifespan of a crisis. A public apology also can minimize negative legal and financial consequences.

Strategists also are quick to point out the dangers of a **non-apology** ("I'm sorry if you took offense"), *an insincere attempt to apologize without really doing so.*

MATTEL TOYS

Like all strategies, an apology must be considered in light of both the public and the cultural context. That was the issue as concern grew about the safety of Mattel toys made in China, including lead paint in some of the toys.

A top Mattel official met with China's product-safety official to issue an apology to consumers. Mattel said it was sorry for the recall of millions of toys and that it would try to prevent future problems—at least, that's the version reported in Europe and North America.

The Chinese version went more like this: "Mattel is sorry for having to recall Chinese-made toys due to the company's design flaws and for harming the reputation of Chinese manufacturing companies."

Actually, the Chinese version got it right. It was a design flaw that had caused the recall of more than 17 million toys. Only 2 million of those were recalled because the Chinese firms used lead paint, which is prohibited in the United States.

China had previously been stung by a series of recalls undermining confidence in its manufactured goods (pet food, toothpaste, packaged seafood, and baby cribs).

China needed the public apology, and it needed for the explanation to be clear that the fault was with Mattel which, critics agreed, deserved the bigger blame because of corporate policies to cut costs and speed up production.

REACTIVE STRATEGY 6: RECTIFYING BEHAVIOR

A **rectifying behavior strategy** is *a positive response to opposition and criticism that involves action by an organization to repair the damage.* One such strategy is **investigation** ("We are looking into the cause of this problem"), *in which an organization promises to examine a situation and then act as facts warrant.*

Corrective action ("Here's how we will fix this problem") *involves taking steps to contain a problem, repair the damage, and/or prevent its recurrence.* This was part of Johnson & Johnson's response to the classic crisis of the cyanide murders associated with Tylenol. The company, clearly a victim along with its customers, took responsibility for repackaging the product to prevent future tampering, thus setting a new standard for the entire pharmaceutical industry.

More recently, McDonald's swiftly pulled its Quarter Pounder from about 20 percent of its restaurants in 2024 after an E. coli outbreak across ten states in the US killed one person and sickened dozens of others. The burger chain's investigation pinpointed slivered onions from one supplier as the source of the problem with the Quarter Pounders.

Another rectifying behavior that serves the interests of both the organization and its publics is **restitution** ("Here's how we will make this right"), *which involves making amends by compensating victims or restoring the situation to its earlier condition.*

The strongest type of rectifying behavior is **repentance** ("We did something wrong, and here's what we are doing to make sure it never happens again"). *This strategy signals an organization's full atonement because it becomes an advocate for a new way of thinking and doing business.*

DENNY'S

The story of Denny's restaurant chain is one of transformation from a symbol of corporate racism to a model of workplace diversity.

Denny's faced lawsuits for racial discrimination at several restaurants during the 1990s. One of the most notorious cases involved 21 members of the Secret Service. While 15 white agents were served quickly, a waitress and manager delayed serving six Black agents for nearly an hour, allowing their food to get cold.

The ensuing publicity highlighted a series of lawsuits for similar acts of discrimination at other Denny's restaurants: Asian American students refused service and beaten by customers, Hispanic customers refused service, Muslim customers served pork after asking for a vegetarian menu, men of Middle Eastern descent kicked out of a restaurant and a blind woman refused service because she was accompanied by her service dog.

Denny's eventually paid $54 million (£39.8 million, €47.2 million) in legal settlements. The company's chief diversity officer later looked back on that "historic low point" in the company's history as presenting "huge opportunities. We had no place to go but up."

Dramatically, the company seems to have embraced the strategy of corporate repentance. It adopted an aggressive antidiscrimination policy that included hiring minority managers, training employees and firing those who discriminated. Denny's increased minority franchise ownership from 1 to 109 over five years (currently 40 percent of all Denny's franchises, and 44 percent of its board of directors are minorities and/or women).

The company launched a $2 million (£1.5 million, €1.7 million) antidiscrimination advertising campaign. Each year it purchases goods worth more than $100 million (£73.8 million, €87.4 million) from minority vendors. It supports the King Center in Atlanta, civil rights groups, and the United Negro College Fund and has worked with the Hispanic Association on Corporate Responsibility and the NAACP.

A result of this turnaround is that Denny's ranked No. 1 in Fortune magazine's listing of best companies for minorities, two years running. It received similar awards from Black Enterprise, Essence, Asian Enterprise and Hispanic Business magazines.

This story is not without its irony. So successful is Denny's commitment to diversity, some white-nativist organizations called for boycotts because the company has become "too multicultural."

REACTIVE STRATEGY 7: DELIBERATE INACTION

Sometimes, the best response is *no response*, a reactive strategy known as **deliberate inaction**. **Strategic silence** is a *reactive strategy of not responding to criticism, though it may take follow-up action.* That was the case with Perrier, the upscale European company that produces bottled water. When cancer-causing benzene was discovered in some of the water, the company pulled millions of bottles from store shelves but refused to give any information to the news media.

A related approach is **strategic ambiguity**, *the refusal to be pinned down to a particular response.* This involves the artful dodging of a question, though often it's more a clear evasion of responding.

The final category is **strategic inaction**, *where the organization simply waits out a situation and allows it to fade.* While this may be a useful approach if the stakes are not too high, some problems do not fade away, especially those fanned by the opposition. By doing nothing, the organization risks allowing the problem to fester.

STATE DEPARTMENT

For years, the United States has walked a tightrope regarding the political status of Taiwan. China claims the island, but the United States and a handful of other countries refuse to recognize this claim.

US diplomats have been deliberately vague, using strategic ambiguity to provide at least a semblance of options over the international dispute. The State Department uses terms such as "acknowledging" rather than "recognizing" a single Chinese political entity. US, UK, and Canadian diplomats "take note of" rather than "support" Beijing's claim to be the legitimate government of China.

WORKSHEET FOR STEP 6: CHOOSING PROACTIVE AND REACTIVE STRATEGIES

Step 6 dealt with the "doing" part of a public relations campaign—what the organization does proactively or reactively. It grows from the notion that actions speak louder than words, reminding you to build your public relations message (in the next step) on a solid foundation of deeds.

Here are the basic questions to guide your planning for this step:

Proactive Strategies

1. If the organization is proactively initiating a public relations campaign, what kind of action or adaptation is appropriate?
2. What approach to news and information can be developed?

Reactive Strategies

1. If the organization is responding to forces in its environment, to what extent is pre-emptive action appropriate?
2. … offensive response?
3. … defensive response?
4. … diversionary response?
5. … vocal commiseration?
6. … rectifying behavior?
7. … deliberate inaction?

PLANNING EXAMPLE FOR STEP 6

University Exchange is confident that its performance level is high. There have been no mishaps or embarrassments in recent years, and "graduates" of the engagement and exchange programs consistently give positive feedback. Additionally, the program involves careful training of staff and volunteers to provide high levels of service.

One strategy that University Exchange will undertake is to enhance *audience participation* by involving business leaders in planning for international activities. Another strategy is to forge strong *alliances* with like-minded organizations, particularly college and university exchange programs (which generally are long term) and shorter-term visits arranged through professional organizations.

University Exchange also will proactively seek to generate *newsworthy information* for social media and local news media.

The one potentially negative incident involved a small but vocal group of single-issue dissidents in the community who rail against any international engagements because of an exaggerated sense of patriotism. Their message is that this country is No. 1 in its culture and thus does not need to engage with other countries. University Exchange will adopt a strategy of *strategic silence* toward these vocal opponents, who have shown from past incidents with other organizations that they are incapable of civil discussion and that, when they attract media attention, they discredit their own cause by their blatant and simple-minded diatribes against organizations that would participate in the international community.

STEP 7: DEVELOPING THE MESSAGE STRATEGY

Having identified publics (Step 4), established objectives (Step 5), and set into motion the way the organization is preparing to act to achieve those objectives (Step 6), it's time to turn your attention to the issue of how to communicate.

Effective public relations campaigns involve the sharing of information. Generally they also involve advocacy and attempts to persuade. Sometimes they aim for understanding, consensus building, conflict resolution, and improved relationships. Communication is central to each of these models.

One way to approach communication planning is to look to the threefold analysis developed 23 centuries ago by Aristotle: Effective communication involves **ethos**, *the character of a speaker and common ground shared by speakers and audiences*; **logos**, *the rational appeal of messages*; and **pathos**, *appeal to sentiment with positive or negative emotional appeal.* That is, effective communication rests on a credible speaker, logical arguments, and a sympathetic approach to storytelling.

ETHOS: SELECTING MESSAGE SOURCES

Years of research have produced a snapshot of an effective message source: someone who is credible, has charisma, and exercises some kind of control over the audience.

Credibility is *a message source's power to inspire belief.* Even audiences that don't understand an issue well often will accept a message from someone they think is believable. Credibility rests on how the audience perceives several qualities:

- The speaker is seen as an expert in the discipline being addressed.
- The speaker has a certain organizational or professional status.
- He or she is competent in speaking, remaining calm under pressure and able to articulate clearly.
- Finally, the credible speaker is perceived as being honest, both unbiased on the topic and not having a vested interest in it.

Charisma is *a message source's magnetic appeal or personal charm.* It's a matter of perception, varying from one person to another. Charisma has several components:

- A charismatic speaker is familiar to the audience.
- She or he is liked by the audience, at least to the extent that the audience thinks it knows the person.
- Generally, an effective charismatic speaker is similar to the audience, sharing (or appearing to share) its interests and values, and often reflecting demographic factors such as age, sex, race, ethnicity, religion, culture, sociopolitical perspectives, and so on.
- Finally, and least importantly, a charismatic message source is seen as someone the audience considers to be physically attractive.

Control is *the extent to which a speaker has some command over the audience and the perceived willingness to exercise that power.* It has three components:

- An effective speaker can exert a certain power over the audience, such as the ability to reward or punish.
- He or she may be in a position of authority, which implies that the audience more or less willingly has granted the right of control and thus will give obedience. The authority may be based on family, occupational, religious, or some other important set of relationships in the life of audience members.
- The persuasive speaker has the ability to examine, giving scrutiny over members of the audience.

With this understanding of effective message sources, public relations strategists try to identify appropriate spokespersons to present their organizational message.

Some campaigns rely on celebrity spokespersons. Celebrities are often charismatic and familiar, but they aren't necessarily perceived as being credible. Nonprofit organizations such as charities for cancer and other diseases find that celebrities can attract attention to their cause. Social causes such as those focused on human rights, environmental issues, and humanitarian concerns also find that star power can attract other supporters and donors.

But celebrities have baggage. Many organizations, both corporations and nonprofits, have been publicly embarrassed by their celebrity endorsers. Think of Tiger Woods, one of the highest-rated celebrities who annually earned $105 million (£77.5 million, €91.8 million) in endorsements before the scandal of his extramarital relationships.

Also, celebrities sometimes wish to avoid being linked with controversial products or partisan issues. Few celebrities would promote tobacco products, for example. While some feel strongly enough about politics to lend their name, others follow the example of Michael Jordan who, when asked to endorse a Black Democrat in a Senate election, refused "because Republicans buy sneakers too."

Some organizations rely on company spokespersons, on the notion that people close to the organization will be viewed as more expert. But expertise may not outweigh a perceived lack of credibility. Also, some company executives may not have the "stage presence" to be effective public spokespersons.

Your job at this point in the planning process is to identify the person (or perhaps several persons) to carry your message to the key publics.

CELEBRITY ENDORSERS

Businesses and nonprofit organizations have found that they need to exercise discretion in identifying celebrity spokespersons. Fame draws attention, but that attention is not always positive.

Soccer great David Beckham lost endorsements when British tabloid press reported that he had cheated on his wife. After the scandal died down, he emerged with multiple endorsements including a $10 million (£7.4 million, €8.7 million) contract with Gillette, followed by a $161 million (£118.9 million, €140.7 million) lifetime deal with Adidas.

Golfer Tiger Woods was earning $1 billion (£737.8 million, €874.5 million) in endorsements before his fall from grace (car accident, call girls, extramarital affairs, public apology, messy divorce), which left him without his car, home, wife, and endorsement contracts with AT&T, Gatorade, Accenture, and Gillette. However, other companies stood by Woods, notably Nike, which ultimately partnered with him for 27 years.

Other corporate sponsors have been embarrassed by their spokespersons: football star Michael Vick (dropped by Nike, Coke, Hasbro, Reebok, and Kraft for illegal dog fighting), model Kate Moss (dropped by Chanel, Burberry, and H&M Clothing after snorting cocaine on camera at a fashion show), and swimmer Michael Phelps (dropped by Kellogg's after he was photographed taking a hit from a bong).

Cyclist Lance Armstrong was stripped of his Tour de France and Olympic titles and banned from the sport for life following numerous allegations of doping. Nike, Giro helmets, Trek bicycles, Oakley sunglasses, Radio Shack, and Anheuser-Busch canceled endorsement contracts worth an estimated $150 million (£110.6 million, €131.2 million). He also resigned as chairman from his own cancer foundation, Livestrong.

Meanwhile, the social and political activism of some celebrities—Angelina Jolie, Sean Penn, Bono, and Susan Sarandon, for example—has limited their commercial value as corporate spokespersons.

Some examples of wayward celebrity spokespersons fall into the "What were they thinking?" category. PETA publicly fired volunteer supermodel Naomi Campbell, who had pledged not to wear natural fur, after she wore it for fashion ads in Europe. And when Brylcreem sales dropped 25 percent after its celebrity hairdo guy David Beckham shaved his head, the soccer celeb lost his contract worth $7.9 million (£5.8 million, €6.9 million).

LOGOS: APPEALING TO REASON

Having selected the spokesperson, strategic planning next focuses on the content of the message. What will be said, and how will the message be framed?

Effective messages are built on solid reasoning, with clear claims and supportive evidence. *The primary idea in a speech, editorial, advertisement, TV program, or other type of communication*—and there should be only one idea per message—is a **proposition**. There are four kinds of propositions:

- **Factual propositions** *state that something exists based on provable evidence*, such as urban air pollution.
- **Conjecture propositions** *state that something probably exists based on a reasoned conclusion drawn from physical evidence*, such as likely outcomes of particular economic or political alternatives.
- **Value propositions** *assert the virtue or merits of something*, such as school arts programs.
- **Policy propositions** *identify courses of action and encourage adoption*, such as advocating to change the legal drinking age.

Each proposition should be supported by evidence. *When evidence is clear and indisputable*, it's called **physical evidence**, and the proposition is easily provable. For example, if a city is spending more than it takes in, it clearly is dealing with an economic problem of major magnitude. As a factual proposition, that's an easy one.

But the parallel policy proposition—what to do about it?—may not be so easily resolved. Consider the various alternatives: raising taxes, selling off city-owned land, cutting services, reducing the workforce, reducing quality. Each of these impacts various principles and priorities, and there may be no clear solution on which everyone can agree.

Arguments for these alternatives rest on **verbal evidence**, *which is less clear than physical evidence and open to varying interpretation.* Verbal evidence takes various forms: analogy ("This problem is sort of like …"), comparison ("This problem is similar to another"), example ("Here's an illustration of this problem"), statistics ("This data sheds light on the problem"), endorsement ("I'm famous, and I recommend this to you") and testimonial ("I've used this, and I recommend it to you").

PATHOS: APPEALING TO SENTIMENT

Human beings are not mere thinking machines. Much as we'd like to believe that we make decisions logically and based on evidence, we also rely heavily on feelings. Effective communication strategists take this into account and build an emotional appeal.

Some emotional appeals are positive. Here are a few types.

- A **love appeal** *can be based on an aspect of love such as family, nostalgia, compassion, romance, pity, or sympathy*. Pleasant images lead consumers to remember the persuasive message because it makes them feel good.
- A **virtue appeal** *can evoke any of the various values that society or individuals hold in esteem, such as justice, loyalty, bravery, piety, or social tolerance*. Consider how natural disasters such as earthquakes and floods inspire volunteerism, blood donations, and financial contributions to relief agencies.
- A **humor appeal** *harnesses the power of comedy and amusement to gain attention and make the speaker more likeable*. But humor gets old fast. In today's 24/7 news cycle, it's risky when politicians or organizational spokespersons repeat jokes that were previously communicated to a wide audience. Additionally, for humor to be effective, it should be relevant, tasteful, perhaps self-deprecating but

not disparaging of others, and above all funny (not an easy thing to achieve when what's funny to one person may be unfunny to others).

- A **sex appeal** is *an appeal based on gender, nudity, or sexuality*. Messages with sex appeal can be effective in gaining attention, though whether the attention is positive or negative depends on the audience. But sex appeal is notoriously bad at linking the message with long-term retention and eventual action.

Persuasive messages sometimes are based on one of two negative emotions. Used in moderation, these can be powerful advocacy tools.

- A **fear appeal** *is intended to arouse anxiety or worry among audiences.* Political messages often are based on fear (such as pending economic doom, high taxation, erosion of rights, and freedom). So, too, with advertisements for some health products (tooth decay) and grooming aids (body odor). For fear appeals to be effective, they should be moderate in the amount of anxiety they generate, and they should be capped with an easy-to-achieve resolution of the problem (buy this product, vote for my candidate, use that medicine).
- A **guilt appeal** is *a common persuasive technique that attempts to arouse remorse or acceptance of responsibility*, particularly in the area of marketing communication and fundraising. Like fear appeals, this approach is best done in moderation. For example, seeking support for refugees by making readers uneasy in their relative comfort can become a turnoff if the guilt level becomes too intense. Also, like fear appeals, guilt-based messages should feature solutions to the problems that they raise.
- A **hate appeal**, though sometimes effective in a short-term situation, *is unethical at its base and is not used by true public relations professionals.*

EFFECTIVE VERBAL COMMUNICATION

Both kinds of appeals—logical and emotional—can be communicated verbally or nonverbally. **Verbal communication** *is communication occurring through written or spoken words, and the right use of those words*. Here are some of the elements associated with effective verbal communication.

- **Message Structure**. Research suggests that one-sided arguments are useful in reinforcing opinions, especially among friendly audiences with low knowledge levels. Two-sided arguments that present both pros and cons are more effective with better-educated or undecided audiences. A common technique is to sandwich the message, first presenting your positive message, then refuting opposing points, and finally restating your theme.
- **Message Content**. Effective messages have several common elements. They use simple language that can be clearly understood by the audience. They offer what advertisers call the **unique selling proposition**, that *clear statement of the benefit to the audience.* They involve **grabbers**, *power words that get attention and are easily recalled* ("eco friendly," "job creators," "human rights"). They also feature memorable quotes and strong product or program names. Finally, they use ethical language that does not stretch beyond the breaking point, as well as language that respects legal issues such as defamation and privacy.

Nonverbal communication *occurs through actions and cues other than words*. Some estimates are that 80 percent of what we learn comes to us nonverbally.

A whole range of body language issues can communicate information to us. These include eye behavior, facial expressions, touch, and space between people. There also is a wide range of external aspects of visual communication. Here are some of these.

- **Symbols** can be powerful emotional elements of communication. Some are general, such as the national flag and wedding rings. Others are issue-specific symbols such as baby harp seals and pink breast-cancer ribbons. Certain photos take on a symbolic value, such as the attack on the World Trade Center or the iconic Vietnam-era photo of the running girl who was burned by napalm.
- **Corporate logos** identify businesses, nonprofit organizations, and other groups. Some, such as the Nike swoosh or the Olympic rings, have become so descriptive that often they no longer need the words.
- **Music** often has a symbolic value, such as the singing of a national anthem or songs associated with birthdays, holidays, and religious events, even sports.

- **Language** itself takes on symbolic tones, often when it is used within religious traditions or in discussions of official national languages, such as some of the language issues in Quebec, many of the Southwestern states in the US, and among indigenous peoples throughout the world.
- **Physical artifacts and clothing** sometimes become symbolic—a judge's gavel, burning of a religious book, or wearing of a police uniform or religious garb. Clothing has symbolic significance in many countries and cultures.
- **People** such as a king, the Dalai Lama, and the pope sometimes are used symbolically.
- **Mascots** sometimes serve as symbols, such as Ronald McDonald or Smokey Bear, or more generically, the koala or the panda.

BRANDING THE STRATEGIC MESSAGE

A concept drawn from marketing, **branding** means *the creation of a clear and consistent message for an organization.* The purpose of branding, which is rooted in a strategic communications plan, is to foster understanding and goodwill and to encourage participation and support.

Corporations have been using branding for years. A car dealership has "the greatest deals in town." This toothpaste cleans "better than all the rest." That medical facility is "the hospital preferred by women."

Note that these branding statements have an implied comparison with the competition. Would it be appropriate for an educational institution to claim to be "the state's best university" or an environmental action group to proclaim itself "more effective than all the other tree-huggers put together"? Probably not, but the university may want to be known as "a top educator for science and technology" and the conservation group as having "proven results in saving the woodlands."

This step of the strategic planning process ends with attention to the message package. It may involve a **slogan**, *a catchphrase developed as part of a communication campaign.* Nokia is about "Connecting People." At Allstate insurance, "You're in good hands." "Take action for the climate" is what Greenpeace wants.

Note that branding takes us back to the positioning statement in Step 4, where we began thinking strategically about the public relations situation and desired outcomes.

WORKSHEET FOR STEP 7: DEVELOPING THE MESSAGE STRATEGY

In Step 7, you have considered the practical elements of the message: who will serve as spokesperson, how you might appeal to both logic and sentiment, how you can be effective in both verbal and nonverbal communication.

Here are the basic questions to get you started:

1. Who will be the spokesperson for this campaign? Why?
2. What is the logical part of the message (the proposition and evidence for it)?
3. What emotional appeal(s) can be used in this campaign?
4. How does this come together with a slogan or branded message?

Follow-up questions regarding the message source might deal with ways to enhance the perceived credibility of your spokesperson. When considering message appeals, consider the appropriate balance between the two.

Finally, flesh out verbal communication by giving your attention to creating a clear and understandable message and using powerful language in your message. Give attention to the various elements of nonverbal communication—symbols, logos, music, and so on—that can enhance your message.

PLANNING EXAMPLE FOR STEP 7

There will be two *spokespersons* for this campaign.

- Sophie Mercier is the University Exchange executive director. She is articulate in speech, professional in demeanor, and quick with information and anecdotes about the exchange and engagement program and the benefits that past participants and companies have enjoyed.
- Kito Kawa-Jones is a young engineer with Serene Gardens Landscape Design in this community. He participated in a four-month exchange program in Japan, allowing his company to expand its professional services and increase its customer base.

The *logical element* of the message consists of facts and data about the low-cost, high personal benefits to participants and parallel benefits to employers in terms of productivity, professional networking, and enhanced service to customers.

The *emotional element* consists of messaging about the value of personal development, the adventure of international work, and significance of an added professional credential.

Branding will consist of several variations, from the humorous "Help your boss. Leave the country" to the more serious "Forging global alliances for local businesses." UE's corporate logo and its symbolic colors, white and purple, will be used on the website and in all campaign materials.

NOTE

1 The author wishes to thank Buffalo State master's in public relations student Chelsea Allen for her work on the Adidas case involving Ye.

WORKS CITED

Anderson, M., Toor, S., Olmstead, K. Rainie, L., & Smith, A. (2018, July 11). Activism in the social media age. *Pew Research Center.* www.pewresearch.org/internet/2018/07/11/activism-in-the-social-media-age/

Bestvater, S., Gelles-Watnick, R., Odabas, M., Anderson, M., & Smith, A. (2023, June 29). #BlackLivesMatter turns 10: Social media, online activism and 10 years of #BlackLivesMatter. *Pew Research Center.* www.pewresearch.org/internet/2023/06/29/blacklivesmatter-turns-10/

Cadelago, C. (2018, October 2). Nickname and shame: Trump taunts his 2020 Democratic rivals. *Politico.* www.politico.com/story/2018/10/02/2020-democrats-trump-nicknames

Fischer, S. (2022, October 5). Adidas drops partnership with Ye amid outcry over antisemitic remarks. *Axios.* axios.com/2022/10/25/adidas-partnership-ye-antisemitic

Fuentes, M.A. (n.d.) Digital activism. Brittanica. www.britannica.com/topic/digital-activism

Hawkins, E. (2023, May 5). Brands bounce back after scandal. *Axios*. www.axios.com/2023/05/25/adidas-ye-balenciaga-backlash-disney-reputation-ranking

McConnell, D. (2009, October 17). David Letterman confesses to affairs with female staff after becoming victim of $2 million extortion plot. *Daily Mail*. www.dailymail.co.uk/tvshowbiz/article-1217618/David-Letterman-confesses-affairs-female-staff-victim-2million-extortion-plot.html

Wu, S. (2020, August 28). It's about time Democrats stop stereotyping and shaming. Especially if they want to win. *Harvard Political Review*. harvardpolitics.com/its-about-time-democrats-stop-stereotyping-and-shaming-especially-if-they-want-to-win

PUBLIC RELATIONS PLANNING

PHASE 3: TACTICS

The tactical phase of the planning process focuses on the tools of communication. This chapter gives you an overview of the many and varied ways to present the organization's message and engage its publics.

Tactics are *the specific communication tools through which an organization interacts with its publics*. They are the visible elements of a strategic plan: social media posts, websites, blogs, emails, news releases, media kits, special events, advertisements, and more.

PR PROFILE: GARY MCCORMICK, APR, FELLOW PRSA

Introduction: For more than four decades, Gary McCormick, APR, Fellow PRSA, has provided strategic communications for the government's largest public information/community relations programs, as well as corporate and nonprofit clients. In addition, his consumer experience with Scripps Networks, parent company of cable networks HGTV, Food Network, DIY Network, Cooking Channel, Travel Channel, and Great American Country provides a wide range of experience in marketing and entertainment promotion, as well as issues management.

DOI: 10.4324/9781003521211-9

Gary served as the Chair/CEO of the Public Relations Society of America in 2010, the President of the PRSA Foundation in 2005 and 2006, and the co-chair of the Champions for PRSSA since 2003. Gary has been recognized by PRSA with its Gold Anvil Award in 2023, the Patrick Jackson Distinguished Service Award in 2015, and the David Ferguson Award for Outstanding Contribution to Public Relations Education in 2006. His alma mater inducted him into the inaugural class of Colorado State University's Media Hall of Fame in 2011.

Why did you decide on a public relations career? I originally planned on majoring in journalism/media but after taking an introductory class on public relations in my freshman year in college, I realized that I was more interested in working for companies and causes to tell their story than simply being on air and repeating someone else's words.

What's your favorite part of the job? I think I always leaned toward the human behavior side of our business—understanding the issues or obstacles that are presented to a client or company and working to develop a strategy and plan for helping them to tell their story. Doing the research and finding out the motivations or cause and then working to resolve it is both exciting and rewarding. I love to build the strategy and approach to an issue/problem and watch the implementation help move the company/client to success.

Where do you see the public relations industry in 10 years? I believe that in 10 years our industry will have matured to focus more on strategic communications and reputation management than press releases and party planning. There is need for a communications function within companies to ensure that they are building and returning investment on the relationships that they have with their employees, their customers, their stockholders, and the public.

What advice to you have for graduating students launching their own PR careers? Begin building your network of connections throughout the country and the industry. Our principal currency is relationships and working to ensure that we deliver value to customers and clients. Connections are career insurance as well as the key to success in our industry. For that reason, invest your time and start building your personal network that you can go to for advice, career development, building relationships, and delivering value to your clients.

STEP 8: SELECTING COMMUNICATION TACTICS

Consider tactics in light of your goals and objectives, matched to the needs of the organization and its publics, and chosen with an eye toward time and budget constraints. Many communication professionals use the **PESO model**, *an integrated communication model using paid media, earned media, shared media, and owned media.* First articulated by Gini Dietrich in *Spin Sucks* (2014), here are the PESO model's categories:

- **Paid media** are *communication channels that are purchased by an organization.* This includes advertising and other promotional tactics for which an organization must pay.
- **Earned media** are *journalism-based communication channels that provide opportunities for the credible presentation of organizational messages to large audiences through the news media.* With earned media, information about organizations' activities and issues needs to warrant coverage.
- **Shared media** are *communication channels, not controlled by an organization, providing user-generated messages that are shared on a social media platform, usually for free.*
- **Owned media** are *communication channels that are produced or published by the organization, which controls the message content as well as its timing, packaging, distribution, and audience access.*

"PESO" is an easy-to-remember acronym, but that doesn't mean you would necessarily begin with paid media! Organizations have found that it makes more sense to start with "free" media—their owned media—followed by earned media, then shared media, and finally paid media, so that's the order we will follow here.

OWNED MEDIA TACTICS

Many communication vehicles are managed ("owned") by an organization and are used at its discretion. These media generally are controlled, internal, non-public media in five categories: digital media, electronic media, interpersonal communication, print and online publications, and direct mail.

When should you rely on owned media? When your publics are too widespread or too large to interact on a more personal level, but when you want to keep control of the content of the message, timing, and distribution. Also realize that owned media are used by **information-seeking publics**, *people who have gone out of their way to interact with the organization.*

When would you *not* use owned media? When your audience is too small to warrant it, so scattered that dissemination would be next to impossible, when you need the higher credibility associated with earned or shared media, or when greater visibility might be possible through paid media.

Digital media is *a category of owned media focusing on computer-based electronic media vehicles*. Examples include email, mobile devices, QR codes, websites, blogs, online fundraising, and crowdfunding. To help people find a website, organizations turn to **search engine optimization (SEO)**, *the process of improving the visibility of a website to get traffic from organic (free) results on a search engine, such as Google.* To improve a website's rankings in search engines, publish high-quality content and update it regularly, identify specific keyword phrases for each web page, make sure content is fast-loading, add relevant links, and consider blogging to provide additional content that contains keyword phrases.

Electronic media are *media delivered primarily through electronic vehicles*. Examples include audio media (podcasts, robocalls), video media (corporate video, videoconferences, drones, streaming video), and presentation software, a computer program used to show information, usually as a slideshow, increasingly with video or web links (examples include Microsoft PowerPoint, Prezi, Canva, Apple Keynote, and Google Sides).

Organizations need to watch for **deepfake videos** featuring their leaders, *fake videos that use a form of artificial intelligence called deep learning to replace one person's likeness with another in video and other digital media*, and **deepfake audio**, *the use of artificial intelligence to replace one's voice with that of another.* Deepfakes can be used to commit fraud and to misrepresent an individual's statements, a growing concern especially in politics.

Clues that you are watching a deepfake video: the subject never blinks, blinks far too often, or blinks unnaturally; lighting looks unnatural; lip-synching might be bad; the person's skin tone might be patchy; and details such as hair, teeth, and jewelry are hard to render well.

Interpersonal communication involves *tactics offering face-to-face opportunities for personal involvement and interaction.* These are among the most persuasive and engaging of all communication tactics and can have a strong impact on audiences, although they may not reach as many people as social media, advertising, websites, or newspaper and TV news reports. These tactics are particularly useful with information-seeking publics.

Some types of interpersonal communication tactics focus on **personal involvement**, *tactics involving direct interaction between an organization and its publics.* When the organization wishes to provide information and education or to engage in persuasion or dialogue, it often turns to tactics of personal involvement. Examples include organizational site involvement (e.g., plant tours, open house events, trial memberships) and audience site involvement (door-to-door canvassing, in-home demonstrations).

Interpersonal tactics also include **information exchange**, *various types of face-to-face encounters between an organization and its publics.* Meetings provide such face-to-face opportunities, including educational gatherings, product exhibitions and trade shows, annual stockholder meetings, rallies and demonstrations, and speeches. A concept related to speeches is the **speakers bureau**, *an organizational program to promote availability of knowledgeable and trained employees or volunteers to give presentations.*

Another category of interpersonal communication tactics involves **special events**, *activities created by an organization mainly to provide a venue within which to interact with its publics.* This commonly-used category includes civic events (parades, fairs, festivals, carnivals, swearing-in ceremonies), sporting events (tournaments, marathons, triathlons, track meets, field days, rodeos, runs), contests (science fairs, beauty pageants, talent contests, spelling bees, cook-offs), holiday events, progress-oriented events (groundbreaking ceremonies, dedications, grand openings), historic commemorations (founders' days, anniversaries, plays, pageants, reenactments), social events (luncheons, awards dinners, banquets, fashion shows), artistic events (concerts, dance recitals, plays, film festivals, art shows, photo exhibits), fundraising events (auctions, murder mystery dinner theater events, fashion shows, house or garden tour tasting parties, antiques shows), and publicity events (photo ops).

Print and online publications, another type of owned media, *are materials published and printed by the organization.* Increasingly, organizations are replacing print publications with online versions, which can be archived or updated as additional information becomes available. This category includes serial publications (newsletters, bulletins), stand-alone publications (brochures, fliers, booklets, FAQs (Frequently Asked Questions), fact sheets, reprints, annual reports, user kits, and research reports).

Direct mail is *a category of owned media featuring written messages disseminated to individual recipients.* This category includes letters (business letters, appeal letters, marketing letters), memos, postcards, invitations, and catalogs.

EARNED MEDIA TACTICS

Earned media tactics are *journalism-based communication channels that provide opportunities for the credible presentation of organizational messages to large audiences through the news media.*

These include **print media**, *media delivered primarily through print vehicles, such as newspapers and magazines*, and **electronic media**, *media that are delivered primarily through electronic vehicles, such as television and radio*. Many print media and electronic media outlets also offer digital media opportunities to organizations through their own websites and shared media. Collectively, they present many opportunities for public relations.

Journalists and public relations practitioners have a reciprocal, symbiotic relationship. Journalists need public relations practitioners to provide information and access so that they can report news, while public relations practitioners need journalists who can provide a venue for information about their organizations.

The advantage of working through news media is that they generally feature large and/or highly involved audiences. They offer significant credibility to organizations they report on through **third-party endorsement**, *the added credibility that comes with the endorsement of an* *outside, unbiased agent, such as a reporter or editor.* This means that media **gatekeepers**—*editors, reporters, or news directors who determine what gets reported in the media*—have considered all the information available to them and selected this information to share with their audiences. This vetting process gives credibility and prestige to organizational information disseminated through the news media.

A second major benefit of the news media is that publicity is free. There is no charge to the organization when an editor, reporter, or news director decides to report news about the organization.

The downside is that the content of publicity is not controlled by the organization. With the benefit of third-party endorsement comes the loss of control over the content, timing, and context. Even the decision of whether the information is published or broadcast at all is left to the media gatekeeper.

News reports generally are much briefer than the organization would write about itself.

The biggest limitation of working through the news media is that the information must be **newsworthy**—*information that media gatekeepers consider of relevance to their audiences*, not merely information or data that the organization hopes to publicize.

Public relations practitioners provide media with **news subsidies**, *information provided to media organizations by public relations professionals.* News subsidies can be subdivided into two categories: **direct news subsidies**, *information presented to the media in ready-to-use format*, and **indirect news subsidies**, *information presented for media guidance but not meant to be published or aired.*

Here is a listing of various earned media tactics:

DIRECT NEWS SUBSIDY

- News release (news story written by a public relations practitioner and given to media gatekeepers to use edited or unedited; types include announcement, response, hometowner, and news brief)
- Fact sheet (bulleted newsworthy information: who, what, when, where, why, how, quotes, background info)
- Event listing (brief about upcoming activity or event)
- Interview notes (transcript of interview with organizational expert)

- Feature release (story on background aspect of the news, written by a public relations practitioner and given to media gatekeepers to use edited or unedited; types include biography, history, backgrounder, question-and-answer piece and service article/how-to piece)
- Actuality (sound bite for radio)
- Audio news release (radio release with actuality)
- B-roll (sound bite for television)
- Video news release (TV release with B-roll)
- Email release
- Social media release (news report prepared for blogs, websites, and other online forums)
- Media kit (collection of news releases and related material on a particular topic or news event)
- Online newsroom (organizational website with current and archived news releases and other direct information subsidies)

INDIRECT NEWS SUBSIDY

- Media advisory (note to media gatekeepers about upcoming news opportunity)
- Story idea memo (news-oriented tip sheet informing gatekeepers of interview subject or topic)
- Query letter (promotional letter urging media gatekeepers to do an interview or use something written by a public relations practitioner)

OPINION SUBSIDY

- Position statement (factual background with opinion-based conclusion; types include position paper, white paper, position paragraph, and contingency statement)
- Letter to the editor
- Guest editorial or op-ed piece

INTERACTIVE MEDIA ENGAGEMENT

- News interview (question-answer session by reporter one-on-one with organizational news source)

- News conference (organizational announcement with group interview of organizational news source by various reporters)
- Studio interview (hybrid between interview and news conference; often reporter or commentator with individual or panel of news sources and opinion commentators)
- Satellite media tour (in-studio interview mediated by satellite, with reporter/commentator in one location and interviewees elsewhere)
- Editorial conference (meeting between organizational news sources with editors and editorial boards of newspaper or other news media)

SHARED MEDIA TACTICS

Shared media are *communication channels, not controlled by an organization, providing user-generated messages that are shared on a social media platform, usually for free.*

Who uses shared media? Nearly everybody, it seems. Not only celebrities but world leaders—presidents, kings, queens, prime ministers, governors, and members of Congress— not to mention organizations of all kinds and millions of individuals around the world.

Shared media have been a crucial tool for emergency communication during wildfires in California, bushfires in Australia, hurricanes in Florida, blizzards in New York, tornadoes in Oklahoma, floods in the United Kingdom, and earthquakes in Nepal, among many others.

How does this use of shared media impact public relations? It enhances our toolbox with a powerful and wide-reaching new family of media. It also enhances credibility. The Nielsen Report found that only 55 percent of Americans trust advertising, but 78 percent trust recommendations on shared media by other consumers.

When selecting social media platforms for an organization, realize that you don't need to be on every platform. Research your key publics. Where are they having conversations on social media, what type of content are they looking for, and are they passive consumers or content creators? Think about their **demographics**, *key public factors such as age, income, gender, socioeconomic status*, and **psychographics**, *key public factors such as lifestyles, opinions, interests, and behaviors*. Read the latest reports on social media use from organizations such as the Pew Research Center (https://www.pewresearch.org/).

Categories of shared media are fluid and constantly evolving. Many platforms used to focus on one function, such as photo sharing or social networking. Now, most platforms have expanded to incorporate features such as livestreaming, augmented reality, social audio, and more, so there may be some overlap.

Here are the main categories of social media.

- **Social networking sites**—*shared media that allow people to build online relationships with others having similar personal or career interests, backgrounds, or activities.* Examples: Facebook, LinkedIn.
- **Microblogs**—*shared media that mix instant messaging and blogs for posting short messages, photos, and video links.* Examples: X (formerly Twitter), Bluesky, Threads, Weibo (China's second largest social media platform).
- **Video sharing platforms**—*shared media that allow users to upload full-length TV shows or movies as well as short clips, ads, and video blogs (vlogs) to the internet.* Examples: TikTok, YouTube, Vimeo, Instagram Reels, YouTube Shorts.
- **Photo sharing platforms**—*shared media that allow users to upload, manage, and share photos privately or publicly.* Examples: Instagram, Pinterest, Google Photos.
- **Livestreaming**—*broadcasting live video to many viewers, ranging from one person on screen to organized panels with multiple speakers.* Examples: TikTok, Twitch, YouTube, Vimeo, Facebook Live, Instagram Live Rooms.
- **Disappearing content platforms**—*shared media that are useful for publishing timely, in-the-moment content for an organization's followers for up to 24 hours.* Examples: Snapchat, Instagram Stories, Facebook Stories.
- **Instant messaging**—*shared media that allow users to send real-time messages through a software application.* Examples: WhatsApp, Facebook Messenger, WeChat (China).
- **Discussion forums**—*shared media that can be used for asking and answering questions, networking, and forming a community about a particular topic.* Examples: Quora, Reddit.
- **Social audio platforms**—*shared media that allow people to listen to live conversations on specific topics.* Examples: Clubhouse, Spotify.
- **Wikis**—*collaborative websites where all users can edit and update content.* Example: Wikipedia.

- **Closed or private community groups**—*shared media that enable organizations to bring together members of their community*. Examples: Facebook Groups, Slack, Discourse.

PAID MEDIA TACTICS

If your organization is paying to put its message somewhere, it's using **paid media**—*communication channels purchased by an organization that are associated with advertising and promotion*. **Advertising** is *persuasive communication through paid media to promote a product, service, or idea on behalf of an identified organization or sponsor.*

The advantages of paid media: they can provide a large and/or highly specialized audience, and the organization can control the content, timing and presentation style.

The disadvantage: paid media can be the most expensive of all of the categories of communication tactics, although costs vary dramatically depending on the type of advertising. For example, a full-page black-and-white ad on a weekday in *The New York Times* can cost $158,000, £30,000 for the *Daily Mail* in the United Kingdom, or AUS$51,000 for *The Australian*. However, if you integrate paid media with owned, earned, and shared media, paid media can be very effective.

When you're planning a paid media campaign, do research at the beginning to discover the communication "channels" your key publics are using. Are they using TikTok, Instagram, or Facebook? Are they also watching network television shows, local TV newscasts, or streaming shows on Netflix? What about radio, newspapers, or magazines? Your key publics are probably using a combination of communication channels, so learn what they're using so that you spend your advertising dollars wisely.

Categories of paid media including the following.

- **Digital media advertising** (*advertising to a key public through digital platforms*). This includes search engine marketing (use of paid search platforms to drive targeted traffic to a website), remarketing ads (ads served by a company through search engines to previous visitors of a company's website), social media ads, influencer marketing (a collaboration between an organization and an online influencer to market an organization's product or service), affiliate marketing (referral of an organization's product or service by sharing it on a blog social media platform, podcast, or website), display ads, email ads, guerrilla marketing (marketing that uses surprise or unconventional interaction interactions to advertise a product or service), and native advertising (advertising that looks like the media format in which it appears).

- **Television and radio advertising**—television commercials, radio commercials, cable television advertising, virtual ads for TV audiences, product placement and product integration into storylines of TV shows and films, and long-form television and radio advertising such as **infomercials**, *program-length television advertising.*
- **Print advertising**—newspaper ads (display ads, which feature illustrations, headlines, and copy blocks; and classified ads, brief, all-text messages), or magazine ads (full or partial page, center spread, advertorial, or breakout ads that vary with geographic region or audience profile).
- **Out-of-home advertising**—outdoor posters (billboards, painted bulletins, and digital billboards), out-of-home videos (at sports arenas, movie theaters, and concert halls), signage, transit advertising (in bus shelters, subway stations, airports), aerial advertising, and inflatables.
- **Promotional items**—clothing (e.g., T-shirts and caps), costumes, office and home accessories (e.g., coffee mugs, key chains).

WORKSHEET FOR STEP 8: SELECTING COMMUNICATION TACTICS

In Step 8, you created a list of communication vehicles to carry your organization's message to your publics, selecting among various tactics associated with owned media, earned media, shared media, and paid media.

Here are the basic questions for this worksheet:

1. What owned media tactics will be part of this strategic plan?
2. What earned media tactics?
3. What shared media tactics?
4. What paid media tactics?

PLANNING EXAMPLE FOR STEP 8

University Exchange will use the following owned media tactics:

- Weekly podcast about UE's international programs.
- Updated website with exchange information, testimonials, and placement opportunities, with keywords for improved search engine optimization.
- Email blasts to young business professionals and college students who have attended UE events.
- Virtual meetings on Zoom with prospective students interested in upcoming UE international internships and exchange programs.
- Online 10-minute video presentation about UE programs.
- Quarterly online newsletter about UE's international programs.
- Workplace seminars about the exchange program.
- Speeches before business and civic organizations.
- Sponsorship presence at golf tournament for junior and midlevel business professionals.
- Historic commemoration luncheon for 25th anniversary of the first University Exchange-sponsored exchange.
- Annual progress report for donors, sponsoring organizations, and prospective exchange candidates.
- Survey with follow-up research report on attitudes and opinions of area leaders in business, nonprofits, higher education, and government on the value of international insight and experience.

Earned media tactics:

- News release to local newspapers, business publications, business radio programs, and television stations announcing exchange opportunities (three per year).
- Story idea memo for interview opportunity with returning exchange participants.
- Feature release focused on returning exchange participants.
- Guest editorial on value of international experience for local businesses.
- One-on-one news interviews with local journalists.
- Appearances on radio and TV public affairs programs.
- Studio interviews during TV newscasts.

- Photos with captions to weekly newspapers about UE internship and program participants.
- Editorial board meeting with local daily newspaper.
- Fact sheet about UE for distribution to potential program participants and news media at UE events.
- Calendar of events listings about UE events to local news media.
- Media kit for news media at UE events.

Shared media:

- Social media posts on UE's Instagram, LinkedIn, and Facebook pages about UE's internships and upcoming programs.
- Weekly features about UE participants on UE's LinkedIn page.
- Video testimonials from UE participants on Instagram, YouTube, and TikTok.
- Livestreaming of UE events on YouTube and Instagram.

Paid media:

- Social media advertisements for UE programs on Instagram, LinkedIn, and Facebook.
- Advertisement in local business newspaper.
- Influencers in travel and international business.
- Promotional items such as lanyards, pens, coffee mugs, and T-shirts.

STEP 9: IMPLEMENTING THE STRATEGIC PLAN

Now that you have a full plate of ways to present your message and engage your publics, turn your attention to implementing these tactics. Try to turn the inventory of tactics into a logical and cohesive program that will appeal to the organization's publics. When you read a restaurant menu, you often make selections based on a particular culinary focus: Japanese, Tex-Mex, Southern, Italian, Middle Eastern, and so on.

It's unlikely that you would start with tuna sashimi, feature jalapeño chili relleno as main course, add sides of grits and ravioli, and end with a flaming cherries jubilee for dessert, served with ouzo and Pepsi. Gastric nightmare!

Rather, you'd probably develop a culinary theme. You would creatively package your choices to concoct a special dining experience that's appropriate for the occasion and your dining companions.

The same is true with strategic communication planning. Package your tactics to achieve your objectives. Consider how various tactics can be woven together.

Think creatively as you approach this step. For example, if you have a new organizational logo to unveil, consider making it a real unveiling. How about a ceremonial removal of a sequined cloth covering the logo? One nonprofit organization introduced a new logo by involving five local political and media celebrities who each gave a short testimonial about the organization and then, one by one, placed together cut-out pieces of a giant jigsaw puzzle to create the new logo.

Some organizations have specially designed vehicles used for promotion and other public relations objectives. United Parcel Service has a miniature delivery truck to give its "Big Brown" branding visibility with potential customers. UPS uses these trucks in athletic arenas to deliver a coin for the ceremonial coin toss, such as at the start of football games.

Some award-winning campaigns have found their success through such creativity. Here are some other examples.

SPECSAVERS—"THE MISHEARD VERSION"

People avoid hearing tests for up to ten years because hearing loss terrifies them and it makes them feel old. The British company Specsavers aimed to create a hearing test that people actually wanted to listen to, so it teamed up with public relations agency Golin London on an awareness campaign.

They asked singer Rick Astley to re-record his hit "Never Gonna Give You Up" with its famously misheard lyrics—as researched by Specsavers and Golin London—and then released the new version of the song in the United Kingdom.

That caused chaos on social media, the story made news in 95 percent of the UK's major news organizations, and it ignited a national conversation in the UK about hearing loss.

The "misheard version" was played over 20 million times in the first eight hours after its release, driving a 138 percent increase in "hearing loss" internet searches and making "hearing aid" the UK's number one trending topic on Google. This led Specsavers' hearing test bookings to increase a record 1,220 percent above target. "The Misheard Version" public relations campaign won six Cannes Lions awards, including two Grand Prix awards, making Golin London the first-ever PR agency to win a PR Lions Grand Prix for a creative idea.

UN WOMEN AUSTRALIA

Australian girls, like those around the world, are surrounded by conversations about gender equality. They aren't old enough to march or petition the government, but they are on TikTok creating dances to band together.

Based on this information, UN Women Australia worked with Edelman Australia on a campaign focusing on the creation of a special TikTok dance featuring basic self-defense moves. The #EmpowerMoves dances brings together music of Australian singer-songwriter Wafia, the movements of choreographer Karla Mura, and the She Fights Back self-defense program. On October 11, 2021—the International Day of the Girl—UN Women Australia revealed to the news media the meaning behind the dance, which was becoming more and more viral.

Across seven days, the #EmpowerMoves hashtag was viewed more than 70 million times on TikTok. The campaign secured more than 40 news stories and a cumulative reach of 3.3 million.

CONFUSED.COM

A public relations agency in England helped raise brand awareness of Confused.com, an auto-insurance company. Goals included driving traffic to the company website, increasing visibility and generating requests for insurance quotes.

Company statistics identified the most accident-prone street in the United Kingdom: Somerville Road in Worcester. Eight people worked 12 hours to bubble wrap the entire street. Nearly 1,800 square yards (1,500 square meters) of bubble wrap covered cars and trucks, houses, bicycles, dog houses, swing sets, trees and shrubs, even garden gnomes.

The light-hearted publicity event carried a serious message about the dangers of winter driving, raising it well above the level of a mere publicity stunt. Rather, it was a means of attracting media attention to a serious issue of public safety.

The public relations planners contacted established news media, including major national newspapers. They engaged social media by posting photos on Twitter, Flickr, and Facebook.

The combined buzz attracted more than 125 million viewers to blogs and articles, and the story was picked up by international news media in Australia and North America. The company website saw a 20 percent increase in visitors on the first day of the publicity event, which passed its objective of generating an additional 4,000 requests for insurance quotes.

In a final burst of publicity, the bubble wrap was donated to Oxfam, the international NGO, which used it to package aid being sent to earthquake victims in Haiti.

OXFAM

Oxfam is an international confederation of organizations that responds to humanitarian crises, works on the long-term development of sustainable livelihoods, and campaigns for changes in policies that reinforce injustice and poverty.

To call attention to an international conference on global climate change in Copenhagen, Oxfam wanted to highlight the danger of climate change in a creative way.

The organization set up the scene of a family living underwater, with a living room installed at the bottom of a shark tank at the London Aquarium. It was a typical family enjoying a meal together, except that parents and kids were wearing scuba masks and air tanks.

Oxfam invited news organizations and photographers to record the spectacle. The creative tactic was a top news story on BBC, Al Jazeera, and Sky News beamed throughout the world. Blogs and internet news sites featured it, as well as newspapers in the US, China, and Australia.

PUTTING THE PROGRAM TOGETHER

Review the information gathered during the Research Phase (Steps 1, 2, 3, and 4), and the first part of the Strategy Phase (Step 5). Then think of several different ways to package the tactics you have chosen. Consider the most distinctive element of your program, and select the format that is likely to make the best impression on your colleagues, boss, or client.

- **Packaging by Media Category**. This approach lists each tactic according to the outline of media categories from Step 8 (owned, earned, shared, and paid media tactics). With each tactic, list the relevant publics and objectives. This format may be a good starting point in organizing the tactics and in making sure that all publics and objectives are covered. But it usually is not the most creative approach.
- **Packaging by Public**. If the main focus of the campaign is appealing to several different publics, it may make sense to package the campaign that way. List the objectives and associated tactics for Public A, then for Public B, Public C, and so on. This format clearly distinguishes among the various publics (for example, a hospital fundraising campaign that is reaching out both to former patients and to donors).
- **Packaging by Goal**. If the plan has two or more significant goals, look at that as the distinguishing characteristic. For example, if a nonprofit organization has a campaign to increase visibility for a new program and to raise funds to support it, list the publics, objectives, and tactics associated with each of the two goals.
- **Packaging by Objective**. Similarly, if the plan is built around a single goal, perhaps the various objectives supporting it provide the best framework. List publics and tactics for each objective (awareness, acceptance, and action).

- **Packaging by Department**. Sometimes the internal structure of the organization suggests a way to distinguish among the distinctive elements of the plan. Consider identifying goals, objectives, publics, and tactics as they relate to various departments, divisions, or organizational programs.

CAMPAIGN PLAN BOOK

The **campaign plan book** is *the formal written presentation of your research findings and program recommendations for strategy, tactics, and evaluation.* This report should be concise in writing, professional in style, and confident in tone.

The plan book should include a title page, executive summary, an optional table of contents (if the plan book is detailed enough to warrant this), situation analysis (summarizing Steps 1, 2, 3, and 4), strategic approach (summarizing Steps 5, 6, and 7), tactical program including schedule and budget (Steps 8 and 9), and evaluation plan (Step 10).

The book often ends with the consultant's credentials and resources, and sometimes includes a statement of principles indicating the philosophy and professional ethics that undergird the campaign.

Here's an example of a hypothetical outline for one tactic, an open house as part of a campaign proposal for a new graduate program in architecture at a university in a mid-sized city. This shows the internal linkage between the tactic, previously identified publics, already determined objectives and strategy, administrative details such as budgeting, and subsequent evaluation methods.

- *Public*: Professional architects (specifically, approximately 145 practicing architects within a three-county area).
- *Objective*: To increase the understanding of professional architects about the new program (50 percent of the professional community prior to beginning the academic program; with 25 percent attending open house).
- *Strategy*: Attract attention of the professional community and create a core of opinion leaders; give specific attention to leading architects, particularly those who have received recognition from the Midstate Association of Professional Architects.

- *Tactical Elements*:
  1. Publicity elements including news release, fact sheets, posts on Instagram, LinkedIn, and Facebook, email invitations (no cost).
  2. Advertising: Outreach to appropriate bloggers ($100), 1/8-page ad in local business/professional weekly newspaper ($500 value; actual cost $350 with nonprofit/education discount).
  3. Promotional video: an eight-minute video ($15,000 value; actual cost $1,000 with in-house production by Media Production university students).
  4. Information packet for visitors, with same information at website ($200).
  5. Open House logistical support including reserved space and parking arrangements ($100 for two student police aides).
  6. Open House hospitality: snacks and beverages ($1,000 value; actual cost $500 with catering by university students majoring in Culinary Arts as a promotion for their new catering service).
- *Budget*: $16,900 value; actual cost $2,250.
- *Evaluation Methods*: Attendance figures; follow-up mini-survey as part of a follow-up telephone call thanking people who attended.
- *Oversight*: Assistant Director of Community Relations.

In a complete proposal, each tactic would receive similar treatment. Even individual tactics might have multiple components. For example, the open house noted earlier might have additional publics, perhaps donors or potential students. Each of these would require its own statement of objectives and strategies, though the budget and evaluation methods may remain constant.

CAMPAIGN SCHEDULE

Implementing the strategic plan calls for establishing a timeline of when various activities need to be done. This involves two considerations: (1) the pattern and frequency of the communication tactics and (2) the actual timeline of tasks to be accomplished as the tactics are implemented.

Two concepts drawn from marketing and advertising are helpful in the implementation stage of a public relations plan. **Message frequency** deals with *the number of times and the pattern (continuous,* *pulsing, and so on) in which messages are presented to a particular public.* **Message reach** refers to *the number of different people who are exposed to a single message.*

Research into message frequency shows that one presentation is never enough. That's why public relations practitioners look for multiple, overlapping ways to communicate with their publics. The same message should be repeated and reinforced through various media and over time. Too-frequent repetitions seem unnecessarily redundant, but messages that are given only infrequently often fail to build awareness.

Your decision here is about how much and how often to communicate. If you aren't sure, err on the side of too much.

Planners also develop timelines of tasks, often working backwards from a key implementation date. For example, if a brochure is to be mailed by June 1, it may need to be received from the printer by May 21, with time remaining to add address labels and prepare it for mailing. To achieve this, copy would have to be delivered to the printer May 15, final copy approved May 10, first copy draft completed May 1, writing and design work begun April 15, and approval for objectives and budget by April 7. Thus planning would need to begin no later than April 1.

CAMPAIGN BUDGET

Identifying resources needed for each tactic is an important part of the implementation stage. At every turn of the planning process, you need to be practical. Consider budget constraints and limitations so the recommendations will be realistic, practical, and doable.

Budgeting is about more than money. It deals with all needed resources, including personnel, material, media costs, equipment and facilities, and administrative costs. Here's how each category factors into the final budget.

Personnel items in a budget include the number of people and the amount of time needed to achieve the results expected of the tactic and the cost of this. Include both organizational and outside people (consultants, agency staff, subcontracted specialists, and freelance workers). Make sure to account for salaried public relations staff within the organization. Though they may already be on salary, the value of their time associated with each particular tactic should be included in the full campaign budget.

Material items in a budget are the tangible "things" associated with each tactic. This may be paper for brochures, banners and food for an open house, media kits for a news conference, software for an online newsroom, and so on. Each of these carries a price tag. A good budget itemizes each separately, allowing planners to make adjustments if the total cost estimate comes in over the expected budget.

Money needed to purchase time and space for advertising is part of the media cost. These costs are set by the publication, station, or other advertising venue. The basic cost (such as the per-column-inch rate in newspapers or the per-second cost for airtime) varies as placement frequency increases.

Budgets often include a 15 percent surcharge as a commission or agency fee or to cover in-house overhead expenses. Public relations agencies sometimes bill all out-of-pocket expenses at cost plus 15 percent.

There also may be costs for equipment and facilities. This budget category includes the cost of new computers needed for a newsletter, for example, or software to create a blog. Because these often are one-time expenditures, they might be calculated on a percentage basis to amortize the cost over potential uses after this campaign is completed. This category might also include expenses such as transportation fees for a portable outdoor stage or the cost of renting a banquet hall.

Finally, administrative items also are included in the budget. These include the cost of telephone, delivery, photocopying, and travel costs. Some organizations add a 15 percent surcharge to cover standard office expenses, often with a separate category for travel-related costs.

Make sure to include the full cost of all the tactics, even if some do not have a specific price tag. Note donated or contributed services, such as the value of volunteer time. Also figure financial support that nonprofit organizations sometimes receive, such as support from a corporation that offers to print its brochures, discounted consulting fees, or the actual cost of a video production that is produced pro bono by a media sponsor.

Also, try to provide a range of costs for tactics. This will help if the organization needs to trim costs. Rather than eliminate entire tactics, a cost range might allow the organization simply to choose some less-expensive options. For example, you might cost out a brochure for both one color and full color.

Finally, determine just how much success is necessary. Calculate this as the break-even point. Identify the total project cost; determine the dollar value for each desired outcome; and divide the total cost by that value. Let's say a private college will spend $160,000 of its recruiting budget for brochures, an informational video, paid radio commercials, and billboards. Let's add $10,000 for salaries and freelance fees associated with the projects. Add another $10,000 for postage, travel, and other administrative costs. That's $180,000 for the total project cost.

Now let's presume that tuition at this college is $35,000. Apply the formula: cost $180,000 divided by outcome value $35,000 equals five-plus. That's the break-even point. Thus the brochure/video/commercial/billboard program has to recruit six new students just the pay for itself. After that, the income is profit.

Another useful tool is the per capita cost, the total cost associated with the number of people needed to cover that cost. Using the college scenario, divide the project cost by the number of new recruits (let's say that's 1,600). Apply the formula: $180,000 divided by 1,600, which equals $113—the amount of money the college spends to recruit each new student through these tactics. That's about a third of a penny for every dollar received in tuition.

DEVELOPING A LONG-TERM BUDGET FOR PUBLIC RELATIONS

Budgeting is more than merely adding up the costs of various tactics for specific projects. It's part of the strategic management of an organization.

The question often comes up: How much should an organization spend on public relations? There is no simple answer, no one-size-fits-all formula. That's because so much depends on variables: the nature of the issue being addressed, the current relationship of the publics, the objectives sought, the tactics employed and so on.

Here are some various approaches to budgeting for public relations:

- **Competitive Parity**. This approach bases the budget on the level of similar activity by major competitors. Hospital A may set its budget for attracting new patients by matching the apparent budget of neighboring Hospital B. That involves guesswork, and it doesn't take into account the varying circumstances of each hospital.

- **Same-as-Before Budgeting.** This approach looks at how much the organization spent on a similar recent project and allows the same budget, perhaps adjusted for inflation. This presumes the first project was successful and worth imitating. It also assumes that the two projects are similar enough for the first to be a benchmark for the second.
- **Percentage-of-Sales Budgeting**. Drawn from marketing, this approach uses a percentage of income. For example, a university may earmark 2 percent of this year's tuition for next year's recruitment drive. The problem is that this can create a downward spiral. If recruitment was weak last year, probably more effort at more cost is needed, not less, as this approach would provide.
- **All-You-Can-Afford Budgeting**. This approach works best in good times, providing more resources when the organization's financial condition is stronger. Again, the real need may call for just the opposite, more funding when the organization is weak.
- **Cost-Benefit Analysis**. A budget based on this approach identifies the cost of implementing each of the tactics, and then compares this to the estimated value of the expected results. If an animal protection group trying to raise $500,000, for example, calculates that spending money on social media could yield the same results as a more expensive TV advertising campaign, it would make sense to go with the social media approach.
- **What-If-Not-Funded Analysis**. This approach forces the planner to look at expected outcomes and to consider alternative ways to reach the same objective, or to re-think the relative priority of the objective in light of limited available funds.
- **Stage-of-Lifecycle Budgeting**. This approach looks closely at the phase of development of the issue. Starting new programs, for example, generally requires more financial resources than maintaining existing programs.
- **Zero-Based Budgeting**. This technique is rooted in current needs rather than past expenditures. Each tactic is ranked according to its importance. The cumulative cost of the tactics is calculated,

and a cutoff line of a predetermined budget indicates the point at which the client or organization has run out of money. The disadvantage of this approach is that it allows preset budgets and calculators or computer formulas to determine what tactics can be undertaken, though an advantage is that zero-based budgeting can serve as a catalyst in reevaluating priorities.

All of the above approaches to budgeting have problems. Some are arbitrary. Some fail to consider important variables. Some don't provide a way to rework a budget when the total is too high. But there is another way to budget that respects the decisions and priorities already made in part of this planning project.

This approach, more enlightened for public relations planning, is called **objective-based budgeting**, *a preferred approach to budgeting based on implementation of tactics designed to achieve agreed-upon goals and objectives of an organization.* It aligns with decisions already made by the organization or client.

Because the tactics simply provide ways to achieve what already has been adopted as the objectives, the cost of these tactics is not seen as additional budget items for the organization. Rather, the budget is an extension of these prior strategic decisions.

This suggests that the organization will assign the resources needed to carry out tactics that will achieve those objectives. Or the organization may need to scale back objectives. Either way, objective-based budgeting puts the responsibility on the organization or client to establish objectives that it will support with appropriate tactics.

WORKSHEET FOR STEP 9: IMPLEMENTING THE STRATEGIC PLAN

In this step, you develop the creative theme that pulls together each of your proposed tactics and packages them in an effective way for both dissemination of information and eventual measurement of their impact.

Here are the basic questions for this worksheet:

1. What is the creative theme that links all the tactics?
2. How will be tactics be packaged?

3. What is the schedule for implementing the plan?
4. What is the budget for each tactic?
5. What is the total budget, both its full value and its actual cost to the organization?

PLANNING EXAMPLE FOR STEP 9

University Exchange will present a comprehensive program focused on each of the three key publics identified in Step 4: Young professionals; businesses, nonprofits, and professional organizations; and news media. It will unfold as a year-long program for the upcoming calendar year.

PUBLIC: YOUNG PROFESSIONALS

1. **Weekly podcast**. UE will host a weekly podcast for young professionals and businesses, nonprofits, and professional organizations highlighting various UE international internships and programs.
   - Time: Weekly.
   - Cost: No cost.
2. **Updated website**. UE will enhance its website, including keyword phrases for improved search engine optimization, with a relaunch for its 25th anniversary. The new website will add a media/information page that will house contact information, news and feature releases, editorials, and other opinion matter. The site also will catalog all past exchange programs with names of organizations and individual participants (with some testimonials), as well as a current list of exchange opportunities.
   - Time: April, with continual updates.
   - Cost: $600 value. No cost to organization (board members will solicit pro bono web designer from participating organization to work with UE staff on website project).
3. **Email blasts**. UE will send emails about upcoming events to young business professionals and college students who have attended previous UE events.

- Time: Throughout the year.
- Cost: No cost.

4. **Zoom meetings with college seniors and young professionals**. UE will host periodic Zoom meetings for college seniors and young professionals interested in specific upcoming international internship and program opportunities.
   - Time: Throughout the year.
   - Cost: $14.99 per month for Zoom pro membership; total cost $179.88 per year.
5. **Video**. UE will invite a local university media production class to create a 10-minute video to showcase the organization's exchange programs. This video will be posted at the UE website as a YouTube video and will be used in speeches and seminars sponsored by University Exchange.
   - Time: January–March.
   - Cost: Pro bono $5,000 value.
6. **Social media posts**. UE communications staff will post on UE's Instagram, LinkedIn, and Facebook pages about UE's international internships and upcoming programs. Audience: college seniors, young professionals, organizations, news media.
   - Time: Three times per week.
   - Cost: No cost.
7. **Weekly features on LinkedIn**. UE communications staff will post features about UE participants on UE's LinkedIn page. Audience: college seniors, young professionals, organizations, news media.
   - Time: Weekly.
   - Cost: No cost.
8. **Video testimonials**. UE will solicit video testimonials from past participants to post on Instagram, YouTube, and TikTok.
   - Time: Twice per month.
   - Cost: No cost.
9. **Livestreaming of UE events**. UE will livestream events on YouTube and Instagram.
   - Time: Varies.
   - Cost: No cost initially, but UE may opt to invest $500 to $1,000 for lighting, cameras, and microphones in the future.

10. **Quarterly online newsletter**. UE will write and upload a quarterly newsletter about its programs and events for college seniors, young professionals, and organizations.
    - Time: January, April, July, October.
    - Cost: No cost.
11. **Workplace seminars**. University Exchange will solicit speaking invitations from area businesses and nonprofit organizations that employ young professionals and graduating university seniors. PowerPoint presentations will include question-answer periods.
    - Time: Six to be scheduled in consultation with businesses.
    - Cost: No cost.
12. **Speeches before business and civic organizations**. UE will solicit invitations to provide speakers for business and civic organizations with a significant proportion of young professionals. This will provide opportunities to discuss exchange programs with young professionals who are seeking ways to enhance their professional lives.
    - Time: Varies; Rotary International, March. Urban League Young Professionals, July. Jaycees, October.
    - Cost: $300 for handouts and miscellaneous costs.
13. **Golf tournament**. University Exchange will sign on as a sponsor for a local golf tournament marketed primarily for junior-level business professionals.
    - Time: May.
    - Cost: $3,000 value ($1,500 sponsorship fee; $1,500 hors d'oeuvres). (May be no cost; board members will ask their corporations to underwrite the costs.)
14. **Social media advertising**. University Exchange will advertise its upcoming events (Zoom meetings, anniversary luncheon) on LinkedIn, Instagram, and Facebook.
    - Time: Varies.
    - Cost: $2,000.
15. **Newspaper advertising**. UE will purchase a 2×4-inch ad in the weekly business newspaper to invite participants to its anniversary luncheon.
    - Time: Late December.
    - Cost: $1,600 value; actual cost $1,080 with nonprofit/educational discount.

16. **Influencers in travel and international business**. UE will partner with three influencers in travel and international business to write about UE's international internships and exchange programs on their LinkedIn and Instagram accounts.
    - Time: January.
    - Cost: $500 per post, three posts per influencer; total cost $4,500.
17. **Promotional items**. UE will purchase lanyards branded with the UE logo to give away to college seniors and young professionals at its speaking engagements.
    - Time: Throughout the year.
    - Cost: $1.06 per lanyard, 500 lanyards; total cost $530.

PUBLIC: BUSINESSES, NONPROFITS, AND PROFESSIONAL ORGANIZATIONS

1. **Anniversary luncheon**. University Exchange will invite approximately 250 current and past corporate representatives and exchange "alumni" to a luncheon, with an expected turnout of 150. The luncheon will commemorate the 25th anniversary of the business exchange program.
    - Time: Late January.
    - Cost: $4,000 for food; $500 entertainment; $1,200 value for venue rental (no cost if luncheon/meeting space can be successfully solicited from participating corporate sponsor).
2. **Progress report**. UE will research, write, and publish a progress report, with emphasis on the past year and current activities, including a summary of the organization's 25 years.
    - Time: February.
    - Cost: $1,000 for 500 copies (may be no cost; board members will seek corporate underwriter). $100 distribution cost.
3. **Survey**. UE will conduct a survey on attitudes and opinions of area leaders in business, nonprofits, higher education, and government on the value of international insight and experience among professional employees. Board members will be asked to identify a researcher from a local business or university to do the survey pro bono.
    - Time: July–September.
    - Cost: Pro bono $4,000 value.

PUBLIC: NEWS MEDIA

1. **News release.** Various topics including survey report, golf tournament, progress report, anniversary luncheon, upcoming public events and corporate/organizational presentations, application dates for exchange programs, and other relevant topics of newsworthy activities.
   - Time: Varies.
   - Cost: No cost.
2. **Story idea memo**. University Exchange will provide ideas for interviews and feature stories to reporters at the local metropolitan daily newspaper, weekly business newspaper, business radio programs, and television newsrooms.
   - Time: April, September.
   - Cost: No cost.
3. **Feature release**. University Exchange will write and disseminate feature releases about local young professionals who are returning from an exchange visit. Following direct distribution to news media, feature releases will be posted at the UE website.
   - Time: Varies.
   - Cost: No cost.
4. **Guest editorial**. University Exchange will solicit an invitation from the local metropolitan daily newspaper to write a guest editorial on the advantages that international exchange activities offer to local businesses. Following publication (or if publication is denied) University Exchange will post the editorial at its website.
   - Time: Varies.
   - Cost: No cost.
5. **One-on-one news interviews, appearances on radio and TV public affairs programs, studio interviews during TV newscasts**. University Exchange will periodically meet with journalists one-on-one, on public affairs programs, and for studio interviews to promote its upcoming events and programs.
   - Time: Varies.
   - Cost: No cost.

6. **Photos with captions**. UE will send out photos with captions to area weekly newspapers after events.
   - Time: Varies.
   - Cost: No cost.
7. **Editorial board meeting**. University Exchange will solicit invitations from the local metropolitan daily newspaper and the weekly business newspaper to meet with editors to explain the organization's work and the benefits it offers to the local community.
   - Time: Varies.
   - Cost: $100 for leave-behind materials.
8. **Fact sheet**. UE will prepare and distribute fact sheets to potential program participants and news media at UE events.
   - Time: Varies.
   - Cost: No cost.
9. **Calendar of events listings**. UE will send out calendar of events listings to local news media.
   - Time: Monthly.
   - Cost: No cost.
10. **Media kit**. UE will prepare a media kit containing fact sheets, news releases, biographies of UE leaders, and other materials for distribution to news media at UE events.
    - Time: Varies.
    - Cost: $100 for two-pocket folders.

BUDGET TOTAL

- Value: $15,400.
- Actual cost to organization: $14,290–$28,610 depending on University Exchange board's success in obtaining personnel, free venue for anniversary luncheon, and sponsorships from participating organizations.

8

PUBLIC RELATIONS PLANNING

PHASE 4: EVALUATION

Measurement and evaluation research are critical in a public relations campaign. They help document a campaign's successes and provide valuable information to share with management about how the campaign contributed to the organization's bottom line. In this chapter, you turn once again to research techniques, this time to evaluate the effectiveness of the tactics of Phase 3 in achieving the objectives you identified in Phase 2.

Books on strategic planning for public relations extol the virtue of evaluation. Awards competitions by national professional organizations such as the Public Relations Society of America expect to see evaluation as part of winning campaigns. Surveys of public relations practitioners in all kinds of settings—agencies, corporations, and nonprofit organizations—show that professionals see the need for evaluation.

Yet far too often, this phase of the planning process is overlooked. Why? There are many reasons.

- It sometimes is hard to know what to evaluate and how to do so, in part because many practitioners have not studied research techniques.

DOI: 10.4324/9781003521211-10

- Public relations measures may not be as precise as those used in areas such as finance, operations, and safety.
- Public relations campaigns and projects do not exist in a vacuum. Other forces are working on key publics while the organization is mounting its public relations activities, making it difficult to isolate the influence of public relations.
- Everything may be in motion, clouding the possibility of an accurate count of the evolving consequences of public relations activity.
- Some public relations measures are negatives—to what extent did criticism not happen, or how many negative opinions were minimized?
- Research takes time, resources, and creative energy.

PR PROFILE: ROSANNA FISKE, APR, FELLOW PRSA, GLOBAL HEAD OF CORPORATE AFFAIRS, SIGNATURE AVIATION

Introduction: Rosanna "Ro" Fiske has more than 25 years of experience developing strategic communications and brand-building initiatives both in the US and around the world. She leads corporate communications, change management, human resource activities related to mergers, acquisitions and divestitures, and community impact for Signature Aviation.

As the former Global Chief Communications Officer for Royal Caribbean Group, Fiske led the company's external and internal corporate communications worldwide. Before that, she was Senior Vice President and Corporate Affairs Leader at Wells, Fargo & Co., Executive Vice President and Chief Strategy Officer at a top ten advertising agency, and head of the master's program in Global Strategic Communications at Florida International University (FIU). Her expertise includes campaigns with several multinational brands, such as American Airlines, Charles Schwab, GE Financial, Absolut Vodka, Google, and MTV Networks.

Fiske received the highest individual lifetime honor in public relations, the Public Relations Society of America (PRSA) Gold Anvil, in 2024. She was inducted into PRWeek's Women of Distinction/ Hall of Femme, PR Daily's Top Communicators Hall of Fame, and

PRovoke Media's Top 100 Influencers/Top CMOs and CCOs in the world in 2022. She was also named the PR industry's Diversity Champion by PRWeek in 2014 and has led several teams to win six Silver Anvils (known as the Oscars of the PR industry).

A former PRSA Chair and CEO, Fiske attended the University of Florida and FIU and received a bachelor's in journalism and a master of science in integrated communications. She serves on the Accrediting Council on Education in Journalism and Mass Communications and is a member of the University of Florida's Business Advisory Council and the Arthur Page Society.

Why did you decide on a public relations career? I'm one of those lucky professionals who found a mentor—or maybe I should say, a mentor found me—early in my journalism career. As a reporter, I had no idea what public relations was, nor that there were public relations professionals. As I began my work as a reporter and came to know several PR professionals, I understood more about the profession. But it was my first mentor, who was one of my reporter sources and a CEO of a Fortune 100 company, who said I should consider going in-house and be part of a corporation's communications department. He gave me my first job in corporate marketing, and as I rose through the ranks, PR and corporate communications became part of my responsibilities. I joined PRSA at that point, and I found great affinity between my journalism training and background and my PR/communications responsibilities.

What's your favorite part of the job? There are two aspects of my job that I love: 1. The opportunity to do something different every day. I get exposed to just about every facet of the business and the company. It is so exciting to have the opportunity to connect with so many team members, from engineers to safety experts to financial analysts to guest experience professionals. One minute we're talking about aviation and the different planes in our hangars, including celebrities' planes, and the next we're talking about sustainability and our commitment to provide Sustainable Aviation Fuel (SAF). 2. The opportunity to learn something new every day. Working in PR and communications allows me to learn about things I never thought I'd learn about—the making of spirits, audience dynamics and programming, hospitality, and private aviation and planes.

Where do you see the public relations industry in 10 years? I know our profession will become even more needed as companies evolve and AI continues to expand. The mix of insight, research, ethics, analytical and critical thinking skills combined with a moral compass is not easy to find. If you have strong and sharp PR professionals on your team, they'll bring all of those qualities and knowledge. In 10 years, what many call the "soft skills" will be the "essential skills," and these will become even more relevant and significant. Our industry will be that much better for it.

What advice to you have for graduating students launching their own PR careers? Find a role that allows you to learn as much as you can. Think of your career as knowledge stepping stones. If every step you take leads you to expand your learning, you'll be better for it. A career trajectory is not linear. Sometimes the best career moves are those that take you a step back or to the side.

STEP 10: EVALUATING THE STRATEGIC PLAN

In this final step of the process of strategic communication planning, we look at various aspects of evaluative research: what, when, and—most important—how, to evaluate.

WHAT TO EVALUATE

Public relations evaluation begins with a clear understanding of what it means to be effective. Your research plan needs to consider several issues: the criteria to gauge success, timing of the evaluation, and specific ways to measure each level of objectives (awareness, acceptance, and action). The plan also may prescribe particular evaluation tools.

The first decision point for an evaluation program focuses on **design questions**, *the aspect of program evaluation that considers what criteria should be evaluated.* What information is needed to make an assessment? Who has this information, and how can it be obtained? Who will receive the final evaluation, and how will it be used?

Next come the **evaluation criteria**. These are called **metrics**, *the standards of measurement to assess the outcome of a program or project.* Each metric should be realistic, feasible, ethical, and socially responsible. Here are some examples.

- **To evaluate awareness objectives**:
  Metric: Media coverage and calculation of media impressions.
  Metric: Post-campaign awareness survey.
- **To evaluate acceptance objectives**:
  Metric: Number of likes, comments, retweets, and shares on social media.
  Metric: Post-campaign attitude/opinion survey.
  Metric: Post-event audience feedback.
- **To evaluate action objectives**:
  Metric: Measures of sales, attendance, or donations.
  Metric: Organizational or environmental change.

WHEN TO EVALUATE

There are three stages in the process of program evaluation related to timing.

Implementation reports *document how the tactics are being carried out.* Such a report may include a schedule of work to date and an indication of the work remaining. Implementation reports do not evaluate the quality of the work, only that it has or has not taken place according to schedule.

Progress reports are *preliminary evaluations in which planners can make strategic modifications as they further implement the program.* Such mid-course corrections can keep the project functioning at peak efficiency.

The **final report** *provides a comprehensive review and overall evaluation of the program.*

RESEARCH DESIGN

How should you structure the evaluation in relation to the measurement standards? There are several possibilities.

The simplest research design is the **after-only study**, *a study where you implement a tactic, measure impact, and presume that the tactic caused* *this impact.* This approach is particularly appropriate for action objectives with relatively simple metrics, such as measuring attendance, votes, contributions, or purchases.

But the simplicity of this approach is also its weakness, because this design presumes a cause-and-effect relationship that may not be accurate.

One way to overcome this flaw is to conduct a **before-and-after study** (also called a **pretest/post-test**), *where you observe a key public before any public relations program is implemented, then expose the public to the tactic, and then measure the public again.* Any change in the public's awareness, acceptance, or action is likely due to exposure to your tactic.

But remember, public relations activities don't take place in a vacuum. Not every change in your key public can be linked, cause-and-effect fashion, to your programming, because the public most likely has been exposed to other messages from other organizations as well.

Therefore, a more sophisticated evaluation tool is a **controlled before-and-after study**, *a study that involves two sample groups drawn from the same key public—one that receives the message, the other that does not (the control group).* Measure each group again and compare the results of both groups.

The control group is likely to remain unchanged, while any change you find in the exposed group presumably can be linked to exposure to the public relations tactic.

How to accomplish the controlled study? Let's say you are working on a ridership campaign for an urban transit system. Identify a city similar to yours, and conduct the pretest both there and in your city. If both places are similar, ridership influences such as the price of gasoline, time of year, suburban sprawl, and so on should make the results similar. The group in the other city serves as the control group for this study. After conducting your program in your city, retest both groups. Presumably there would be little or no change in the control group in the other city.

HOW TO EVALUATE

At the beginning of Step 10, you were asked to identify what information is needed in order to evaluate a program's effectiveness. Here are several levels of evaluation that can help you answer that question.

Judgmental assessment is *an evaluation made on hunches and personal experience.* This sometimes can be pretty useless feedback: "The boss liked it." "The client asked us to continue." "Hey, we won an award for this project." To make judgmental assessment more useful, seek input from industry experts or public relations colleagues. The knowledge they have of the situation helps compensate for the informal way of gathering information.

While practitioners should draw on their personal insights, they should try to base program evaluation on more careful analysis. Thus, another way of evaluating public relations activities is by measuring **communication outputs**, *tactics implemented during a public relations campaign.*

Output evaluation may focus on **message production**, *the number of messages produced*, such as the number of news releases written, brochures printed, and blog entries written. A bit more effectively, it may focus on **message distribution**, *evaluation focusing on the frequency and manner of message dissemination*, such as the number of news releases sent or blog entries posted.

Some outcomes focus on **message cost**, *evaluation focusing on the amount of money spent producing messages*—the presumption being that cost equates to value, not always a good indicator of success.

Related to this is **advertising value equivalency** (AVE), *a discredited approach to evaluation that pretends to calculate the value of publicity by estimating how much it would have cost if the same amount of time or space in a news report had been purchased as advertising.*

For example, you could focus on a story about your organization in a local newspaper. If the story totals 21 column inches (headline, story and photo), multiply 21 by the cost per column-inch of advertising (let's say $165 per inch). This calculation suggests that the publicity is worth $3,465.

But it's all smoke and mirrors. Publicity is not advertising. Actually, publicity has more credibility with audiences, though it offers less control for public relations.

Public relations experts from around the world met in Barcelona, Spain in 2010 to articulate standards and common approaches for evaluating public relations. One of the main principles of the Barcelona Declaration of Measurement Principles was a clear rejection of advertising equivalency. Some call it a game changer for public relations and a death knell for attempts to fix a dollar value on public relations by falsely comparing it to advertising.

So if judgmental assessment is too subjective and measurement of communication outputs of dubious value, what should be the basis for evaluating public relations? The answer is to look back to Step 4, where you established objectives. Now in Step 10, measure each of those objectives: awareness, acceptance, and action.

Awareness evaluation *focuses on the content of the message.* One way to do this is to measure **message exposure**—*evaluation based on the number of people in key publics who were exposed to a message*, such as by counting the number of people who log onto a website or who watch a TV news report. Focus also on **message content**, *evaluation based on the extent to which a message was accurate and positive.*

Another useful measurement tool is a **readability measure**—*calculating the reading level of a message, usually translated into the level of education needed to easily understand the written content.* There are a number of formulas for this, most notably the Gunning Readability Index, also called the Fog Index.

Message recall, a practice drawn from advertising, is another useful technique for evaluating awareness objectives. *This involves interviewing people to learn the extent to which they recall a message, associate it with the organization and are able to describe the basic information provided in the message.*

Acceptance evaluation looks at the second category of objectives. It goes one better than awareness evaluation by *considering how publics internalize a public relations message.*

Common techniques for this include **audience feedback**, which is *based on the voluntary reaction of an audience.* This often is linked with a measure of audience interest. Additionally, acceptance can be measured with a **benchmark study**, which is *a more formal technique that provides a baseline that serves as a standard for comparing program outcomes.*

Action evaluation *considers the impact of a public relations program on bottom-line issues for an organization*—the ultimate form of measurement. One thing to measure is **audience participation**, *evaluation based on measuring outcomes such as attendance figures.* But be careful in interpreting this. Just because people attend a political speech doesn't necessarily mean that each person in the audience will vote for the candidate.

You also might consider **direct observation**, *research based on measures of program effectiveness, such as money raised or members recruited*, as a way to measure program effectiveness. If your candidate wins the election, your objective was achieved. If you sought financial contributions of $12 million (£8.9 million, €10.5 million), count the total of donations and pledges.

Other examples of direct observation include passage (or defeat) of a piece of legislation, increased use of seatbelts, and audience turnout. The outcomes for the legislation and audience size are easy to measure, but how would you measure the results of a seatbelt campaign? One way might be to place observers in highway tollbooths and at busy street corners. Over time, you also could monitor police and insurance data.

A final method of evaluating action objectives looks at **relative media effectiveness**, *evaluation that compares one medium to others, attempting to help the organization determine venues for future editions of its campaign.*

"SPOT HER" WOMEN'S HEALTH CAMPAIGN

Solid evaluative research played a major role in "Spot Her," a successful campaign to create greater awareness about endometrial cancer symptoms in Black women. They are especially vulnerable to the disease due to delayed diagnoses, more aggressive tumor types, and other healthcare disparities.

Eisai Inc. created two objectives: to elevate awareness and educate women ages 40–65 about common risk factors and potential symptoms of endometrial cancer, especially in US communities of color, with women ages 20–39 as a secondary key public.

Planners launched a campaign website, distributed "Spot Her" fanny packs, created social media content and a #SpotHerforEC hashtag, collaborated with four influencers who have personal connections to the issue, and planned a "Spot Her" virtual walk. The planners also set up media interviews with the campaign's national spokesperson about her own endometrial cancer scare as well as a doctor from Memorial Sloan Kettering Cancer Center in New York, and aimed for at least 138 million total media impressions.

Evaluation found that the campaign had exceeded many of the original objectives, creating greater awareness about endometrial cancer in the key publics:

— SpotHerforEC.com was visited more than 39,200 times, exceeding the original objective by 61 percent.
— 4,000 "Spot Her" fanny packs were distributed, exceeding the original objective by 100 percent.
— #SpotHerforEC was used 433 times across social media, exceeding the original objective by 24 percent.
— Virtual walk participants walked more than 11,500 miles (243 participants).
— Owned social content with paid support resulted in 188 clicks (exceeding the original objective by 34 percent) and over 1 million total impressions (20 percent of original objective to date).
— Influencer content received more than 50,000 impressions, exceeding the original objective by 150 percent.
— Total media impressions resulted in more than 577 million impressions, exceeding the original objective by 300 percent.
— Media interviews resulted in 66 stories, exceeding the original objective by 230 percent.

DATA ANALYSIS AND REPORTING

Having gathered the data through various measures, it's now time to analyze the data carefully and match results to your objectives from Step 5.

If the program failed to meet some objectives, try to determine if this was the result of over-ambitious objectives, flawed strategy that undergirded the program, or tactics that were inappropriate or poorly implemented. Consider also if there might be a flaw in the evaluation techniques used to gather the data.

Most program evaluations call for a written report, usually with an **executive summary** that *outlines in one or two pages the more detailed findings in the full report.* The evaluation often concludes with recommendations, such as the feasibility of continuing or expanding the program or applying a similar strategy to other situations.

WORKSHEET FOR STEP 10: EVALUATING THE STRATEGIC PLAN

In Step 10, you have considered the various ways to measure the success of the campaign. Evaluation centers on determining the extent to which previously agreed objectives were met.

Here are the questions for this worksheet:

1. How will you measure awareness objectives?
2. How will you measure acceptance objectives?
3. How will you measure action objectives?
4. What recommendations (if any) stem from this evaluation?

PLANNING EXAMPLE FOR STEP 10

Objectives for Public #1 (individual professionals):

1. To have an effect on the *awareness* of young professionals about University Exchange (UE), specifically to increase their understanding of the advantages that University Exchange offers by 50 percent within one year.

   This objective will be measured by tracking attendance at UE seminars and presentations, number of attendees on weekly podcasts, open rate on email blasts, number of website hits, and social media metrics (likes, shares).
2. To have an effect on their *acceptance*, specifically to increase their interest in the engagement/exchange programs by 25 percent within one year.

   This objective will be measured by tracking the number and content of questions at UE presentations, email requests for follow-up information, and comments on social media.
3. To have an effect on their *action*, specifically to generate ten applicants for long-term exchange programs and 40 for short-term engagement programs within one year.

   This objective will be measured by counting the number of applicants throughout the year.

Objectives for Public #2 (organizations):

1. To have an effect on *acceptance*, specifically to increase the awareness of corporate executives and human resources staff about University Exchange program opportunities (50 percent of identified organizations within one year).

   This objective will be measured by tracking the number of organizations that act on information sent to them, such as by acknowledging receipt or requesting additional information.
2. To have an effect on their *acceptance*, specifically to generate feedback and inquiries from these organizations (15 percent within one year).

   This objective will be measured by tracking the number of organizations that express some interest in scheduling presentations about the exchange program throughout the year.
3. To have an effect on their *action*, specifically to generate invitations for University Exchange to meet with organizational leaders (25 organizations within one year).

   This objective will be measured by tracking the number of organizations that actually schedule a seminar or presentation during the year.

Objectives for Public #3 (news media):

1. To have an effect on their *awareness*, specifically to increase their knowledge about University Exchange programs (journalists at 50 percent of identified news media and news blogs within one year).

   This objective will be measured by tracking the output of information in the form of media advisories and releases throughout the year.
2. To have an effect on their *acceptance*, specifically to generate inquiries from these journalists (25 percent of identified news venues within one year).

   This objective will be measured by tracking media requests for interviews and information throughout the year.
3. To have an effect on their *action*, specifically to see publication/broadcast of positive/neutral pieces by 10 percent of identified news venues within one year.

This objective will be measured by tracking local media references to University Exchange throughout the year, then conducting content analysis at year's end.

WORKING THE PLAN

This concludes the strategic planning process for public relations. In the four phases of Part II of this book, you have learned how to gather information (Phase 1), and you have made decisions about what you will accomplish (Phase 2). You learned to create a plan effectively and creatively to use various communication vehicles toward your objectives (Phase 3) and finally you learned to evaluate the campaign once it is completed (Phase 4).

Thus, these ten steps have broken down this comprehensive process into manageable segments. This process is used throughout the world by effective public relations strategists. It works for small cultural and charitable organizations with few resources as well as for multinational corporations with million-dollar budgets.

You've seen the warning: "Don't try this at home." Toss away all such thinking—you *should* try this for yourself! This process provides you with a guide.

Certainly this is only a bare-bones approach to strategic planning for public relations, but it covers all the bases. The questions posed in these steps allow you to answer them in many different ways. There are no preconceived right or wrong answers, only responses that reflect your organization—its needs, resources, and self-understanding of its personality and vision.

It's a template for you to create a public relations campaign for your company or nonprofit group. Feel free to adopt this planning process for your own needs and purposes. Let it guide you through the process of planning an efficient and effective public relations campaign.

[For more information, see another book by this author, with the late Ronald D. Smith, *Strategic Planning for Public Relations*, 7th edition, 2024, Routledge.]

APPENDIX: CAREERS IN PUBLIC RELATIONS

Public relations is a growing field in all parts of the developed world with many opportunities for employment and advancement. Labor analysts predict that the demand for public relations practitioners will grow faster than average for all occupations.

That's good news for public relations students and for graduates seeking entry-level jobs. The job search may take time, but it should be successful.

GLOBAL OUTLOOK FOR PR JOBS

Around the world, public relations has a bright future. That's because all kinds of businesses and nonprofit organizations, large and small, turn to public relations to build markets, attract customers, and serve their clientele.

In the US, the Labor Department's Bureau of Labor Statistics predicts that jobs in public relations are growing faster than average, with an expected increase of 6 percent through 2033. Growth areas for jobs in public relations are in digital and social media, crisis communication and reputation management, data-driven and analytics-based PR, corporate social responsibility, internal communication, health care, pharmaceutical, and technology. The bureau expects competition to be keen for entry-level jobs.

Similar predictions come from Canada, the United Kingdom, Australia, Mexico, India, Russia, Japan, China, and the European Union, where France, Germany, and the Netherlands continue to drive the PR scene, while Eastern European countries are emerging with strong talent and innovative work. There is steady growth in public relations jobs in the Middle East, especially in cities like Dubai, Riyadh, and Abu Dhabi. The outlook for PR jobs in South America is bright, too, especially in countries such as Brazil, Chile, and Colombia. Africa's PR market is among the fastest-growing globally, fueled by countries such as Kenya, Nigeria, and South Africa.

The public relations industry has bounced back from the COVID era, growing 9 percent in 2022, although growth has slowed somewhat since then with the threat of an economic downturn. Research from The Holmes Report, an industry analyst, estimates that the top 250 PR firms in the world reported fee income of $17.3 billion (£12.8 billion, €15.2 billion) in 2023.

Public relations is a lucrative international profession. In 2024, the largest global agency, Edelman, generated about $1.03 billion (£762.3 million, €906.1 million) in fees and employed 6,116 people.

Other global top 25 agencies include: Weber Shandwick, BCW, FleishmanHillard, and Real Chemistry (all US-based); Vector Inc. (Japan); Ketchum (US); Brunswick (UK); FGS Global (US); Media Consulta (Germany); Ogilvy PR (US); MSL (France); Inizio Evoke (US); FTI Consulting (US); Hill & Knowlton (US); BlueFocus (China); Golin (US); APCO (US); Teneo Holdings (UK); SEC Newgate SpA (Italy); D&S Media (China); Finn Partners (US); WE Communications (US); Pomilio Blumm (Italy); and Ruder Finn (US).

SALARIES

Salary comparisons are notoriously imprecise, especially with international comparisons. The salary information here was gathered from various governmental, professional, academic, and other sources. It is presented with the following cautions.

Salaries vary regionally. Even within the same country, they often differ geographically. Higher salaries are associated with larger metropolitan areas. For example, North American salaries are higher in larger cities (e.g., New York, Los Angeles, Washington, DC, Chicago, Toronto, and Vancouver) than in smaller cities. Similarly, salaries in London and Southeast UK are higher than in Scotland or Wales.

Likewise, salaries vary within different organizational settings: public relations agencies, public relations divisions within marketing or advertising agencies, and in-house public relations departments. Within the latter, they diverge greatly depending on the type of organization—at the higher end for science, high-tech manufacturing, investor relations, and high-performing industries such as pharmaceuticals and energy; at the lower end of the salary scale for nonprofit organizations, cultural groups, travel/tourism, education, and religion.

Salaries also vary among groups of practitioners. Men still earn more than women, though the gender gap is not significantly different than in other professional areas.

In the United States, entry-level public relations jobs generally have salaries of about $40,000 (£29,600, €35,187) with approximately 27,000 job openings each year. Experienced practitioners earn an average of $85,000 (£62,867, €74,773).

In the UK, entry-level salaries are about £25,000 ($33,800, €29,734). Salaries for experienced public relations managers are about £67,000 ($90,600, €79,710).

In Australia, starting salaries are about AUS$46,333 a year, (US$30,097, £22,253, €26,475), with seasoned professionals earning approximately AUS$135,308 (US$87,896, £64,988, €77,317).

ENTRY-LEVEL JOBS

Who's hiring in public relations? Here are some places to start looking for an entry-level job in the field:

- Public relations agency (general or specialists).
- Public relations section of advertising, marketing, or fundraising agency.
- Public relations department in company: business, manufacturing, sports, health care, entertainment, travel/hospitality, industry association.
- Public relations/communication department in nonprofit or nongovernmental organization: education, charity, religious, arts, professional, advocacy.

- Public affairs unit in government or military: press secretary, public information, public affairs, communications specialist.
- Independent public relations consultant.

There are two categories of public relations practitioners: technicians and managers. Students can expect entry-level positions that emphasize competence in writing and editing at the technician level, such as writing news releases, social media posts, speeches, and newsletter articles, and producing videos.

Look for openings with job titles such as public relations writer, public affairs or public relations specialist, media relations assistant, account assistant, and publications or web editor. Also look for generic job titles such as staff associate, coordinator, and associate director.

Use an entry-level position as a springboard toward the next level, communication managers, who are the communication decision makers. Cultivate interpersonal and problem-solving skills. Develop an expertise in a particular specialty such as social media, public affairs, crisis communication, research, or employee relations.

Consider joining a professional organization such as the Public Relations Society of America, which lists multiple resources for early-career professionals on its website at prsa.org.

HIRING CHARACTERISTICS

What characteristics are employers seeking in entry-level PR practitioners? A 2023 survey of public relations practitioners by the Commission on Public Relations Education found the following top 10 desired traits ranked as follows: writing performance, teamwork ability, internship or work experience, public relations coursework, currency in professional trends and issues, strong references, a diverse/multicultural perspective, a public relations portfolio, activity on social media, and the candidate's diversity.

Lower on their list were: capability for hybrid/remote work, a degree in PR, business coursework, activity in PR organizations, activity in student media, an online portfolio, leadership experience, and volunteer work.

Note the importance of writing skills, perennially at the top of surveys of employers who are hiring entry-level public relations employees. This is because PR professionals must be able to write well-organized news releases, social media posts, speeches, and other items.

In addition, public relations practitioners, educators, and government labor analysts note that successful public relations practitioners should possess the following qualities:

- Interpersonal skills, since public relations specialists deal with the public and the media regularly;
- Organizational skills, because they are often in charge of managing several events or communications at the same time;
- Problem-solving skills, because public relations specialists sometimes must explain how a company or client is handling sensitive issues;
- Speaking skills, because they regularly speak on behalf of clients or their organization.

You will move ahead faster in public relations if you also have these skills and abilities: listening skills, management ability, planning skills, research ability, and an understanding of media, communication technology, and organizational behavior.

EDUCATION

The most useful advice for obtaining a job in public relations is to get the best education possible. Some people begin in the profession through workshops and short courses, while others transition from other areas such as journalism, teaching, and law.

Increasingly, however, many people obtain a bachelor's degree in the field. The following categories of courses and knowledge/skill areas may help you plan your academic career.

PUBLIC RELATIONS COURSES

The Commission on Public Relations Education (2023) recommends six specific and separate courses for undergraduates in a public relations major, minor, or sequence:

- Principles of Public Relations;
- Public Relations Research Methods;
- Public Relations Writing;

- Public Relations Campaigns or Public Relations Case Studies;
- Supervised Work Experience or Internship;
- Public Relations Ethics.

Employers rank ethics highly among the most desired knowledge, skills, and abilities for entry-level employees because PR professionals are likely to encounter ethical challenges in the workplace, such as disinformation and misinformation, deceptive practices, lying, and conflicts of interest. Students need to be prepared to address such ethical challenges when they enter the workplace, rather than relying on workplace ethics training.

Other areas of study that future PR practitioners should investigate include:

- Critical strategic thinking skills—In survey after survey, public relations practitioners have repeatedly ranked critical and strategic thinking as a most sought-after skill for entry-level career success.
- Data insights and strategy—Public relations students don't need to become data scientists, but they must have a solid grounding in quantitative and qualitative research. The need for early-career public relations practitioners to understand the basics of analytics metrics and data analysis is clear, especially with the advent of AI.
- Artificial intelligence—As noted in Chapter 2, AI is here to stay. Organizations are adopting AI systems because they offer a powerful combination of efficiency, automation, and innovation. Many entry-level, routine PR tasks such as basic audience and topic research, media monitoring, written, audio, and visual content development, evaluation, and more are amenable to AI applications. Entry-level practitioners will need to be familiar with AI's potential and to make judgments about the AI systems they use.
- Diversity, equity, and inclusion—Although the term "DEI" was in flux as this book went to press, the need for public relations practitioners who understand the importance of inclusiveness and diversity remains unchanged. PR professionals play a critical role in ensuring that their organizations appreciate human differences, treat all people fairly, and making sure that individuals in their organizations feel valued.
- Public relations as a driver of social change—Entry-level practitioners should understand the role of public relations in addressing

issues such as gender identity, sexuality, racism, ableism, and poverty. Public relations has a role as a catalyst to advance the human condition in the communities it serves.

- Networking and experiential learning—In addition to internships and service-learning courses where students serve the community while learning course content, students should consider joining student organizations, especially those related to public relations, which provide opportunities for professional training. The Public Relations Student Society of America, which is affiliated with PRSA, has chapters on more than 300 campuses. IABC, the International Association of Business Communicators, also has established student chapters, and many colleges and universities have independent student public relations groups not formally aligned with either organization. Parallel organizations in other countries also have student members, such as the Canadian Public Relations Society, the Chartered Institute of Public Relations in the UK, Communication and Public Relations Australia, and organizations in many other nations.

GRADUATE EDUCATION

The minimum academic qualification for a job in public relations is a bachelor's degree. Increasingly, competition for jobs includes people with master's degrees. Many universities throughout North America and Europe offer advanced studies in public relations, organizational communication, and related areas.

Offering an international perspective, the Commission on Public Relations Education has recommended the following areas of study as part of a master's degree, culminating in a project or thesis: strategic public relations management, basic business principles and processes, communication/public relations theory, research methods, ethics, and global influences on the practice of public relations.

CERTIFICATION AND ACCREDITATION FOR DEGREE PROGRAMS

Public relations organizations in many countries have created a certification or accreditation program for universities offering programs of study in public relations.

For example, in the US, public relations degree programs are included in the accreditation of most of the 120 institutions affiliated with the Accrediting Council on Education in Journalism and Mass Communications, and 47 universities hold a Certification in Education for Public Relations offered by the Public Relations Society of America.

Communication and Public Relations Australia offers an accreditation program that blends theoretical concepts, professional skills, and industry engagement for universities in Australia. In the UK, the Chartered Institute of Public Relations recognizes university courses, while the Public Relations Institute of Ireland offers accreditation for university public relations programs.

JOB SEARCH

There is no easy formula for landing your first job or getting a foothold in the profession of your choice. However, some techniques have been used by many job seekers to land jobs in public relations. Here are several suggestions.

PERSONAL ASSESSMENT

Before you plunge into the job search, do some soul searching.

- Do you like continual change or a routine and stable environment?
- Do you thrive on pressure, or does it grind you down?
- Are you willing to relocate for a job with potential?
- Do you have most of the skills needed for success in a job and can you learn the rest?

Many types of personal inventories are available at career development offices in colleges and universities. These can help you assess your personal interests, aspirations, and work styles, using the information to direct your career path.

EMPLOYMENT ASSESSMENT

Research the field. Learn who is hiring and where the jobs are. Investigate opportunities in other sections of the country or in other parts of the world. Look into job possibilities in related fields such as marketing, research, advertising, and technical writing. Explore possibilities in both corporate and nonprofit organizations, as well as with agencies. Don't be afraid to ask for an informational interview with a senior person in the public relations profession.

NETWORKING

Network, network, network! Let everyone know that you are looking for a job. Ask friends to pass along your name to their friends and colleagues who may know someone looking for an eager public relations employee. Join the student chapter of a professional public relations organization, and transfer your membership to a professional chapter when you graduate. Participate in both local chapter meetings (join a committee in your chapter) and national conferences.

Build an expanding network of professional contacts through your internships, class projects, shadowing and mentoring programs with practitioners, visitors to your campus, and contacts with your university's alumni who work in your areas of interest.

COVER LETTER

A cover letter is your first introduction to a prospective employer. Make a strong first impression.

- *Ensure accuracy and professionalism.* Proofread it carefully before sending it. Make sure there are no misspellings or other imperfections. Present a professional tone that reflects you without being humorous, overly confident, cute, or avant-garde.
- *Address the cover letter to a real person.* This is more effective than sending it to a nameless office holder such as Personnel Director or Public Affairs Manager. A search of the organization's website or a telephone call to the receptionist should yield the name you need.
- *Indicate your interest in the position.* State where you heard about the opening, indicate why you are interested in this job, and express confidence that you can do it effectively. Keep the focus on what you can do for the organization rather than on your need for a job.
- *Briefly describe your philosophical approach.* Indicate what you think about this type of work, its importance, and your commitment to it.

- *Summarize your qualifications.* Tell how they relate to the particular job for which you are applying. Restate from your résumé the two or three items that highlight your competence for this particular position.
- *Address each advertised qualification the employer is seeking.* The job posting will signal that the employer is looking for some very specific skills and experiences. Many applicants with otherwise excellent backgrounds will be overlooked because they appear not to have each qualification the employer is seeking. You are likely to be stronger in some areas and less experienced in others, but do not simply skip over one of those weaknesses. Address each in some way. For example, if the employer is looking for someone with experience in running focus groups, you may realize that you not have done this on your own. But perhaps you can indicate that you helped lead focus groups as part of a team in one of your classes or that beyond class you have studied on your own about how to conduct focus groups—and that you are eager to conduct focus group research for this company.
- *Ask for an interview.* End the cover letter with a specific request to obtain a response or to meet with the employer. If it is appropriate, offer to telephone for an appointment, or ask for a formal application.

PORTFOLIO

Every applicant for a public relations job should have a comprehensive portfolio of writing samples, graphic designs, research projects, and other relevant materials. Preferably, the portfolio should be available both in hard copy and online.

At a minimum, the portfolio should include news releases, social media posts, website copy, a fact sheet, a brochure, and a newsletter article. Additionally, the portfolio should include a report on one of your research projects, particularly applied research using a focus group, survey, or content analysis.

Display the portfolio in a professional-looking binder. Make sure that the online version of your portfolio can be accessed from your online résumé.

In addition to the portfolio, make copies of a couple of the more impressive pieces to leave behind with the search committee.

RÉSUMÉ

Every job seeker needs a high quality résumé, which is a listing of your professional credentials and experience. This should be tightly written to highlight your strengths.

- *Keep the résumé to a single page.* This is sufficient for new graduates and other entry-level job seekers. To do that, use résumé language that features action statements such as "edited newsletter" or "conducted focus group research" rather than complete sentences.
- *Use a summary rather than an objective.* Traditional résumé objectives focus on what you want, such as "position in public relations" or "challenging writing position with opportunity for advancement." Instead, consider using a personal summary highlighting what you have to offer. For example: "Recent graduate and agency intern familiar with research techniques. Strong writing skills. Proficient in social media. Experience with PRSSA accounts. Degree in public relations."
- *Design the résumé for eye appeal.* Especially in the field of public relations, where appearance is important and design ability is expected, would-be employers expect résumés that look professional. Use quality paper. Bold or underlined section heads with bullet items can be useful. People read from the left, so use the left side of the sheet for the most important information; save details such as inclusive dates for less-prominent positions.
- *Avoid gimmicks.* Neon-colored paper, personal brochures, techno typeface and bizarre graphics may be attention getters, but they often fail to generate a positive response. Stick with conventional and professional styles.
- *Avoid hype words.* Control the urge to call yourself "a dynamic, self-motivated go-getter" and avoid other such hyperbolic statements. Instead, use objective words, numbers, and strong verbs. Give examples of past success.
- *Use buzzwords.* Showing that you know the language can attract the attention of the person initially screening applications. Consider what is expected for the job you are applying for, and then use words to address those expectations. High on the list of most public relations employers are the following words: analyze, design, edit, evaluate, plan, research, and write.

- *List professional experience.* Include paid employment, internships, volunteer work, and military service. Indicate the company or organizational name, job title, and dates (years, or months and years) of employment. If you have many part-time or summer jobs unrelated to public relations, summarize these under one generic heading. List your professional experience concisely, using bullets and brief action statements. Focus on tangible tasks rather than broad job categories, and use strong action verbs. Indicate not only your work projects but also their results. For example: "Increased student agency accounts by 35 percent." Many résumés present experience in reverse chronological order focused on jobs. An alternative is to focus on areas of skill or achievement, such as separate sections on writing, editing, and research, followed by a brief work history.
- *List educational achievements.* Include the name of your school, major, degree, awards, and any special concentrations of study. Note if the major is accredited or certified in public relations. Indicate your grade average if it is noteworthy (3.0 or better on a 4.0 scale). List your most recent education first. Do not list high school unless it adds a particular credential, such as Academy for Visual Arts if you are citing experience in design. If you do not have much work experience, list relevant courses, using generic course titles, and don't overlook non-major courses in business, language, and other disciplines.
- *List professional affiliations and memberships.* Even in an entry-level job search, you can show involvement with job-relevant organizations.
- *Provide an email contact.* You may have to establish a new email, if you have been relying on one provided by your college or university. It's probably a good idea to create an email account just for job search and professional uses. Remember to check it often. Also, be careful about the name you choose. SuperKrak, LilMama, and StudMonkey17 may be okay for e-mails to friends, but they don't create the professional impression you need for business purposes.
- *Identify special skills.* Language fluency, computer skills, and other personal capabilities relevant to employment should be listed. List organizational and volunteer activities if they are relevant to public relations or if they show leadership experience.

- *Monitor your social media pages.* Expect would-be employers to look at your social media pages, even if you try to limit access to your virtual friends. Be careful what you post online. Many job applicants have been scrubbed from the interview list because the company saw unflattering photos or negative information on their Instagram or Facebook page. Google your own name (quotation marks around the name, plus city) and see what employees would find about you online.
- *Be selective with personal information.* Hobbies, political involvement, and religious affiliation generally have no place on a résumé, unless your hobby relates to the potential job or if the position deals with political or religious matters. Marital status and other such personal information are out of bounds in a job search.
- *Do not list personal references.* Save these for a separate sheet including names, postal addresses, email contacts, and telephone numbers for people who have indicated their willingness to give you a good recommendation. Always ask permission to list a reference, and don't be shy about asking if that person feels comfortable about giving you a positive recommendation. Don't waste space on the résumé with the obvious note that references are available on request. Instead, be prepared to give this when you get an interview.

INTERVIEW PREPARATION

Employers receive hundreds of applications for a single job opening. Obviously, the cover letter and résumé are the initial screening devices. The competition is tough, but a few of the standouts make it through. If you are lucky enough to get an interview, make the most of it.

- *Research the organization before the interview.* Find out all you can from the organization's website about the organization: its mission, reputation, activities, and successes. Do an online search to see if the organization has been in the news lately. Look at the organization's social media accounts if they exist. Check into biographical materials for information on its leaders.

- *Arrive early*. If anyone has to wait for the interview to begin, it should be you. Learn ahead of time how to get to the interview site and how long the trip will take. Plan to be in the building and on the correct floor at least 10 minutes before the scheduled time of the interview.
- *Dress professionally*. This should go without saying, but too many employers complain that job applicants dress in a way that suggests they aren't taking the interview seriously. Err on the side of being more formal than may be necessary. This doesn't mean to wear your best party dress, nor does it require purchasing an expensive business suit. But for most jobs, conservative professional attire means a suit and tie for men and parallel clothing for women.
- *Be an active listener*. During the interview maintain eye contact, look for nonverbal cues, concentrate on the discussion, and evaluate questions before you respond.
- *Ask your own questions*. Prepare a list of questions relevant to the prospective position, questions that show you to be a person eager to make a contribution. Let these questions indicate that you will work hard, learn fast, and quickly become a contributing member of the organization. Hold questions of salary, benefits, vacations, and other personal concerns until you have a job offer.
- *Show your portfolio*. Bring your portfolio to the job interview so you can show your work rather than merely talking about it. Offer it early in the meeting so the interviewer can glance at it during the discussion.
- *Have some leave-behinds*. Bring copies of the most appropriate portfolio items to leave with the organization. Also, provide a sheet with a link to your online résumé and portfolio.
- *Expect a writing test*. As part of the interview process, many employers hiring writers want to see how candidates perform under pressure. You may be given a set of facts and asked to prepare a news release.
- *Expect a current affairs test*. Many graduates tell, often with regret, of feeling that they did poorly on a current affairs test that was administered as part of a job interview. Public relations professionals are expected to know what's happening in their community and beyond. You should develop a habit of following the news every day. When you go for a job interview, make sure you are

aware of current happenings and that you know the names of key governmental and professional leaders.

- *Have an air of confidence and professionalism.* Maintain eye contact with your interviewer, and control any anxiety you may have. Remind yourself that this organization thinks you are good enough to consider hiring you. Dressing professionally can be an ego boost, and knowing that you are prepared can go a long way to calm your nervousness.
- *Follow up with a thank-you letter.* Immediately after the interview, mail a note or card that expresses appreciation for the opportunity to be considered for the position. Send a real card, not an email note. Use this as another opportunity to restate your interest in the job and to reiterate your main qualifications.

WORKS CITED

Bureau of Labor Statistics. (2025, April 18). "Public Relations Specialists." *Occupational Outlook Handbook*. U.S. Department of Labor. https://www.bls.gov/ooh/media-and-communication/public-relations-specialists.htm

Chartered Institute of Public Relations. (n.d.). *About university course recognition*. https://cipr.co.uk/CIPR/Learn_Develop/Qualifications/About_university_course_recognition.aspx

Commission on Public Relations Education. (2023). *Navigating change: Recommendations for advancing undergraduate public relations education*. https://www.commissionpred.org/wp-content/uploads/2023/11/CPRE-50th-Anniversary-Report-FINAL.pdf

The Holmes Report. (2024a). *Global Top 250 PR Agency Ranking 2024*. PRovokeMedia. https://www.provokemedia.com/ranking-and-data/global-pr-agency-rankings/2024-pr-agency-rankings/top-250

The Holmes Report. *2024 Agency Rankings: Global PR Industry Growth Stalls Amid Challenging Conditions*. (2024b). PRovokeMedia. https://www.provokemedia.com/long-reads/article/2024-agency-rankings-global-pr-industry-growth-stalls-amid-challenging-conditions

GLOSSARY

The number in parenthesis indicates the chapter in this textbook (Chapters 1–8) where the primary reference is located.

Acceptance evaluation: (8) approach to evaluation research that considers how an organization internalizes a public relations message

Acceptance objective: (6) category of objectives dealing with what an organization wants people to think about it, thus focusing on interests and attitudes

Accreditation: (1) a process that involves the public relations profession setting and maintaining its own standards, rather than having them imposed from the outside

Action evaluation: (8) approach to evaluation research that considers the impact of a public relations program on bottom-line issues for an organization

Action objective: (6) category of objective dealing with how an organization wants people to act toward it, thus focusing on opinion and behavior

Activism: (6) a confrontational proactive strategy focused on persuasive communication and advocacy

Actuality: (4) see **sound bite**

Acute stage: (3) stage in crisis communication when the crisis breaks forth on the public stage

Adaptation: (1, 5, 6) the ability of an organization to make changes on the basis of what its publics want and need

Advertising: (7) persuasive communication through paid media to promote a product, service, or idea on behalf of an identified organization or sponsor

Advertising value equivalency: (8) a discredited approach to evaluation that pretends to calculate the value of publicity by estimating how much it would have cost if the same amount of time or space in a news report had been purchased as advertising

Advocacy letter: (4) a format for direct-mail or internet release that promotes a cause or supports an issue

Advocacy model: (2) approach to public relations focusing on the use of two-way communication to modify attitudes and influence behavior; often used by competitive business organizations, causes, and movements

After-only study: (8) a type of evaluation where you implement a tactic, measure impact, and presume that the tactic caused this impact (compare with **before-and-after study**)

Agenda-setting theory: (4) theory that states that the media don't tell us what to think but rather tell us what to think about; also see **priming**, **framing**, and **herd mentality**

Alliance: (6) informal relationship among organizations that compounds their influence and often generates media attention as the organizations work toward a goal (compare with **coalition**)

Announcement release: (4) type of news release that announces an upcoming activity or a new program or product

Appeal letter: (4) direct-mail piece sent to potential donors by a nonprofit organization engaged in a fundraising campaign

Apologia: (4) formal defense of an organization's actions (not to be confused with an apology)

Apology: (6) a vocal commiseration response strategy where an organization publicly accepts responsibility and asks pardon; also see **non-apology**

Artificial intelligence (AI): (2) the ability of a computer or computer-controlled robot to perform tasks commonly associated with human beings

Attack: (6) a reactive strategy of claiming that an accusation of wrongdoing is motivated by an accuser who is negligent or malicious

Audience: (5) a group of people who pay attention to a particular medium of communication

Audience engagement: (6) proactive public relations strategy involving two-way communication between an organization and its publics

Audience feedback: (8) aspect of acceptance evaluation based on the voluntary reaction of an audience; often considered a measure of audience interest

Audience participation: (8) aspect of action evaluation based on measuring outcomes such as attendance figures

Augmented reality: (2) a technology that superimposes a computer-generated image on a user's view of the real world, thus providing a composite view; also see **metaverse** and **virtual reality**

Awareness evaluation: (8) approach to evaluation research focused on the content of messages

Awareness objective: (6) category of objective dealing with what an organization wants people to know about it, dealing with visibility and reputation

Background information: (4) information in a news release that provides context

Balance theory: (4) theory that states that unbalanced mental stances create tension and force an individual to try to restore balance; also see **consistency theories** and **congruity theory**

Before-and-after study: (8) a type of evaluation research where you observe a key public before any public relations program is implemented, expose the public to the tactic, and then measure the public again (compare with **after-only study**)

Benchmark study: (8) aspect of acceptance evaluation based on a baseline that serves as a standard for comparing program outcomes

Benefit statement: (4, 5) a statement that clearly articulates the benefit or advantage that a product or service offers to a public

Biographical release: (4) narrative about a person significant to an organization; also known as a **bio**

Blog: (3) website featuring short articles called blog posts, often with videos, photos, and links to other blogs or websites, with reader comments

Branding: (6) creation of a clear and consistent message for an organization; see **positioning**

Breaking news: (4) hard news that is happening even as the media are covering it; see **hard news**

Campaign plan book: (7) the formal written presentation of your research findings and program recommendations for strategy, tactics, and evaluation

Channel: (4) the specific vehicle through which a message is communicated from sender to receiver

Charisma: (6) message source's magnetic appeal or personal charm

Closed or private community groups: (7) shared media that enable organizations to bring together members of their community. Examples: Facebook Groups, Slack, Discourse

Closed system: (1) type of system in which organizations and publics cannot interact easily and frequently

Cluster sample: (5) sophisticated approach to sampling that subdivides a complex population, drawing elements from each demographic subsection for the final sampling

Coalition: (6) a formal, structured relationship between organizations (compare with **alliance**)

Cognitive dissonance: (4) theory that states that when people realize they hold contradictory attitudes or beliefs, they try to reduce the psychological discomfort, usually by changing one of their attitudes or beliefs

Communication audit: (5) an analysis of the strengths and weaknesses of the public relations concerns of an organization

Communication output: (8) a tactic implemented during a public relations campaign

Communication theory: (4) field of study that tries to make sense of how people communicate

Community relations: (3) specialty within public relations that manages the organization's relationship with people who live in the geographic or social community in which it operates

Concern: (6) vocal commiseration response strategy in which an organization expresses distress but doesn't admit any culpability

Concession: (6) diversionary response strategy where an organization tries to rebuild its relationship with aggrieved publics by giving them something they want, drawing attention away from the problem that remains

Condolence: (6) vocal commiseration response strategy in which an organization expresses grief over someone's loss or misfortune without admitting guilt

Congruity theory: (4) consistency theory with aspect of measuring attitudes; also see **consistency theories** and **balance theory**

Conjecture proposition: (6) type of proposition stating that something probably exists, based on a reasoned conclusion drawn from physical evidence

Consistency theories: (4) theories that describe how people deal with information contrary to existing information, attitudes, and biases; also see **balance theory** and **congruity theory**

Consumer: (1, 3, 5) people who obtain and use the products or services of an organization, also known as **customers**

Content analysis: (5) a quantitative research technique based on unobtrusive, after-the-fact analysis of a set of media artifacts, such as a newscast, editorials, tweets, blogs, or articles on a particular topic

Control: (6) a message source's command over an audience and the perceived willingness to exercise that power

Controlled before-and-after study: (8) type of evaluation that involve two sample groups drawn from the same key public—one that receives the message, the other that does not (the control group)

Convenience sample: (5) type of nonprobability sample in which respondents are selected mainly on their availability

Corrective action: (6) a rectifying behavior strategy that involves taking steps to contain a problem, repair the damage, and/or prevent its recurrence

Corporate public relations: (1) type of public relations that provides the vehicle for businesses to publicize products, gain customers, motivate productivity and maintain a communication link with investors, regulators and industry colleagues

Corporate social responsibility: (2, 3) an aspect of community relations and strategic philanthropy in which an organization contributes to the betterment of society

Corrective action: (6) reactive public relations strategy in which an organization takes steps to contain a problem, repair damage and/or prevent its recurrence

Credibility: (6) a message source's power to inspire belief

Crisis: (3, 5) a major, negative, public, sudden, and unpredicted event that can seriously disrupt an organization's activity and potentially hurts its bottom line or mission

Crisis communication: (3) process by which an organization plans for, deals with, and communicates in out-of-control issues

Crisis management: (5) process by which an organization deals with out-of-control issues

Cultivation theory: (4) theory that suggests that the media (notably television) shapes or cultivates people's conception of social reality

Culture: (3) how people live their lives; includes shared experiences and activities such as language, religion, dress, food, the environment, history, and government that binds a region or country together as a distinct social system

Customer: (1, 5) people who obtain and use the products or services of an organization, also known as **consumers**

Cyberactivism: (6) see **online activism**

Cybernetic theory of communication: (4) a theory that identifies a model for two-way communication, moving from sender to receiver and returning via feedback

Decoding: (4) a process by a message receiver in interpreting the intended message of the sender

Deepfake audio: (7) the use of artificial intelligence to replace one's voice with that of another; regarded as unethical by public relations professionals

Deepfake video: (7) fake video that uses a form of artificial intelligence called deep learning to replace one person's likeness with another in video and other digital media; like deepfake audio, regarded as unethical by public relations professionals

Deliberate inaction: (6) a reactive strategy where an organization intentionally decides not to respond

Demographic noise: (4) communication disruption caused by differences between message sender and receiver based on ethnicity, age, social status

Demographics: (7) key public factors such as age, income, gender, socioeconomic status; compare with **psychographics**

Denial: (6) a defensive response strategy where an organization refuses to accept blame by claiming innocence ("We didn't do it"), mistaken identity ("You've confused us with someone else"), or shifting blame ("So-and-so did it")

Dependency theory: (4) theory that states that audiences, the media, and society in general are in a three-way relationship

Design questions: (8) aspect of program evaluation that considers what criteria should be evaluated

Diffusion of innovations: (4) theory that identifies the role of opinion leaders as models in the process of mass adoption of new products or ideas

Digital media: (7) a category of owned media focusing on computer-based electronic media vehicles; examples include email, mobile devices, QR codes, websites, blogs, online fundraising, and crowdfunding

Digital media advertising: (7) advertising to a key public through digital platforms

Direct news subsidy: (7) information presented to the media in ready-to-use format

Direct mail: (7) a category of owned media featuring written messages disseminated to individual recipients; examples include letters (business letters, appeal letters, marketing letters), memos, postcards, invitations, and catalogs

Direct observation: (8) aspect of action research based on measures of program effectiveness, such as money raised or members recruited

Disappearing content platforms: (7) shared media that are useful for publishing timely, in-the-moment content for an organization's followers for up to 24 hours. Examples: Snapchat, Instagram Stories, Facebook Stories

Disassociation: (6) a diversionary response strategy in which an organization tries to distance itself from the wrongdoing associated with it

Discussion forums: (7) shared media that can be used for asking and answering questions, networking, and forming a community about a particular topic. Examples: Quora, Reddit

Disinformation: (2) false information intentionally created to confuse, misinform, and harm a person or group; **fake news** is a type of disinformation. Also see **misinformation**

Diversity: (2) the idea of appreciating human differences; also see **equity** and **inclusion**

Diversionary response strategy: (6) a reactive strategy that tries to divert attention away from an organization and the problem it is associated with

Donor relations: (2, 3) specialty within public relations, similar to **investor relations**, that manages the organization's relationship with donors and with regulators and watchdog organizations

Doubledown: (6) a reactive strategy in which an organization reiterates its action or position as a matter of principle and stands firm

Earned media: (7) journalism-based communication channels that provide opportunities for the credible presentation of organizational messages to large audiences through the news media

Electronic media: (7) media delivered primarily through electronic vehicles, including audio media (radio, podcasts, robocalls), video media (television, corporate video, videoconferences, drones, streaming video), and presentation software (e.g., Microsoft PowerPoint, Canva)

Embarrassment: (6) an offensive response strategy in which an organization tries to lessen an opponent's influence by using shame or humiliation

Employee relations: (3) Principle that states that an organization is likely to be successful when employees are informed, motivated, and on board with its mission; also known **internal relations**

Enabler: (1, 5) type of public that helps organizations exist and prosper, such as regulators, opinion leaders, allies, and the media

Encoding: (4) a process in creating a message with a specific meaning that can be interpreted by a receiver with approximately the same meaning

Environmental noise: (4) sound pollution from the outside including construction, transportation, and loud music

Equity: (2) treating all people fairly; also see **diversity** and **inclusion**

Ethos: (6) principle identified with Aristotle that focuses on communication effectiveness based on the character of a speaker and on the common ground shared by speakers and audiences (compare with **logos** and **pathos**)

Event listing: (4) a writing format that provides basic information for use in calendars on websites of media outlets and the organization's own website

Excuse: (6) a defensive response strategy in which an organization tries to mitigate wrongdoing; types of excuses include provocation, lack of control, accident, victimization, or association.

Executive summary: (8) formal summary accompanying a public relations plan or evaluation report that outlines in one or two pages the more detailed findings in the full report

Expectancy-value theory: (4) theory that observes that people make media choices based on what they want, what they expect from the media, and how they evaluate the ability of the media to meet those expectations

External impediments: (5) aspect of an organization's external environment involving other political, social, or economic factors that might impede a public relations program

Fact sheet: (3) brief, generally one-page outline of information usually presented as bulleted items

Factual proposition: (4, 6) type of proposition stating that something exists, based on provable evidence

Fake news: (2) purposefully craft, sensational, emotional charged, misleading, or totally fabricated information that mimics the form of mainstream news; also see **misinformation**

Fallacy: (1) erroneous statement

Fear appeal: (6) type of negative emotional appeal intended to arouse anxiety or worry

Feature lead: (4) type of lead used in feature stories

Feature release: (3, 4) news release that emphasizes personalities and human-interest angles rather than hard news

Feedback: (4) communication by a message receiver sent back to the sender

Final report: (8) type of evaluation report that provides a comprehensive review and overall evaluation of a program

Financial public relations: (3) see **investor relations**

Focus group: (5) a qualitative research technique involving conversation among several participants, guided by a monitor and recorded for later analysis

Follow-up release: (4) type of news release in which the organization responds or adds to prior news reporting

Formative research: (5) research that results in data on which a communication program can be built; the first phase of the communication process; also see **strategic research** and **tactical research**

Framing: (4) the way news media treat a particular topic

Gatekeeper: (3, 6, 7) editor, reporter, or news director who determines what gets reported in the media

Gatekeeping theory: (4) theory that states that even journalists trying to be objective will make reporting choices based on their own biases about the presumed interests of their audiences

Goal: (6) a statement rooted in an organization's mission or vision, sketching out how the organization hopes to see an issue settled (compare with **objective**); part of strategy

Government relations: (1, 3) an organization's efforts to build and maintain a working relationship with elected or appointed government officials through dissemination of information and sometimes lobbying; see **public affairs** and **lobbying**

Grabber: (6) power word that gets attention and is easily recalled

Greenwashing: (2) dissemination of misleading publicity by an organization with the aim of presenting an environmentally responsible public image; also see **sustainability**

Guest editorial: (3) opinion piece published as a solicited or approved editorial presenting the view of a person or organization not affiliated with the publication; compare with **op-ed commentary**

Guilt appeal: (6) type of negative emotional appeal attempting to arouse remorse or acceptance of responsibility

Handout: (3) an inappropriate slang term for **news release**

Hard news: (4) information dealing with momentous events, such as accidents, crime, death, scandal, and activities with immediate results such as elections, trials, and sporting events

Hate appeal: (6) type of negative emotional appeal that is unethical and not used by public relations professionals

Herd mentality: (4) a news media organization feels compelled to report on something just because its competitors are focusing on the same topic

How-to article: (4) a feature release that tells readers how to accomplish a certain task; also known as a **service article**

Humor appeal: (6) type of positive emotional appeal using comedy and amusement to gain attention and make the speaker more likeable

Hypodermic needle theory: (4) see **powerful-effects model**

Identity: (1) the way an organization consciously projects itself visually as an expression of its personality

Identity system: (1) tools used by an organization to project its identity, including name and logo, brochures, news releases, advertisements, social media sites, and other means of communication

Image: (1) a short-term evaluation of an organization's messages, drawn from the way an organization projects itself toward its various publics; compare with **reputation**

Image restoration theory: (4) theory that explains how organizations can understand and emerge from crisis situations

Implementation report: (8) type of evaluation report that documents how tactics are being carried out

Inclusion: (2) ensuring that individuals in organizations and communities feel valued; also see **diversity** and **equity**

In-depth interview: (5) a qualitative research technique involving lengthy, detailed, and systematic interviews conducted individually with several respondents

Indirect news subsidy: (7) information presented for media guidance but not meant to be published or aired

Infomercial: (7) program-length television advertising

Information-action statement: (4) part of a news release that offers a way to mobilize readers and viewers

Information exchange: (7) category of communication tactics involving various types of face-to-face encounters between an organization and its publics

Information model: (2) approach to public relations focusing on use of one-way communication to disseminate newsworthy information; often used by government, nonprofit organizations, and business organizations

Information theory: (4) theory that focuses on the content and channels of communication

Information-seeking public: (7) people who have gone out of their way to interact with the organization

Ingratiation: (6) a diversionary response strategy, which raises ethical questions, that involves giving a public something insignificant under the pretense that it has value

Inoculation theory: (4) theory that suggests that unchallenged beliefs and attitudes can be swayed with persuasive information, while attitudes that have been tested are more resistant to change

Instant messaging: (7) shared media that allow users to send real-time messages through a software application. Examples: WhatsApp, Facebook Messenger, WeChat (China)

Integrated marketing communication: (1) a blend of public relations and marketing that allows organizations to strategically use every possible communication tool to engage and communicate with their customers and other significant publics

Intercessory public: (5) a public that bridges the organization and its publics

Intercoder reliability: (5) the degree to which various coders in content analysis agree on their interpretation of a unit of analysis

Intergovernmental relations: (3) specialty within public relations through which government agencies engage their counterparts in other nations; see **public diplomacy**

Internal impediments: (5) aspect of an organization's internal environment involving organizational obstacles that might impede a public relations program

Interpersonal communication: (7) tactics offering face-to-face opportunities for personal involvement and interaction

Interview notes: (4) a news release that provides reporters with an unedited transcript of an interview that they can use to develop a story

Investigation: (6) a rectifying behavior strategy in which an organization promises to examine a situation and then to act as facts warrant

Investor relations: (3) specialty within public relations that manages an organization's relationship with shareholders, regulators, financial journalists and bloggers, investors, and both sell-side and buy-side analysts; also known as **financial public relations**

Issues management: (3, 5) process by which an organization tries to anticipate emerging issues and respond to them before they get out of hand

Judgmental assessment: (8) an evaluation made on hunches and personal experience

Justification: (6) a type of defensive response strategy in which an organization admits to a deed but explains it did so for a good reason, such as good intention, context, idealism, or mitigation

Key public: (5) a specific public that is identified as being most important to an organization's public relations activity; also known as a **strategic public**

Lead: (4) the most important paragraph in a news release

Lead-in: (4) a transition in a broadcast news release that introduces a sound bite; also called a **throw**

Limited effects model: (4) theory that sees communication as being a weak influence in affecting people's attitudes, opinions, and behaviors

Limiter: (1, 5) type of public that undermine an organization's success, including competitors, opponents, unfriendly media, watchdog organizations, and opinion leaders who hold negative views of the organization

Linkage: (1, 4) aspect of systems theory dealing with the patterns in which an organization interacts with its publics

Litigation public relations: (3) specialty of public relations through which defense attorneys manage communication before and during legal disputes

Livestreaming: (7) broadcasting live video to many viewers, ranging from one person on screen to organized panels with multiple speakers. Examples: TikTok, Twitch, YouTube, Vimeo, Facebook Live, Instagram Live Rooms

Lobbying: (1) persuasive campaigns to support, defeat, or amend legislation that's necessary to an organization's own interests; see **government relations**

Logos: (6) principle identified with Aristotle that focuses on communication effectiveness based on rational appeal of messages (compare with **ethos** and **pathos**)

Love appeal: (6) A positive emotional appeal based on an aspect of love such as family, nostalgia, compassion, romance, pity, or sympathy

Magic bullet theory: (4) see **powerful-effects model**

Market: (5) a segment of a population including people with characteristics (e.g., age, income, lifestyle) that can help an organization achieve its consumer-oriented goals

Mathematical theory of communication: (4) a theory that identifies a model for one-way communication, moving from sender to receiver

Mean world effect: (4) aspect of cultivation theory observing that people who use the media heavily tend to be more fearful and more susceptible to social paranoia and conspiracy theories; see **cultivation theory**

Media advisory: (4) a memo written by a public relations practitioner that notifies reporters about an upcoming activity; also called a **media alert**

Media list: (4) a list of people interested in covering an organization's news story such as journalists, social media personalities and influencers, bloggers, and podcast hosts

Media pitch: (4) a targeted, compelling message to journalists so that they decide to cover an organization's news, resulting in media coverage; also known as a **pitch**

Media relations: (3) specialty within public relations through which an organization communicates through various media (print, broadcast, electronic, and digital)

Message content: (8) awareness evaluation based on the extent to which a message is accurate and positive

Message cost: (8) output evaluation focusing on the amount of money spent producing messages

Message distribution: (8) output evaluation focusing on the frequency and manner of message dissemination

Message exposure: (8) awareness evaluation based on the number of people in key publics who were exposed to a message; see **message reach**

Message frequency: (7) the number of times and the pattern (continuous, pulsing and so on) in which messages are presented to a particular public

Message production: (8) a type of output evaluation focusing on the number of messages produced

Message reach: (7) the number of different people who are exposed to a single message

Message recall: (8) aspect of awareness evaluation based on the ability of a public to remember a message and associate it with the organization that produced it

Metaverse: (2) a virtual-reality space in which users can interact with a computer-generated environment and other users; also see **virtual reality** and **augmented reality**

Metric: (8) a standard of measurement to assess the outcome of a program or project

Microblogs: (7) shared media that mix instant messaging and blogs for posting short messages, photos, and video links. Examples: X (formerly Twitter), Threads, Bluesky, Weibo (China's second largest social media platform)

Misinformation: (2) false information though not created with negative intent; also see **fake news**

Models of public relations: (2, 4) theoretical approach to the evolution of public relations through four models: publicity, information, advocacy, and dialogue

Moderate effects model: (4) theory which acknowledges that, over time, the media have a cumulative effect on people, moderated by other social influences

Multimedia news release: (4) a news release that includes features such as web links, videos, photos, infographics, live social media feeds, social sharing, and call to action buttons

Multi-step flow of communication: (4) theory that focuses on multiple layers in the communication process, with a strong role for opinion leaders; also see **two-step flow of communication**

News: (4, 6) significant information relevant to a local media audience, presented with balance and objectivity and in a timely manner

News conference: (3) A group interview in which an organizational spokesperson makes a newsworthy announcement and reporters ask follow-up questions

News media: (7) see **earned media**

News peg: (4, 6) a topic currently being reported that overlaps with an organization's mission or interests

News release: (3) news-type article written by a public relations practitioner and given to media gatekeepers

News subsidy: (7) information provided to media organizations by public relations professionals

Newsworthy: (7) information that media gatekeepers consider of relevance to their audiences

Noise: (4) any interference that limits the ability of the channel to carry a message faithfully from sender to receiver

Non-apology: (6) a vocal commiseration response strategy that is an insincere attempt to apologize without really doing so; also see **apology**

Nonprobability sample: (5) series of techniques for selecting samples of a population *not* based on the principle of **probability**

Nonprofit public relations: (1) type of public relations involving education, health care, cultural and religious groups, human service agencies, charitable organizations, and membership organizations

Nonverbal communication: (6) communication that occurs through actions and cues other than words

Nut graph: (4) nutshell paragraph following the lead in a feature story that presents the key point of the story

Objective: (6) a statement emerging from an organization's goal, presented in clear and measurable terms with a deadline (compare with **goal**)

Objective-based budgeting: (7) preferred approach to budgeting based on implementation of tactics designed to achieve agreed-upon goals and objectives of an organization

Obstacle: (5) a public relations situation that limits the organization in realizing its mission

One-on-one interview: (5) an interview in which people are interviewed at their home, office, a research office, or field service location

Online activism: (6) a proactive strategy that uses digital and social media for social engagement; also called **cyberactivism**

Online newsroom: (3) a set of web pages within a website that provides resources for journalists

Op-ed commentary: (3) opinion piece presenting the view of a person or organization not affiliated with a publication but not necessarily solicited by the publication; compare with **guest editorial**

Open system: (1) type of system in which organizations and publics can interact easily and frequently

Opinion leader: (5) a person with a particular influence on an organization's publics

Opinion subsidy: (7) category of earned media tactics including information presenting an organization's point of view, such as a guest editorial or a position statement

Opportunity: (5) a public relations situation offering a potential advantage to the organization or its publics

Organizational identification: (4) a paragraph with standard wording about an organization that routinely is dropped into a news release, usually at the end

Organizational performance: (6) a key type of proactive action that involves assessing and, when necessary, changing the output of an organization; also see **adaptation**

Out-of-home advertising: (7) category of paid media tactics including outdoor posters, out-of-home videos, transit advertising, aerial advertising, and inflatables

Owned media: (7) communication channels that are produced or published by the organization, which controls the message content as well as its timing, packaging, distribution, and audience access

Paid media: (7) communication channels that are purchased by an organization that are associated with advertising and promotion

Pathos: (6) principle identified with Aristotle that focuses on communication effectiveness based on the appeal to sentiment with positive or negative emotional appeal (compare with **ethos** and **logos**)

Personal involvement: (7) category of communication tactics involving direct interaction between an organization and its publics

PESO model: (7) an integrated communication model using paid media, earned media, shared media, and owned media

Petition: (4) request for action circulated among supporters and signed by many people, often urging governmental or other officials to act in some way

Photo sharing platforms: (7) shared media that allow users to upload, manage, and share photos privately or publicly. Examples: Instagram, Pinterest, Google Photos

Physical evidence: (6) in a proposition, evidence that is clear and indisputable

Physical noise: (4) communication disruption caused by inefficient communication channels

Physiological noise: (4) disruption caused by physical distractions in the message receiver

Pitch: (4) see **media pitch**

Policy proposition: (4, 6) type of proposition that identifies a course of action and encourages its adoption

Political public relations: (1) type of public relations that focuses on the process of getting elected and staying in office

Poll: (5) a very short, survey-like method that focuses more on immediate behavior than attitudes and asks only short, closed-ended questions

Position statement: (3) *the formal, public position of an organization on a particular topic* media relations tool for presenting an organization's perspective on an issue; also called **white paper**; categories include **position papers** and shorter **position paragraphs**

Positioning: (1, 6) process of managing how an organization distinguishes itself with a unique meaning in the mind of its publics

Positioning statement: (6) a general expression of how an organization wants its publics to distinguish it vis-à-vis its competition; part of strategy

Post-crisis stage: (3) final stage in crisis communication when an organization focuses on recovery (returning to normal activities, assessing the extent of physical and reputational damage, and planning to prevent a recurrence of the crisis)

Powerful-effects model: (4) theory that presumes that media have direct, immediate, and powerful-effects on their audiences

Pre-crisis stage: (3) early stage in crisis communication when an organization can anticipate and possibly prevent a crisis

Prebuttal: (6) a reactive strategy that presents advance information defending an organization when bad news is inevitable

Press release: (3) an inappropriate term for **news release** that implies a release only for print news media

Primary research: (5) the generation and analysis of new information to address a research question or problem

Priming: (4) how a news topic reminds media audiences of previous information; also see **agenda-setting theory** and **framing**

Principle of disclosure: (3) one of seven principles of crisis communication, focusing on the need to communicate as much information as possible

Principle of existing relationships: (3) one of seven principles of crisis communication, focusing on the need to communicate with employees, volunteers, stockholders, donors and other supportive publics

Principle of media-as-ally: (3) one of seven principles of crisis communication, focusing on the need to communicate with publics through the media

Principle of message framing: (3) one of seven principles of crisis communication, focusing on the desirability of managing the agenda to maintain some level of control over how the story unfolds

Principle of one voice: (3) one of seven principles of crisis communication, focusing on the need to have either a single spokesperson or the coordinated message by designated multiple spokespersons

Principle of quick response: (3) one of seven principles of crisis communication, focusing on the need to communicate quickly with key publics

Principle of reputational priority: (3) one of seven principles of crisis communication, focusing on top priority of shoring up an organization's reputation

Print and online publications: (7) materials published and printed by an organization; a category of owned media. Examples include serial publications (newsletters, bulletins), stand-alone publications (brochures, fliers, booklets, FAQs (Frequently Asked Questions), fact sheets, reprints, annual reports, user kits, and research reports)

Print media: (7) media delivered primarily through print vehicles, such as newspapers and magazines

Proactive strategy: (6) a strategy that enables an organization to take the initiative by launching a campaign under conditions and according to a timeline that best fits the organization's interests (compare with **reactive strategy**)

Probability: (5) each element within the population has an equal chance of being selected for the sample

Probability sample: (5) series of techniques for selecting samples of a population based on the principle of **probability**

Proclamation: (4) formal advocacy message made by some authority

Producer: (1, 5) type of public that makes an organization's product or service, including employees, volunteers, suppliers, and financial backers

Progress report: (8) preliminary evaluation in which planners can make strategic modifications as they further implement a program

Pronouncer: (4) phonetic tip in a news release to help readers correctly pronounce unfamiliar words such as names of people and places; also called **pronunciation guide**

Proposition: (4, 6) primary idea in a speech, editorial, advertisement, TV program, or other type of communication; also see **factual proposition**, **conjecture proposition**, **value proposition**, and **policy proposition**

Psychographics: (7) key public factors such as lifestyles, opinions, interests, and behaviors (compare with **demographics**)

Psychological noise: (4) disruption caused by preconceived notions such as bias, assumptions, reputation, or racial/ethnic stereotypes

Public: (5) a group of people that shares a common interest vis-à-vis an organization, recognizes its significance, and sets out to do something about it

Public affairs: (1, 3) efforts by government agencies to inform their publics about programs and services, to respond to inquiries, and gauge public opinion; also see **government relations**

Public diplomacy: (1, 3) type of public relations involving government use of the media to impact public opinion in another country, nongovernmental organization, corporation, political faction, or nonprofit group; see **intergovernmental relations**

Public information: (3) term for **media relations** used by government agencies and the military

Publicity: (6) proactive strategy of gaining attention through the news media for an organization, person, event, product, or idea

Publicity model: (2) approach to public relations focusing on use of one-way communication to disseminate information and gain attention; often used in entertainment, sports, and marketing

Random sample: (5) a type of probability sample in which everyone has an equal opportunity to be selected

Reactive strategy: (6) strategy through which an organization responds to influences and opportunities from its environment (compare with **proactive strategy**)

Readability measure: (8) aspect of awareness evaluation based on the calculation of the reading level of a message

Rectifying behavior strategy: (6) a reactive strategy that is a positive response to opposition and criticism, involving action by an organization to repair the damage

Receiver: (4) a person or organization obtaining a message

Regret: (6) a vocal commiseration response strategy in which the organization admits its role but doesn't necessarily accept responsibility or admit wrongdoing

Relabeling: (6) a diversionary response strategy that offers an agreeable name to replace a name with negative connotations

Relationship-management goal: (6) a goal that focuses on how the organization connects with its publics

Relationship marketing: (3) an aspect of public relations focusing on an emerging area of marketing that, public relations-like, deals with gaining long-term support

Relationship model: (2) approach to public relations focusing on use of two-way communication toward mutual understanding and conflict resolution; often used by regulated business, government, nonprofit organizations, and social movements

Relative media effectiveness: (8) aspect of action evaluation that compares one medium to others, attempting to help the organization determine venues for future editions of its campaign

Repentance: (6) rectifying behavior strategy that signals an organization's full atonement because it becomes an advocate for a new way of thinking and doing business

Reputation: (1) the general, overall, and long-term impression of an organization on a specific public; compare to **image**

Reputation management: (1, 3) the process of seeking to influence the way publics view and understand the organization

Reputation-management goal: (6) goal that deals with the identity and perception of the organization

Research: (5) a formal program of information gathering; also see **formative research**

Restitution: (6) a rectifying behavior strategy in which an organization makes amends by compensating victims or restoring the situation to an earlier condition

Rhetorical theory: (4) theory associated with Aristotle which observes that effective communication is based on ethos, logos, and pathos

Reversal: (6) A defensive response strategy in which an organization under criticism tries to gain the upper hand

Risk management: (3, 5) process of identifying, controlling, and minimizing the impact of uncertain events on an organization

Sample size: (5) optimum minimum size for a sample to be considered representative of the population

Sampling: (5) selecting relatively few respondents to stand in for the wider population

Sampling error: (5) a measurement of the extent to which a sample does not perfectly correspond with the target population

Search engine optimization (SEO): (7) the process of improving the visibility of a website to get traffic from organic (free) results on a search engine, such as Google

Secondary customer: (5) the customer of an organization's customer

Secondary details: (4) information in a news release that amplifies information in the lead

Secondary research: (5) process of re-analyzing existing information obtained by previous researchers for a new, specific purpose

Selective attention: (4) theory that states that people pay attention to information that supports their attitudes and ignore information opposed to their attitudes

Selective exposure and avoidance: (4) theory that states that people expose themselves to messages they think they will like and avoid what they expect not to like

Selective perception: (4) theory that states that people interpret information based on how it fits their attitudes

Selective recall: (4) theory stating that people are more likely to remember what supports their beliefs

Selective retention: (4) theory stating that people remember information that is of interest and forget information that doesn't seem to be relevant to them

Semantic noise: (4) disruption caused by use of language not understood or appropriately interpreted by the receiver

Sender: (4) a person or organization originating communication

Service article: (4) see **how-to article**

Sex appeal: (6) type of positive emotional appeal based on gender, nudity, or sexuality

Shared media: (7) communication channels, not controlled by an organization, providing user-generated messages that are shared on a social media platform, usually for free

Shock: (6) an offensive response strategy of deliberately agitating publics by presenting information that surprises, causes fear, or disgusts them

SiLoBaTi + UnFa: (4) acronym to identify elements of news: significance, localness, balance, timeliness, unusualness, and fame

Situation: (5) a set of circumstances facing an organization

Situation analysis: (5) the collection of information that managers use to analyze an organization's internal and external environments

Situational theory: (4) theory that looks at publics as being active or passive

Sleeper effect: (4) theory that notes that the persuasive impact of communication sometimes increases as time elapses

Slogan: (6) a catchphrase developed as part of a communication campaign

Social audio platforms: (7) shared media that allow people to listen to live conversations on specific topics. Examples: Clubhouse, Spotify

Social judgment theory: (4) theory that observes that individuals accept or reject messages to the extent that they perceive the messages are corresponding to their internal anchors (attitudes and beliefs) and as affecting their self-concept

Social networking sites: (7) shared media that allow people to build online relationships with others having similar personal or career interests, backgrounds, or activities. Examples: Facebook, LinkedIn.

Soft news: (4) type of news that is light information dealing with upcoming events and new programs, trends, and developments without major consequences

Sound bite: (4) a brief, memorable quote used by a news source for radio and television reports; also known as an **actuality**

Speakers bureau: (7) an organizational program to promote availability of knowledgeable and trained employees or volunteers to give presentations

Special events: (7) activities created by an organization mainly to provide a venue within which to interact with its publics

Specialized news: (4) information of importance to particular publics and particular segments of the media, such as news about business, religion, sports, the arts, agriculture, science, health, home, fashion, and so on

Spiral of silence: (4) theory that suggests that people learn through media reporting what appears to be the majority opinion, and those holding minority viewpoints often silence themselves

Sponsorship: (6) a proactive strategy in which an organization provides financial, personnel and other resources to support a community project

Stage-of-lifestyle budgeting: (7) approach to budgeting that considers the phase of development, such as new versus continuing programs

Staged event: (6) an activity created by the organization as a focal point for public involvement and potential media attention

Stakeholder: (5) person or group that relates to an organization through its potential impact on the organization's mission and objectives; similar to **public**

Strategic ambiguity: (6) reactive strategy in which an organization attempts to dodge an issue by not responding

Strategic counseling: (3) a management function that involves research, analysis and planning, execution of tactics, and evaluation

Strategic inaction: (6) reactive strategy in which an organization waits out criticism and allows a situation to fade

Strategic public: (5) see **key public**

Strategic research: (5) systematic gathering of information about issues and publics that affect an organization; a type of **formative research**

Strategic silence: (6) reactive strategy in which an organization does not respond to criticism, though it may take follow-up action

Strategy: (6) an organization's overall plan

Stratified sample: (5) sophisticated approach to sampling that ranks elements according to demographic factors, then draws elements from each factor to be part of the sample

Structured interview: (5) an interview in which standardized questions are asked in a certain order

Summary news lead: (4) most common type of news lead, providing a one- or two-sentence overview of the information

Survey: (5) a quantitative research technique based on a standard series of questions, which yields statistical results and conclusions

Sustainability: (2) development that meets the needs of the present without compromising the ability of future generations to meet their own needs; also see **greenwashing**

SWOT analysis: (5) strategic planning tool that analyzes an organization's strengths, weaknesses, opportunities, and threats

Systematic sample: (5) type of probability sample in which the researcher selects every nth name on a list

Systems theory: (1, 4) theory that explains an organization's relationship with its publics

Tactics: (7) specific communication tools through which an organization interacts with its publics

Tactical research: (5) information that guides the production and dissemination of messages; a type of **formative research**

Talking points: (4) type of internal position statement used by organizations to encourage consistency among organizational spokespersons

Task management goal: (6) a type of goal that is concerned with getting certain things done

Theory of accounts: (4) theory about the use of communication to manage relations in the wake or rebuke or criticism

Third-party endorsement: (7) the added credibility that comes with the endorsement of an outside, unbiased agent, such as a reporter or editor

Threat: (6) an offensive response strategy that promises that harm will come to the accuser or the purveyor of bad news

Throw: (4) see **lead-in**

Transparent communication: (6) proactive, open, and observable activity that helps publics understand the organization and support its actions

Two-step flow of communication: (4) theory stating that instead of directly changing attitudes, the media may influence opinion leaders, who then influence others through interpersonal means; also see **multi-step flow of communication**

Unique selling proposition: (6) a clear statement of the benefit to an audience

Unstructured interview: (5) interview in which the interviewer has the freedom to determine what additional questions to ask

Uses and gratifications theory: (4) theory that suggests that people make choices in selecting media for particular purposes, including information, entertainment, value reassurance, social interaction, and emotional release

Value proposition: (4, 6) type of proposition that asserts the virtue or merits of something

Value system: (3) what people value or place importance on

Verbal communication: (6) communication occurring through written or spoken words, and the right use of those words

Verbal evidence: (6) in a proposition, evidence that is less clear than physical evidence and open to varying interpretation

Video B-roll: (4) sound bites and raw, unedited footage provided to television stations to use in news reports

Video news release: (4) news release produced specifically for television stations with actualities, presented as an edited story package

Video sharing platforms: (7) shared media that allow users to upload full-length TV shows or movies as well as short clips, ads, and video blogs (vlogs) to the internet. Examples: TikTok, YouTube, Vimeo, Instagram Reels, YouTube Shorts

Virtual reality: (2) a three-dimensional, computer-generated digital and real space in which users interact, while also creating their own experiences; also see **metaverse** and **augmented reality**

Virtue appeal: (6) type of positive emotional appeal that evokes any of the various values that society or individuals hold in esteem, such as justice, loyalty, bravery, piety, or social tolerance

Vocal commiseration: (5) ways in which an organization expresses empathy and understanding about a misfortune

Volunteer sample: (5) type of nonprobability sample in which the researcher invites people to participate if they feel strongly about an issue

Weighted sample: (5) approach to sampling in which each demographic group is sized according to its proportion in the population to compensate for its being a small proportion

Wikis: (7) collaborative websites where all users can edit and update content. Example: Wikipedia

RECOMMENDED READING

Austin, E.W. & Pinkleton, B.E. (2015). *Strategic public relations management: Planning and managing effective communication programs* (3rd ed.). Routledge.

Austin, L.L. & Jin, Y. (2022). *Social media and crisis communication* (2nd ed.). Routledge.

Boyle, M.P. & Schmierbach, M. (2024). *Applied communication research: Getting started as a researcher* (3rd ed.). Routledge.

Center, A.H., Jackson, P., Smith, S., & Stansberry, F.R. (2014). *Public relations practices: Managerial case studies and problems* (8th ed.). Pearson.

Coombs, W.T. (2023). *Ongoing crisis communication: Planning, managing, and responding* (6th ed.). Sage.

Dietrich, G. (2014). *Spin sucks: Communication and reputation management in the digital age*. Que Publishing.

Fearn-Banks, K., with Kawamato, K. (2024). *Crisis communications: A casebook approach* (6th ed.). Routledge.

Freberg, K. (2022). *Social media for strategic communication: Creative strategies and research-based applications* (2nd ed.). Sage.

Freberg, K. (2025). *Discovering public relations: An introduction to creative and strategic practices* (2nd ed.). Sage.

Gregory, A. (2021). *Planning and managing public relations campaigns: A strategic approach* (5th ed.). Kogan Page.

Kelleher, T. (2020). *Public relations: Engagement, conversation, transparency, trust* (2nd ed.). Oxford University Press.

Kim, C.M. & Prince, M. (2025). *Social media campaigns: Strategies for public relations and marketing* (3rd ed.). Routledge.

Lipschultz, J.H. (2024). *Social media communication: Concepts, practices, data, law and ethics* (4th ed.). Routledge.

Luttrell, R. (2022). *Social media: How to engage, share, and connect* (4th ed.). Rowman & Littlefield.

Moss, D., & DeSanto, B. (2022). *Public relations cases: International perspectives* (3rd ed.). Routledge.

Seitel, F.P. (2019). *The practice of public relations* (14th ed.). Pearson.

Silverman, D.A. & Smith, R.D. (2024). *Strategic planning for public relations* (7th ed.). Routledge.

Sriramesh, K. & Vercic, D., eds. (2020). *Global public relations handbook: Theory, research, and practice* (3rd ed.). Routledge.

St. John, B., Martinelli, D.K., Pritchard, R. S., & Spaulding, C. (2019). *Cases in public relations strategy*. Sage.

Stacks, D.W. (2017). *Primer of public relations research* (3rd ed.). Guilford Press.

Stacks, D.W., & Michaelson, D. (2017). *A professional and practitioner's guide to public relations research, measurement and evaluation* (3rd ed.). Business Expert Press.

Swann, P. (2025). *Cases in public relations management* (4th ed.). Routledge.

Tindall, N.T.J., Hutchins, A.L., & Smith, R.D. (2025). *Becoming a public relations writer: Strategic writing for emerging and established media* (7th ed.). Routledge.

Turk, J.V. & Valin, J. (2017). *Public relations case studies from around the world* (2nd ed.). Peter Lang Publishing.

Ulmer, R.R., Sellnow, T.L., & Seeger, M.W. (2023). *Effective crisis communication: Moving from crisis to opportunity* (5th ed.). Sage.

Wilcox, D.L., Reber, B.H., Shin, J.H., & Cameron, J.T. (2023). *Public relations: Strategies and tactics* (12th ed.). Pearson.

Wimmer, R.G. & Dominick, J.R. (2014). *Mass media research: An introduction* (10th ed.). Wadsworth.

INDEX

For Product Safety Concerns and Information please contact our EU
representative GPSR@taylorandfrancis.com
Taylor & Francis Verlag GmbH, Kaufingerstraße 24, 80331 München, Germany

www.ingramcontent.com/pod-product-compliance
Lightning Source LLC
Chambersburg PA
CBHW061717270326
41928CB00011B/2016

* 9 7 8 1 0 3 2 8 6 0 7 4 9 *